BASICS OF SUCCESSFUL BUSINESS PLANNING

Basics of
Successful Business Planning

WILLIAM R. OSGOOD

a division of American Management Associations

Library of Congress Cataloging in Publication Data

Osgood, William R.
   Basics of successful business planning.

   Includes index.
   1.Small business—Management.   I. Title.
HD69.S6085   658.4'02   79-54846
ISBN 0-8144-5420-8
ISBN 0-8144-7579-5 pbk

First AMACOM paperback edition 1982.

DEDICATED TO PAT DAWSON

Preface

Basics of Successful Business Planning is written for people who want to go into business for themselves and aren't sure of what to do, or worse, are already in business and simply do not understand what they are doing or should be doing. There are many books and other publications available that purport to reveal the mysterious secret of success in business. This book too promises to reveal the secret of success in business, but at the same time it demystifies it. In fact, you will see that business planning is a very straightforward systematic process.

Without a logical, coherent plan of action, the business is a victim of fate. Some business managers seem to be quite skilled at reacting to situations and salvaging opportunity out of disaster. This is almost a definition of the all-American entrepreneur. Not being a gambler myself, it has always made more sense to me to anticipate problems and quietly avoid them rather than pull off heroic salvage acts. Good planning helps make this possible. It also greatly enhances the odds for success. Even a good gambler must acknowledge the value of risk reduction.

The book is designed to acquaint the reader with both the theory and practice of business planning. First, a philosophy of planning and types of planning are discussed to encourage the reader to develop the proper attitude toward planning. Then a practical step-by-step approach is presented to assist readers in developing their own business plans. I believe strongly that the greatest benefits of planning accrue to those individuals who do it themselves. Even though they may not be very good at it initially, they will find that their skills develop as they proceed. If they are thoroughly involved in the planning process themselves, they are most apt to benefit from planning as one of their most important management decision-making tools. Accordingly, this book has a very real practitioner orientation. Throughout, I have tried to provide sufficient detail to enable readers to develop an actual plan for a fairly sophisticated business. The text is aimed somewhat above "mom and pop" users, yet somewhat below highly complex emerging technological applications. The real target of the text is the wide range of businesses that have the potential of developing into successful medium-size operations.

It is assumed that the reader has a basic understanding of financial management, the terminology and techniques involved in forecasting, breakeven and ratio analysis, pro forma income statements, balance sheets, and cash flow projections, although working explanations are given for each. It is also expected that the reader has a basic understanding of the general principles of business management. This book is not intended to be a management text, but instead focuses specifically on planning as the most critical function of management.

The planning process as described may seem complex and confusing in places, and the reader may feel the need for some outside assistance in actually performing various aspects of the planning process. This is not surprising and, in fact, is expected. The specific skills involved in business planning are not among those that most people use in any regular and systematic way. However, they can be developed and, once acquired, can certainly be used to advantage not only in business planning but in other situations as well. Business planning is, after all, only a specialized application of the more general planning process everyone must use in everyday life. To some extent, we all attempt to predict or forecast what it likely to occur in the future so that we will have a better idea of what to do when that future becomes reality. Planning is the means by which this may be accomplished.

The primary purpose of the text is to establish a methodology and framework for planning. The need for planning is universal to all businesses, as are the techniques necessary for successful accomplishment of the planning process. Given this universality, planners and practitioners in many different fields of business should find the concepts developed in this book useful in solving problems in their individual situations. In any kind of activity, it is necessary to bridge the gap between intention and action and to make sure that action is firmly grounded in reality. Properly applied, basic business planning will provide these critical linkages. In that sense, then, *planning is the key to business success.*

ACKNOWLEDGMENTS

The writing of this book has been, like its subject *planning,* an activity which developed over time. The result presented here is the product of in-depth analysis of literally thousands of plans for a wide variety of different ventures. My own ideas and observations have been shaped by others who are active in this field as writers or teachers in ways too numerous and sometimes too subtle to acknowledge more directly. Many bankers, students, teachers, and entrepreneurs have been extremely helpful by listening and reacting to my ideas, frequently forcing me to further clarify issues that I had mistakenly thought were making sense. This help has all been greatly appreciated.

More specifically, Professor William E. Wetzel, Jr., of the Whittemore School of Business and Economics at the University of New Hampshire was most generous with his advice in reviewing the sections on financial forecasting and financial management, although I retain responsibility for any errors that may remain. The value of the incredible contribution of time, energy, and patience of my friend and typist, Ann Scanlan, cannot be overemphasized. I am especially grateful to these two valued supporters. The thoughtful and constructive suggestions of Peter Reimold significantly improved the readability of the text. Finally, the sheer amount of time and energy that this project has represented would have been impossible without the support of my family. My sincere appreciation is extended to all.

William R. Osgood

Contents

Chapter 1:
Why Planning?

Planning is the secret ingredient in business success. Recognized by large corporations as a critical activity, planning is included as an integral component of their management systems. While less frequently used, planning is even more critical to smaller organizations, because they typically, almost by definition, lack the resources necessary to absorb the costs of mistakes, errors in judgment, or failure to anticipate change.

Probably the major reason inhibiting the wider use of planning by smaller businesses is the popularly held stereotype that planning is a mysterious and complex activity leading to dubious results of questionable value. However, this stereotype can be broken and should not keep smaller businesses from using this valuable management tool. Planning can be a direct, straightforward, methodical process. This book will show the purposes of planning and the techniques needed to develop useful and effective plans for any size or type of organization.

WHO WANTS TO PLAY "CHICKEN"?

Planning means anticipating what is likely to happen in the future and then determining what must be done in the present in order to take advantage of opportunities and avoid problems that the future may contain. This is done consciously or unconsciously by most individuals for most activities. It is an essential part of decision making that people automatically engage in for normal activities. However, when it comes to applying the same techniques to planning for a business, the individuals who need planning the most—those who start and run their own businesses—back away with a variety of excuses. There isn't time. It's too complicated. I don't know how. These excuses are all due to the fact that the principals really don't understand why they should plan.

Operating a business without planning is very much like playing "chicken" in an automobile—driving along without touching the wheel until the very last moment to avoid an imminent crash. This may be thrilling, but it carries with it a very high risk. One disadvantage of planning is that through risk reduction it also causes the loss of the excitement and the thrill of near-disaster avoidance. With planning, however, the business is far more likely to get where it should be going without an accident. Planning is deliberate avoidance of problems (and disasters).

The business plan is a tool, probably the most important one available to either a new or an existing business. A building contractor would never consider commencing construction of a highrise office building without a detailed set of architectural plans. Most would agree that it would be insane to do so. However, no such consensus exists concerning business development. Otherwise intelligent people plunge ahead into the construction of a new venture without a second thought or a clear idea of what they are doing. Unfortunately, these new creations usually collapse. They become another dreary statistic, another one of the 400,000 new businesses that fail every year.

SOME DANGERS

Planning is frequently seen as a complex process and one that requires great sophistication and skill. But the complexity and sophistication of the plan are more a function of the nature of the business itself than endemic to the planning. In fact, there is a real danger in overplanning, in making complex what is basically simple. Some people seem to be great planners but ineffectual doers. It is possible to plan into oblivion. This is known as "analysis paralysis."

Planning is critical to, but not sufficient for, business success. Doing a good job in planning is not a guarantee of anything, because the planning may be unrealistic. Planning cannot save someone who is a good planner but unrealistic in operational assumptions. To take an extreme example, there are people who have planned for the end of the world. Excellent as their plans may be, they're evidently based on an unrealistic assumption, for there hasn't been any delivery on the world's end yet. In order for business planning to be effective, then, it is essential not only to understand planning techniques, but to have implementation as an objective of planning and make sure that the process stays in tune with reality.

BUSINESS PLANNING AND FINANCING PROPOSALS

A thorough business plan will also contain the information that is required for a financing proposal. This is important to note, because most businesses require some form of outside financing and most lenders or investors require the same documentation and information that is assembled for the business plan. There is an important distinction between a business plan and a financing proposal, however, in that each has different objectives. The objectives of the business planning process are to determine the feasibility of a project and then to lay out a plan of action for its accomplishment. The objective of a financing proposal is, quite simply, to secure financing.

Within reason, it is generally easier to raise whatever amount of financing is required to accomplish the organization's goals and purposes identified in the business plan than to attempt to raise some arbitrarily predetermined amount of funding and then try to create a plan within the constraint represented by the financing so secured. Frequently, individuals preparing to start their own ventures or already in business and seeking to expand frame their development or growth expectations around the amount of capital they think they can raise. Generally, this represents the amount of capital they can collateralize, and it may have nothing to do with the reality of the business situation they are proposing to enter. If they focus instead on the amount of funding required (within reason, of course) to successfully launch the business that emerges from the sequential planning process, the chances of success for that venture are considerably enhanced, as are the chances of raising the required funds.

ESTABLISHING A FEASIBILITY ANALYSIS

Planning, as we noted, involves the anticipation of reality in the future. Clearly, because it is impossible to know what will occur in the future, this must involve a series of abstractions or assumptions, of estimates and predictions. As the venture progresses from a conceptual notion to actual commitment and assumptions are tested against reality and gradually replaced by facts, the plan must be updated. It is essential at the earliest planning stages to be precise and explicit about the nature of the assumptions being made, because it is through an evaluation of these assumptions that a feasibility determination of the business concept will be established. As the business develops, it continues to be important to be able to determine which assumptions are validated and which are not. If any assumptions are invalidated, then by definition the feasibility of the venture must be questioned. A feedback monitoring control loop must be included in the business development process to continually test these assumptions against reality. Feasibility, then, must be evaluated over time. The success of the operation depends to a great extent on a continuous reinforcement of the initial feasibility assessment.

Business planning and development are highly logical rational processes. This cannot be overstressed. Emotionalism, reactive firefighting, seat-of-the-pants decision making, and wheeling-and-dealing problem solving may be fun and exciting for certain types of individuals and may even result in business success. Luck is certainly a valuable component in business development, but success is more surely a function of risk reduction than of wistful hopes for good fortune. Basic business planning is a systematic methodology for reducing risk and enhancing success for any type of business operation.

MANAGEMENT SKILL AND INTEGRATED PLANNING

The single technique most useful in generating success for a new business is applying the general principles of good management. Many functions, including marketing, selling, production, accounting, finance, and personnel, must be balanced in forming and running a new organization. It is essential that the individuals starting a new business recognize from the very outset that as managers, their primary job is to synchronize all these different functions, to coordinate and integrate these different activities into a single coherent whole. In order to successfully accomplish this task, it is necessary to have a framework. The business planning process described in this book provides that framework. A business plan consists of a series of layers of decisions and conclusions, moving from the general to the specific, each decision preparing the way for the next. The final plan naturally emerges as the result of the successful completion of all the preceding steps.

Marketing planning heads the list of planning activities, because a market orientation is an essential predeterminant for the construction of all the other parts of the plan. A marketing orientation helps develop the focus for all aspects of the operation. It provides a means for the conceptualization of the business as a system designed to satisfy wants and needs rather than as an organization producing a product or providing a service.

Thinking in terms of the marketing implications of the organization's activities introduces considerable flexibility in planning for a product line or a family of services. A company founded on a single product with no follow-on products is doomed to a short life, usually due to product obsolescence through the deadly double forces of technological innovation and competition. Merely having a better product or a better technique for doing something does not ensure business success. The ability to perceive customers' needs, to apply technology or ingenuity to the fulfillment of these needs, and to distribute and sell the resulting products or services are the essential ingredients for business initiation, development, and success.

Once the business has been defined as a system satisfying wants and needs, an *operations plan* can be evolved which provides for the optimal provision of appropriate products or services. Since the operations plan follows out of conclusions reached through a marketing orientation, the business is less likely to be bound by the inherent limitations of physical facilities and equipment, and more apt to maintain the flexibility required to be responsive to target customer wants and needs. The traditional approach, which is inherently self-limiting, is to first design a production system, have it produce a product or service, and then look around for ways of getting rid of the product or the service.

The issue is one of focus and emphasis. With a production orientation the focus is on the creation of products or services that the firm feels most qualified or is most interested in producing. With a marketing orientation, on the other hand, the focus is on sales, with the firm producing or providing those goods or services that are most likely to be sold. Very simply, a firm that focuses on sales rather than production is more likely to survive as markets, technologies, and consumer preferences change.

Management has been defined as the process or working with and through individuals and groups to accomplish organizational goals. There are two important factors involved here: people and goals. It is critical that the new business have the right people and that these people have the right orientation. This is a process of organizational planning and involves identifying the right people through functional analysis; that is, management must look at jobs in terms of the functions that are required and then find individuals who have those functional skills. Providing those individuals with the proper orientation toward the organization's goals and objectives represents the motivational aspect of organizational planning and is discussed later within the context of management by exception and management by objectives.

In addition to the planning functions described, a business must have a basic strategy for the future, a long-term concept of what it is in business to do. This long-term concept is best developed within the framework of long-term or strategic planning. The strategic plan helps assure that all the necessary activities will occur in proper relationship to each other in terms of time as well as function and, as far as possible, relieves the risk inherent in most situations.

Planning of any type involves anticipating the future and then doing those things in the present that will permit the business to either take advantage of opportunities that may arise or avoid problems that almost certainly will occur. This concept of futurity represents the philosophy of planning in a nutshell. Futurity means trying to anticipate the consequences in the future of everything that is done in the present. The basic business plan can be seen as having two dimensions: short-term decisions—the specific activities that will occur within an immediate time period of typically one to three years—and the longer-term implications these short-term decisions will have on the business's ability to engage in other activities further into the future. Futurity is concerned with the determination of present activities as either constraints or facilitators of activities in the future.

BENEFITS OF PLANNING

Any business, regardless of its size, faces two problems. First, it has limited resources. For any operation there is a finite supply of money, time, and talent. Second, because the business typically has multiple objectives, it is very likely to experience serious difficulties in allocating its scarce resources to the variety of alternative purposes competing for their use. Matching a company's objectives with its resources is in itself a major task. Ensuring that the objectives are achieved is an even greater task. Proper completion of the business planning activity helps accomplish these tasks.

The planning process helps to maintain a balance between important issues and a sense of perspective relating one area of activity to another. There is always a danger that the management principals will become involved in a mass of detail and fail to recognize that certain aspects of the business operation are more critical than others. The business planning process will help to differentiate between various factors all of which may be competing for the attention of the decision makers and will be particularly helpful in determining which of these factors are most critical to the success of the total operation. The first step of the process, preparing a list of objectives, provides the basis for the establishment of the rest of the strategy framework, and lends a sense of both consistency and perspective to the rest of the planning and business development activities.

There is a need for coordination and communication in any business organization. A written business plan serves this communication function explicitly. When the operational assumptions and details have been made specific, others who interact with the business organization, subordinates, outside advisors, and financing agencies, for example, will find it much easier to coordinate their own activities with those of the business organization. Providing everyone associated with the organization with a clear understanding of the organization's goals and objectives and when and how the organization intends to accomplish its purposes will reduce ambiguity and confusion and greatly improve the opportunities for coordination.

The plan will provide guidelines for day-to-day decision making. It will be clear how specific activities relate to tasks which relate to goals. In addition, once goals, objectives, and the delegations of responsibility and authority have been made explicit, control benchmarks can be established and can be used as a basis for monitoring the progress of the business's development and activities. Goals become the targets or points of reference for measuring progress. When these guidelines are available, deviations can be quickly identified and evaluated and the causes for deviations, whether they are positive or negative, can be determined, thus revealing trouble or identifying opportunity. In these ways, planning will help to avoid problems and exploit opportunities.

SUMMARY

In summary, basic business planning provides a framework, a methodology, not a solution. Planning is a systematic process designed to enable the user to evaluate the feasibility of a contemplated business, to design a framework for its construction and implementation, to anticipate problems that may occur once the venture is under way, and to provide a feedback control system. Planning deals with what will occur in the future, what the business principals would like to have occur in the future, ways of analyzing the feasibility of these occurrences, and the development and establishment of a methodical plan for implementing action toward the achievement of objectives.

Planning cannot foretell the future, but it can systematically and rationally reduce uncertainty. However, there are some things that planning cannot do. Planning cannot make a basically bad deal good. Planning cannot be totally complete. It simply isn't feasible to have complete information about anything. At some point, planning must stop and action begin. Finally, planning must be in tune with reality. An unrealistic plan may be worse than no plan at all.

The business plan serves three important purposes. At the first level, it provides for a feasibility analysis, a full consideration of whether or not the business venture will work. Dry-running a venture on paper may reveal problems which had not been anticipated and which may indicate, before time and capital resources are committed, that the business is inherently infeasible. Second, the plan provides a developmental framework for the venture, both as it is started and as it passes through successive stages of development leading to maturity and eventual success. Third, the plan is a way of communicating both to those who will be involved in the various activities required to turn a plan into an operating reality and to the variety of outside consultants and supporters who may also be involved in the business development process, especially to potential outside funding sources. Basic business planning, in short, represents a fundamental approach for turning a good idea into an operating reality.

Planning is a key to business success. However, essential as it may be, it is not sufficient. Along with planning must go a sense of reality and action orientation.

Chapter 2:
Planning Defined

Dictionary definitions of planning include "a scheme of action or procedure," "a design or scheme of arrangement," and "a project or definite purpose." All these have to do with the aspect of planning as a means of scheduling activities or events. However, there is another dimension of planning that has far more critical implications for individuals and businesses alike, namely, the concept of futurity implicit in the notion of planning activities or events.

Planning involves the anticipation of events in the future. For most individuals, this activity of forecasting or predicting what is likely to occur in the future is a relatively simple process. The events that have occurred in the past are known; the environment is evaluated in terms of any anticipated changes; then, within these considerations, the past is projected into the future. All this can be done with a reasonable degree of certainty, because these projections are based on a great deal of personal experience—the happenings in the individuals' own lives in very narrow, limited areas.

Planning for businesses, especially new ventures, becomes infinitely more complicated. There is a much wider range of influences or factors that are relevant to or affect the activities of the business, both directly and indirectly. One way to conceptualize this problem is to envision the business as an open system and identify the series of exchanges it engages in with various other factors, influences, and organizations within its environment (see Figure 2-1). Then each set of influences or constraints can be indi-

Figure 2-1. Some of the environmental influences on the business.

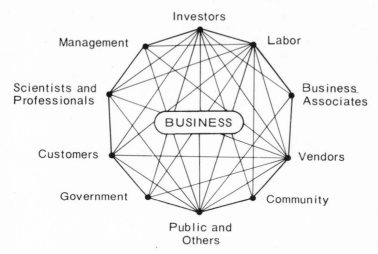

vidually considered to assess its possible impact on the business and its future activities.

The most simple definition of the business plan is that it indicates what the business plans to do, who will do it, when it will be done, and how much it will cost. It should be a record of thought and show the conclusions of the planning process itself.

The short-term implications of the planning process define specific immediate activities of various individuals associated with the new business. Intermediate and long-term planning provide the rational context for the short-term activities and look at the future implications of activities within the framework of organizational objectives. Such analysis may help to reveal, for example, that what appears to be a short-term opportunity for the business could have negative implications at some point in the future.

Developing a good plan, particularly in writing, helps ensure that a complete and integrated examination has been made of the product, market, manufacturing or service delivery process, physical facilities, product cost structure, and the abilities of management. The plan not only forces the clarification of goals and objectives but also provides the framework for establishing the optimal allocation and use of scarce resources available to the firm, especially the scarce resources of time and capital.

It is critical that a balance be established between the different activities of the organization. The planning framework, by forcing a conceptualization of the business as a model, provides the means for keeping the different functions or activities in proper perspective with each other. This in turn provides an opportunity to analyze the concepts and develop a working model of the business operation on paper before committing large sums to what could be a disaster.

REACTION AND PROACTION

There are two polarized approaches to business problem solving: reaction and proaction. Reaction needs very little discussion. The dictionary provides a variety of definitions for reaction, the most important being "action and response to some influence or event" and "the instantaneous response of a system to applied force." Reacting means responding to a situation. In effect, reaction is the victim of other forces; it is controlled or heavily influenced by other factors in a given situation. The vast majority of businesses are operated on a reaction basis. They respond, more or less passively, to changes in the environment.

Proaction, on the other hand, is reaction with a sense of futurity. It requires analyzing likely future occurrences and, on the basis of that analysis, deciding on the course of action in the present which is likely to have the most favorable consequences in the future. Proaction is the anticipation and avoidance of future problems. Proaction is the identification of opportunities in the future and the design of present activities in order to optimally exploit those opportunities when they arrive. Proaction is being in control of a situation rather than being controlled by it. In short, proaction is planning.

A PLANNING ATTITUDE

A critical aspect of planning is the attitude with which individuals approach the process. A positive planning orientation is essential to the development of an objective, rational plan—and any other type of plan is worse than no plan at all. A plan that is based on wistful figments of someone's imagination is likely to result in fallacious conclusions while lending support to the belief of its followers that they know what they are doing. Creating a plan that avoids such problems requires a systematic methodology. Clear objectives are necessary prerequisites to rational activity, and they must be made explicit so that everyone can understand what must be done in order to accomplish them.

Many businesses determine their objectives, purposes, or targets at least in a general way before they commence operations. However, all too frequently, these objectives are merely vague ideas in the minds of the business principals, such as "increasing profits" or "reducing costs." These objectives must be made much more explicit so that others involved in the operation can share in the understanding and accomplishment of them. Formalized, these objectives become the starting point for the development of policy, for planning and developing operating procedures designed to build profits. This important aspect of planning is goal setting, or making explicit where the business is headed. The more specific these objectives may be made, the more useful they are likely to be and the more action-implicit the follow-on planning can become.

Planning specialists have suggested a large number of specific categories where objectives must be developed. These would include market standing, innovation, productivity, physical and financial resources, profitability, manager performance and development, worker performance and attitude, and public responsibility. Variations on these categories can be equally useful. The point is, whatever categories are used, they must be relevant to the general purposes of the organization and the underlying goals and objectives of the owners.

PLANNING INTELLIGENCE

Intelligence is another requirement for effective planning. Intelligence as used here has two significant definitions. The usual definition is certainly a prerequisite: the capacity for reasoning, for understanding, and similar forms of mental activity; aptitude in grasping truths, facts, meaning. The other equally important definition here is, knowledge, information, the gathering or distribution of information, especially secret information about an enemy or a potential enemy (competition); conclusions drawn from such information; the interchange of information. As described in the dictionary, intelligence means acquiring information and having the ability to use that information for decision making, understanding the environment in which the organization will operate, understanding the multidimensional forces that operate within that environment and that influence the behavior within the organization. These forces impose constraints. They may represent parameters that the organization cannot do anything about. Some of the dimensions of that information would involve the technology, the industry's structure, the position of the firm relative to that structure, products, the competitors themselves, the rate of change within the environment, the rate of development, the shifting of markets, the socio-political forces, and the various other internal and external variables that exercise influence upon the organization.

Planners must be tuned to these many different dimensions of information. The ability to acquire this information, process it, and utilize it in the planning effort will be a critical determinant in the quality of that planning. There are a wide variety of sources of this type of information. Some is acquired by simply surviving, listening to news broadcasts and reading newspapers. Talking to others is another important way that this information is acquired. There are libraries and government agencies, trade journals and various other such publications, conventions, meetings, professionals—the list could go on and on. The business can conduct its own research and gather primary data, go out into the marketplace, talk with potential customers, and survey the competition directly. It is important for the business principals to identify the different sources of information that are relevant for their particular kind of operation and then systematically exploit them. Time spent in such research is frequently begrudged by people who are anxiously pursuing development of the business itself. Begrudged though it may be, it is time well spent because it may result in developing understandings that are critical to the organization and have a dramatic influence on its future success.

THE SYSTEMS APPROACH

The concept of systems analysis is very helpful in understanding the position of the business organization in its environment. Looking at the organization as a series of interrelated, interdependent component parts, and looking at the environment as containing still another series of parts or influences, it becomes possible to inspect the operations of the subsystems and, on the basis of these subordinate analyses, better understand the functioning of the complex system in its environment. The better understanding comes primarily through the simplicity of considering only a limited number of effects at any one time, but always with the understanding that each is part of a much more complex situation.

Using the systems approach to planning means designing a system of plans which fit together and complement each other, yet each of which is specifically oriented to the subset of problems that it is designed to deal with. The key that facilitates the integration of these subsystems is the existence of common or shared goals, or goal congruence. This need for such shared goals gets lost in many organizations. They wind up with a multiplicity of subgoals that are not coordinated within a set of shared objectives, and so the potential power of the organization is dissipated by different parts of the organization going off in their own directions.

Along with the required goal congruence goes a need to examine the variety of factors that are direct or indirect influences on the goal-setting process. The decision makers are one set of influences. The owners of the organization may be different from the decision makers; they may be stockholders or investors, and they may have different ideas and goals from those of the decision makers. The environment itself—the economy, the competition, and a variety of other exogenous factors—introduce additional objectives and constraints that further influence decision making and may even inhibit the potential success of the organization.

It is essential to maintain a strong sense of objectivity in assessing these different sets of influences. New businesses, and even many existing businesses, may experience two important problems that limit or compromise their objectivity: (1) the enthusiasm of the business principals may cause them to play down potential problems and hazards, and (2) their ignorance may cause them similarly to overlook or underestimate factors that in reality may be extremely important influences on the business's operations. There is no real cure for these limitations other than maintaining an awareness of their existence.

Finally, the systems approach involves an interrelated, interactive system of plans. For example, strategic planning interacts with operational planning, with the former calling for conceptualizing at an abstract level the generalized activities of the organization and the latter simultaneously developing the specific steps and procedures that facilitate the implementation of the plan. There are a multitude of different types of planning that will be discussed throughout this text, such as strategic planning, long-range planning, profit planning, and contingency planning, to name a few. Each of these, it must be kept in mind, represents a subsystem of the total business planning system.

FEASIBILITY ANALYSIS

Planning is a process of setting goals and targets. It also provides an opportunity for a feasibility analysis—developing a model of the business on paper and identifying potential funding requirements. The development of goals and targets lends direction to the organization. It establishes a point to head for and serves to reduce ambiguity and confusion. Goals lead to objectives, which lead to policies, which in turn lead to activities within the organization.

Feasibility analysis is very simply the process of determining whether or not the business idea makes good sense. If it does not, then there's no reason to pursue it any further. If it does seem feasible, it is important to identify the particular factors or assumptions that contribute to this assessment of feasibility. Identifying exactly why the idea is being deemed feasible provides the capability of quickly identifying deviations from these assumptions which may be encountered during the development process. A thorough feasibility analysis will also provide a great deal of the information needed for the business plan itself. For example, a thorough assessment of the market potential is required in order to determine the project's feasibility. This provides the major substance for the marketing section and becomes part of the business plan.

The process of developing a model of the business operation on paper provides an opportunity for experimenting with organizational relationships and for assessing various cost alternatives. This activity is much like planning the furniture layout for a room on a piece of graph paper before the items are purchased. If something doesn't fit, it's much better to find out on paper before the effort is made to try to squeeze the pieces of furniture into the room itself.

This modeling process provides the principals with the opportunity of confronting the problems in more detail than they may have been able to envision up to this point. Here they must become specific. They must identify exactly who is going to do what. Gaps, overlaps, redundancies, and weaknesses will become evident. All these must be identified before the business is started, because they represent potential hazards to the business operation. If they cannot be satisfactorily resolved before the fact, they become additional evidence of inherent infeasibility.

Planning for the financial requirements of a new business is generally an area that individuals are quick to identify as a need. Frequently, the creation of the business plan is seen as the way of securing financing, of fulfilling the requirements of some banker or venture capital investor. In fact, the implications of the process are more important for the business principals than they are for anyone else. The determination of the required funding may in itself identify a feasibility constraint on the further development of the whole business. The projection of the capital requirements and the summation of the negative cash flows will quickly identify the actual amounts of funding that will be required to launch and stabilize the venture. An analysis of these required investments will often indicate areas where the organization may be able to spend less. For example, it may be possible to lease certain equipment rather than buy it.

It is also important to recognize the potential negative implications of the situation and establish a contingency, or worst-case, plan that shows potential additional working capital requirements. It is essential to look at the full range of capital that may be required, particularly the additional investments that may be necessary if everything doesn't fulfill the possibly optimistic assessment initially made of the business's potential.

Finally, the critical component of feasibility analysis is honesty. It is simply crazy for the individuals involved in developing a venture to go ahead when the signs indicate that it won't work. It is very simple: if the deal won't work, don't do it. There is no nice way of becoming untangled from a business bankruptcy.

GOAL SETTING

Goal setting involves the identification of objectives or targets for the business. These targets are essential in creating a focus for the organization's activities and in measuring the quality of these activities. Once the plan is established, it becomes a benchmark for performance.

Goals or targets must be framed as specifically and objectively as possible. Typical financial targets include net profits, return on capital, return on equity, earnings per share, and price-to-earnings ratio. Other objectives may be related to new market development, market penetration, new product development, or an almost unlimited number of other alternatives.

Goals or targets influence behavior. As the business develops goals, it is important to recognize the possible implications that these targets have for the activities within the organization. For example, if a measure of profitability is employed, it tends to encourage behavior that leads to short-term profits. One way to maximize short-term profits might be to run machinery well beyond its normal servicing patterns. This would reduce the amount of downtime for servicing and the actual costs of servicing, whatever they may be. In the short run, this means that the machinery would be that much more productive. In the longer run, however, it is likely that the machinery will be worn out more quickly and will have to be replaced sooner than it would if it had been properly maintained.

It can be seen, then, that targets need to have a built-in procedure for examining some of their longer-term implications. As the planning horizon is extended into the future, it is quite possible that some of the short-term profit trade-offs are actually necessary for longer-term profits in the future.

Another way the firm can approach the goal- or target-setting process is through the use of performance risk curves. A performance risk curve indicates the potential return for different strategies based on the inherent risk of the strategy. If the world were organized so that events fitted into neat geometric patterns, performance risk curves would be relatively parallel and it would be very easy to see how increases in performance or profitability could be tied directly to risk. In the reality of the imperfect world, however, it is very likely that there is not an arithmetic correlation between risk and performance; instead, there may be a geometric or even an inverse geometric correlation such that performance would tend to fall off or increases in performance might degrade relative to risk. Assuming a valid risk function could be defined, it would be possible then to pick off an optimum point along such a risk performance curve, which becomes a reasonable target for the organization. Different organizations would have different attitudes toward risk, and these different attitudes toward risk influence their desired optimum position along their performance risk curve.

Another approach to goal setting is through a consideration of ethological targets, or the sociological, behavioral, and cultural implications of the business operation. It may be relevant for the organization to have ethological objectives, such as being a good corporate citizen or paying a fair wage or a variety of other similarly subjective desires. However, the subjectivity of such goals may carry an inherent and serious disadvantage in that the measurement of accomplishment of these subjective purposes must somehow be made explicit. These ethological goals may reflect concerns of the stockholders, employees, management, customers, suppliers, or society in general. They may be hard or soft (objective or subjective), and it may be possible to construct a hierarchy of such targets.

It is usually felt that hard objectives are much better than soft objectives, but this is not necessarily true. Hard objectives suggest a great deal more accuracy in terms of their identification and the measurement of their achievement. The accuracy is frequently erroneously imputed. The quantification of almost anything leads it to have more credibility than it might have if it were identified in less objective ways.

The important point to recognize is that we are dealing with information, and information should be presented in the form that it is most useful in. There are ways of handling subjective goals that will make them as useful as objective targets. Subjective goals can become very useful determinants of behavior through a system of management by objectives, for example. Management by objectives requires a consensus on appropriate organizational behavior and goal congruence throughout the organization. These are negotiated agreements between different levels within the organization and represent an opportunity for clear understanding, whether the targets are hard or soft. MBO is further discussed as a meaningful management strategy in Chapter 9.

There may be a range of strategies or different types of strategies that are important to the organization. If that is the case, they can be organized within a priority hierarchy such that they will receive the proper emphasis by different individuals within the organization. The real concern here is to define explicitly the organizational goals. This requirement for specificity will be repeated throughout, because it is essential for effective planning. It is critical to the organization, in terms of furthering its planning activities and communicating its objectives, both internally and externally, to identify its concerns in each of the areas of relevance, and to make these goals explicit as an integral part of the planning process.

THE PLANNING FRAMEWORK

The planning activity is a process and as such can be described as a series of steps:

1. Establish objectives.
2. Develop basic assumptions or premises.
3. Identify alternative courses of action.
4. Evaluate alternative courses of action.
5. Implement the plan.

The foregoing discussion has focused on the development of meaningful objectives for the organization. These objectives should clearly indicate the area of business that will be pursued, the general purposes of the organization, the competitive posture that the business will observe, various goals in terms of market share, plans for new product development, and the future implications of such activities as market segmentation. Critical here are the basic objectives of the managing principals and the relationship between these objectives and other sets of influences in the business's environment, such as competition, technological change, suppliers, customers, and financing agencies. Any other internal or external variables that may represent constraints on the business operation must be explicitly understood. To be fully useful, objectives must be both specific and realistic. Specificity helps to relieve potential ambiguity and confusion. Realism helps to avoid frustration that can come about through adopting unachievable goals and foolish or unrealistic plans.

The basic assumptions or premises being established as the foundation for the planning activity should deal with the variety of conditions—noncontrollable, semicontrollable, and controllable—that may confront the business operation. Noncontrollable conditions include such external factors as business cycles, competitive price levels, population shifts, changes in growth, and any other factors that affect the firm but are essentially fixed as far as the firm is concerned. These external variables are also known as exogenous factors. Semicontrollable conditions represent those events that the firm cannot control but can influence to some degree, such as market share, internal pricing policy, employee productivity, and relative position within the business community. Controllable conditions generally center around those endogenous variables or policy matters that the firm's management can decide largely for itself, such as whether to expand into new markets, selecting a new site for the firm's location, or a major change in product line or pricing strategy. These sets of premises must be realistically constrained or limited to those factors most likely to influence the operation or to affect the achievement of objectives, positively or negatively. It is essential to be completely explicit about the assumptions that underlie the analysis process.

There are usually a number of alternatives available for the accomplishment of any given objective. Frequently, after careful thought and assessment, an alternative that was not immediately obvious may well prove to be the most desirable. It is important to consider all alternatives, because, even though they may at first appear to be foolish or inappropriate, they may lead to the consideration of still others or, after evaluation, prove to be a lot less foolish and a lot more feasible than they seemed to be on the surface. At the same time, the immediate, obviously "best" alternative may, after evaluation, prove to be less desirable than originally anticipated or may even turn out to be infeasible.

Once the various alternatives have been identified, they can be evaluated. The form of the evaluation itself is very likely to include a number of dimensions in order to allow management to fully assess the impact of any given alternative. Some alternatives may prove to be more profitable but too risky, and others may be less risky but incompatible with the firm's major goals. Some alternatives may require additional capital or personnel, which simply may not be available. Still others may turn out to be technologically deficient or may require production or service delivery strategies that are unrealistic. Some alternatives may require additional information before they can be fully evaluated. In some cases it may be necessary to hire an outside consultant or specialist to provide the facts or generally assist with the assessment.

It should be recognized that the variety of assumptions that are made are gradually replaced by facts as activities proceed. Initially, the planning framework will consist almost entirely of assumptions. As the plan becomes an operating reality, it will be based more and more on facts. As the assumptions are replaced by facts, it is critical to continually evaluate the alternative courses of action, especially along those dimensions where the facts have proven to be different from the assumptions that preceded them.

Although planning is essential, at some point the abstract process of modeling must stop and the activity begin. The management principals cannot postpone taking action indefinitely merely because uncertainties and unknowns continue to exist. However, the assumptions or the unknown areas that still remain, especially those that will have a critical impact on the potential success or failure of any of the planning and action, must be made explicit so that if reality deviates from the assumptions, the new information can immediately be introduced into the planning system in order to determine if the alternative that has been put into place remains feasible. Wherever it is possible, it is wise to form both a primary decision and an alternative decision to be used if something changes in the primary plan.

The preceding discussion, which concentrated on the essential steps involved in planning, should not be taken to imply that planning is a strictly sequential process. Planning develops through a series of cycles or iterations that become progressively more specific and more in line with reality as the objectives of the organization become better understood and the reality of the environment becomes better defined. It includes an essential feedback loop that permits the constant testing of the assumptions being used against the reality of the operating environment. The planning system must be kept flexible in order to respond to changes in the operating environment by making appropriate changes within the management planning system.

Careful monitoring of the plan as it develops will keep it in tune with reality and help ensure the optimization of the new firm's objectives. The exact sequence to be followed and depth of analysis used will depend on the nature of the problem, the long-range goals of the organization, the sophistication of the management principals, and the amount of help available to them. Frequently, the success of the plan is a direct function of both the quality of the planning activities and the degree of importance with which they are regarded by the management principals themselves.

TYPES OF PLANNING

Different types of planning frequently referred to include market planning, production planning, sales planning, personnel planning, distribution planning, and product planning. These are all forms of functional planning and are components of the business plan itself. Market planning is the keystone or basis for the other aspects of functional planning and therefore is discussed in some detail in this chapter. Other major categories of planning include financial planning, contingency planning, and long-range or strategic planning. Consistent with the systems approach discussed, each of these different types of planning are subsets of the total plan and must be coordinated within the total framework to ensure compatibility or mutual reinforcement.

Market Planning

Enthusiasm for the new venture is not only wonderful, but a powerful asset for the business as well. Without enthusiasm, the prospect for success is severely limited. However, while enthusiasm is essential, it is not by itself sufficient. To be successful, every business requires a market; there must be a demand for the product or service. The demand must exist, or it must be possible to stimulate it; otherwise, the business is doomed to failure.

One purpose of market research is to provide facts about a potential market which then can become input into the decision-making process and the feasibility analysis. These data will also provide the basis for legitimizing income forecasts or projections. The better the information that can be gathered about the quality of the market, the better the decision making can be. Market research does not guarantee success, but it does provide the basis for rational decision making. It enables the business principals to consider and examine the various factors that will be important when the new business actively begins to sell its products or provide its services.

In order to develop an appropriate marketing system for the new business, an understanding of the nature, size, and other characteristics of the potential target market must be developed. The basic understanding is related to the marketing concept, which has already been discussed. The marketing concept suggests that businesses, to be successful, will design their operations to serve customers' needs. However, in order to do this, certain information must be gathered. It is necessary to identify precisely who the customers will be, where they are located, who among them will be large users, how they will buy the product, and whether there are differences between users and buyers. It is necessary to know the total size of the market in order to predict how many units may be sold over time. It is also important to be able to determine whether the total market is growing or shrinking, and if so, at which rate.

Pricing decisions represent another set of strategic considerations. These must be balanced against the competition's products and prices and the price sensitivity of potential customers. Price testing may be a helpful technique that can be used to establish a demand curve. Distribution systems must be developed and can, at least in part, be based on an understanding of how other firms distribute similar products. In developing distribution systems, the number and type of channel members must be established, with the recognition that each of those channel members needs a slice of the final price. The nature of the competition must be considered, both so that its impact can be assessed and so that ways of minimizing the impact can be considered. Finally, once all these decisions are made, the messages about the products or services must be communicated to the potential customers. Generally, advertising is used for this purpose. Decisions must be made concerning the nature, type, and cost of the advertising and the appropriateness of the messages and media selected for the target market.

The careful collection and analysis of the market data—including purchasing habits of the market customers, projected uses and understanding of the environment the product will be used within, and the sources and channels through which the product will be purchased—will give the business principals some practical understanding of the problems they will need to solve, or the opportunities they can respond to, in establishing their new operation. A careful analysis of the path the product will take as it moves from production into the hands of the ultimate users is a helpful way to make sure that potential problem areas have been identified and provided against. Discussions with other channel members may provide additional insights into potential problems. The development of the market strategy begins to form the framework of a model of the sales activity through which gaps, omissions, or redundancies can be identified.

Market research provides the basis for market strategy. Even though the two topics are treated in the business plan itself as separate subjects, they are interdependent. The evolution of market strategy identifies the needs for market research. Market research, on the other hand, provides the basis for the development of the market strategy. Once the target market segment has been identified, it can be evaluated in terms of its present size, present behavioral characteristics especially relative to the product or service contemplated, and the potential annual sales that each segment represents. Alternatives for marketing and field servicing must be considered, and estimates of potential market share especially relative to the impact of competing products must be included.

Market research involves a series of activities aimed at gathering high-quality market data. It may include literature search, field research, and applied market testing. Sometimes market information can be purchased from one of several excellent organizations engaged in market research. Alternatively, the business principals may engage in a proprietary research project.

The disadvantage of primary research activities is that they can be very time-consuming and may require specialized skills the business principals do not have at their disposal. At the same time, there are many primary research projects that can be defined within a manageable scope and handled with the limited resources available to many developing organizations.

Undergraduate and graduate business school students are one excellent source of labor for this type of primary research. It is frequently possible to get an entire marketing class involved in developing a questionnaire or a test marketing project and to use all the class members as the manpower for putting the field research project into operation. The reward for the students, which is generally quite sufficient, is an opportunity for testing their classroom theory in the real world.

An essential component of marketing that is frequently ignored is a consideration of the distribution system that will be required in order to get the product or service from where it is to where it is needed. This involves an analysis of the marketing or distribution channels available for or needed for the product. The distinction is made between available and needed because even though distribution channels are required, they may not exist. To deal with this gap, many new businesses blithely assume that they will develop their own field sales force. However, to do so generally requires a substantial investment in both time and money. A much more reasonable alternative could be the use of sales or manufacturers' representatives or even developing a cooperative arrangement with some other marketer of an existing but complementary product line. Manufacturers' sales organizations already in existence and selling related products frequently represent the least-cost method of developing initial sales for new products.

No matter what system is selected, the channel costs that will be involved must be carefully considered and incorporated into the cost feasibility analyses. If an incentive program of commission rates is provided, the contribution margin will be reduced accordingly, and the breakeven will rise. Along with distribution issues must be considered the need to provide field servicing support as well. Service and warranty policies may be valuable or even essential in order to induce potential customers to try a new product or service, especially if the offering is from a brand-new company. In any event, the field service required may be provided by the new business's own field staff or by contract with a national service organization. Here, the same decision making involved in choosing between the internal field staff and an external marketing organization may well apply. Initially, establishing a large maintenance support force may simply be infeasible until the business has had an opportunity to develop a market base. Thus contracting initial servicing to outside agencies, although perhaps not the most cost-effective method available, may in fact be the only method possible.

The market share analysis provides the basis for the company's forecasts. Of critical concern here is an identification of the percent of the total market that the company can reasonably secure and the backup data and other information which will support those assumptions.

The sales and market forecasts must be closely integrated under the umbrella of marketing strategy, each influencing the other. The production capacity of the new organization will represent a limit on the total product that will be available for sale. The capacity of the sales force, on the other hand, will represent a limit on the total sales as well. For example, except for entirely new products, figures exist showing the average annual sales per salesman in a wide variety of industries. These figures can provide very useful guides for a new organization. Even though innovative marketing programs may dramatically increase salesmen's productivity, predictions of such improvements are frequently based more on optimism than reality. It is much more reasonable to expect that the performance of the field sales force will be consistent with national averages or even considerably lower as the organization and its new sales force are just getting started.

Finally, a realistic assessment of the competition must be made, both of the different companies involved and of their products. A technique that facilitates comparison is the utilization of a matrix focusing on critical features such as price performance specifications and showing the advantages of competitive products relative to various combinations of products. Comparing the company's proposed products against this matrix can quickly and visually indicate how it stacks up relative to the competition. A brief paragraph on the strengths and weaknesses of each competing company will round out the analysis. Specificity is critical. Assumptions supporting the quantitative information must be included. The sources of any data used must be provided. A range of critical decisions will be made based on the information provided in the market analysis and strategy, so it is especially important that all the data and the information included in this section are as accurate and well reported as possible.

Financial Planning

Financial planning, as implied by the name, is concerned with the profitability of the operation and with the flows of cash, both expenditures and receipts, within the operation. Included under financial planning are capital budgeting, profit planning, and liquidity planning. Capital budgeting refers to the investments in plant and equipment needed by the business to provide the base for operations. Capital expenditures are typically made at the commencement of the business and may be required at additional major periods of growth. These capital assets represent the relatively long-term obligation of funds. In other words, once spent for capital purposes, funds are not easily available for other purposes.

Advanced and sophisticated analytic techniques can be applied to the capital budgeting process as a way of evaluating alternatives in terms of costs versus benefits. For many businesses this alternative analysis may not be particularly relevant, because they will simply require a fixed level of capital investment in order to do business at all. And, on the other side, another important constraint on the investment decision may be the availability and/or cost of funds. Some alternatives, while highly desirable, may simply not be available due to such limitations. Many times smaller and even some larger firms proceed in their decision making without any consideration of potential availability and/or cost of funds. Many times other alternatives may be available to the firm, such as leasing or jobbing, which, though not necessarily the most cost-efficient, may well represent the most viable or available alternative.

This last thought deserves considerable emphasis. Many smaller firms unilaterally reject the notion of leasing, feeling that it is simply too expensive. However, it may represent a highly feasible alternative to capital investment, particularly if the limited capital funds could be employed more productively elsewhere in the business operation. Leasing may introduce a high degree of flexibility, because, as the business grows, the leased equipment may be exchanged or replaced without the dramatic loss in value that could accompany the replacement of similar equipment which the venture itself owns.

The second two categories of financial planning—profit planning and liquidity planning—are critical concerns for any business and are especially important to a new small business. Profit planning is based on the marketing concept, an important part of which suggests that the legitimate goal of the firm is maximization of profits rather than of sales. This means that the business must assess the various opportunities available to it in terms of the net contribution each activity provides to the organization, rather than the aggregate sales that may be available through the process. Decisions made in these areas must be compatible with the overall objectives of the organization.

Liquidity planning is also known as cash flow planning, cash flow forecasting, or cash flow analysis. The objective, very simply, is to make sure that the new business does not run out of cash. It is a real and all too common tragedy to see new businesses beginning to develop and showing sharp increases in sales at a profitable level, and still getting into a financial jam—a liquidity crisis.

This can occur for a variety of reasons. If sales are being made on credit, the problem may well be accounts receivable. If the product is being manufactured for inventory prior to shipment, cash may be tied up in inventory. If the new business is on a cash basis with suppliers and a cash basis with customers, there is still an interval between the time that the product is purchased, manufactured, and distributed—the so-called production time lags.

Consider a service business that pays its workers on a weekly basis and bills its customers on a net 30 basis and discovers that actually the average age of receivables is 60 days. This means that for every new contract the business starts, it must be prepared to absorb eight weeks worth of labor. The dimensions of this problem quickly become geometric, and cash may seem to evaporate within the business even though the sales are showing high levels of profitability.

There are solutions for this potential problem. It may be necessary for the business to repress growth during this period because, to the extent that growth must absorb cash, that cash must come from somewhere, either internally generated by the operations of the business or provided from some outside sources. If the cash is being provided from outside sources, it must be on an intermediate- or long-term basis because the business, by definition, will not have the short-run capability of repaying short-term notes.

Contingency Planning

A planning activity that is frequently ignored by all types of businesses is contingency, or worst-case, planning. The planners, usually the business principals themselves, develop plans based on certain arbitrarily established sets of assumptions. These assumptions, no matter how thoroughly analyzed and carefully considered, may still be wrong. Some important questions may still need to be considered, especially concerning what might happen to the venture if reality does not coincide with all the projections. Contingency planning looks at another set of assumptions that are far less favorable and optimistic than those supporting the development of the plan in general. Realism must be emphasized. Not only should the plan be realistic, but the business developers should make plans using more conservative projections. Prospective investors often ask to see pessimistic projections to see whether the venture remains viable even under somewhat adverse conditions.

The enthusiasm and optimism of the developers themselves frequently distort estimates or projections in favor of the company. However, in reality, everything always seems to take longer to develop than planned. Events seldom come out better than projected; they almost always come out worse. Therefore, any new business should prepare a worst-case plan showing what will happen if the market and the economy hold up but its own business efforts do not come to fruition as rapidly as anticipated. Unforeseen internal contingencies may arise which inhibit the rate of development of the business in spite of the most careful planning, anticipation, and control procedures. It is appalling to see new businesses become the victims of a multitude of tiny glitches that individually may not be very significant but in the aggregate result in a depressed rate of growth for the developing business.

Along with optimistic projections, another very real and very frequent problem is that the principals assume that everyone they come in contact with will share their enthusiasm and dedication to making the new business operational. This is simply not true. Subordinates, bankers, bureaucrats, suppliers, and even customers really do not have any special reason to be committed to the development of the new business and therefore do not have the motivation to invest any extraordinary efforts in dealing with the new organization.

An interesting example of unrealistic assumptions emerges from the planning process of the Battleworks Furniture Company, the sample business plan included in this text. The principal of Battleworks is a big person physically. In his production planning, he carefully considered the process of manufacturing the furniture, the necessary steps in the process, and the amount of labor that would be required to perform each step. He used himself as a test model and figured out what his labor needs would be through each of the production processes. He was appalled to discover, when he actually commenced operations, that the people he hired were not as big as he was and, therefore, that it took more of them to maneuver the large sheets of plywood used in the manufacturing process. His labor costs were 50 percent higher than planned because of this simple difference in handling capability between himself and his employees.

It is often wise to include in the worst-case plan assumptions that not only will the company not grow as fast as the original schedule projects, but the market, the economy, and other exogenous variables will be worse than anticipated. Simply because trends in the past have shown steady growth in various areas does not mean that this growth rate will continue. It is important that the business principals have a realistic assessment of the potential behavior of both their market and the economy and can assess the implications for their business of a downturn in either or both. It is also necessary to consider the introduction of new competition. The same factors that attracted the new business operation to a particular market area may also be attractive to others. Additional potential hazards to the new business are technological or social change—that is, a new product may come along that makes the firm's product obsolete, or changing social patterns and attitudes may cause the rejection of some previously desired product.

These worst-case plans should provide an opportunity for the business principals to make a realistic assessment of the full range of potential hazards that face their business and the economy. In many cases, this assessment process may help them see risks that they had not seen before. In some cases, it may cause them to decide not to take these risks, and so they never launch the newly planned business. Disappointing though such conclusions may be, it is far better to find out these facts before starting a new business than to discover, after capital and other resources have actually been committed to the initiation and development process, that the new operation will not work.

In summary, contingency planning is concerned with developing an alternative strategy that can be used if the first or primary strategy doesn't work or if certain not strongly anticipated negative circumstances occur. There is an important rationale for this kind of planning. Why bother to preserve a venture that is doomed to failure? And once it is started, why jeopardize the venture by sitting back and getting stopped by surprises that could have been avoided? In short, contingency planning provides another good opportunity to apply proaction.

Long-Range or Strategic Planning

Long-range planning has been gaining increasing recognition by business planners for all types and sizes of businesses, primarily due to the need for these businesses to attempt to cope with change. Previously, effective long-range planning for a business meant that it would basically continue doing what it was doing today. This is no longer an adequate strategy, because business environments are dynamic. Even very successful businesses, if they are to remain that way, must stay tuned to environmental changes and change their operations accordingly.

Long-range planning is merely an arbitrary designation along the linear planning continuum which proceeds from this moment onward into the far distant future. Generally, short-range planning is concerned with future periods of up to three or four years, whereas long-range planning involves a period of time 5 to 20 years into the future. As the business planning effort moves further into the future, the goals and objectives become more generalized. However, they must still be identified, because they provide a focus, even though more distant and less specific, for the system of plans that represents the total business plan.

Strategic planning represents the umbrella for the entire planning effort. The strategic plan, as the name suggests, represents a plan of the business's basic strategy. It requires a clear concept of the business, generally framed within the definition of the marketing concept discussed previously. Strategic planning is the process of making choices between alternatives that are available to any business and that are mutually exclusive. It involves the allocation of scarce resources and the strategic coordination of resources once utilized. By definition, there will never be enough of these scarce resources to satisfy all aspects of the business, and so they must be carefully distributed or allocated in order to achieve the maximum total benefit for the organization.

The strategic or long-range plan represents the grand strategy for the business. It is the integrated summary of the variety of substrategies that have been developed, recognizing the system linkages, the interrelationships, and interdependencies between these substrategies. It is a multilevel planning effort in that the strategies must be integrated not only laterally but also vertically. Strategic planning is composed of three important aspects:

1. Determination of basic long-term goals and objectives for the business.
2. The adoption of courses of action oriented toward the achievement of these goals.
3. The allocation of scarce resources necessary for the implementation of the desired courses of action.

Another characteristic of strategic planning efforts is recognition of the importance of clearly identifying the assumptions and premises that must be agreed upon and established as a planning basis for all parts of the company. Agreement is essential here, because the subordinate groups within the organization must accept these goals as valid objectives, or the organization may well become the victim of dysfunctional goal incongruence. The explicit recognition and acceptance of superordinate goals by subordinate groups within the organization represents organizational commitment and fosters subordinate ownership and participation in the goal-setting process. In this manner, activities directed toward the achievement of subordinate goals will simultaneously be oriented or directed to the achievement of the superordinate goals.

SUMMARY

Together, and used sensibly, the planning techniques discussed in this chapter can be valuable tools for business practitioners. The real limitations on any planning techniques that must be clearly recognized are the quality of information available and the imagination and creativity of the practitioners involved. These techniques are simply tools. They do not provide any answers. They can, however, help organize ideas and information in a systematic, logical manner and, in this way, perform a valuable risk-reducing function.

The essence of marketing planning, contingency planning, and long-range planning or strategic planning is thinking systematically about the future and making current decisions on that basis. The secret is not just looking ahead, but looking ahead in a methodical and conscious fashion.

Chapter 3:
A Basic Business Planning Framework

Just as the earlier discussions have dealt with the need for a distinction between abstractions and reality, so the discussion will now turn from the theoretical concepts of planning to their application as a specific framework for the creation of a sensible development strategy for a specific business venture. Throughout the planning process and, indeed, throughout the following discussion, it is very important to keep the objectives of the process in mind. The purposes of the plan are, first, to determine the feasibility of the whole project by testing the concepts against reality in application; second, to provide a plan for the series of activities required to turn that concept into a viable ongoing operation; and third, to communicate the purposes and the activities to others, both within and outside the organization, who may have a need to know what is proposed and how it is to be accomplished.

Whether it is a new venture or the renovation or expansion of an existing operation that is being planned, it is essential to make the goals or expectations of the new project quite explicit. Many times good ideas fail because the objectives have not been properly identified. Investments of time, energy, and funds are thus wasted due to general confusion and lack of focus. A definite schedule must be followed in developing the concept from the idea stage to an operating reality. This is important in that it helps ensure that all possible problem areas are considered, avoided where possible, and provided against where they cannot be avoided.

The purpose of all this is to assure to the greatest extent possible that the business idea is practical and has a good chance of success. That is why this whole part is entitled "Practical Planning." Practicality, good judgment, and common sense are the key requirements for effective business planning.

A STAGED APPROACH TO BUSINESS PLANNING

Business planning is an evolutionary activity. Effective plans are not written at one sitting; they are created over time as a series of ideas is developed. Each part of the plan leads into the next; each influences the other; all the parts are interdependent. As the planning process is pursued, and more is understood about the reality of the actual environment, the original gross assumptions are gradually replaced. As the original ideas in their general form become more refined and more specific, additional problems are revealed, and the process of resolving these problems may reveal still others. While this may be a discouraging and frustrating aspect of planning, the result is enhanced feasibility of the final business venture.

This evolutionary approach to planning involves the following basic steps:

1. Define the business idea.
2. Establish goals and objectives.
3. Evaluate the idea, goals, and objectives.
4. Project cash needs.
5. Identify sources of funds.
6. Write a business development plan.

1. *Define the business idea.* Write a description of the business idea. Get it on paper as succinctly and concisely as possible. Initially, the description may be very informal. This is by far the most important and most difficult part of the business plan. The more precise and specific this description, the easier the rest of the planning process will be. It provides focus for the entire business development process. Spending the time clarifying the business objectives of the project will help avoid ambiguity and confusion later on.

In order to write this description, the business idea must be completely and clearly thought out. Developing a written description forces a clear conceptualization of the whole process. Important conceptual deficiencies will become evident when the description begins to falter. For many, writing out the idea makes it more real and provides a positive incentive as well as a starting point for the development of the plan itself.

A problem with all this is that what is initially felt to be a truly innovative idea may begin to fade under the careful scrutiny required by this activity. Even though this may be personally very discouraging, it is far more desirable to identify business infeasibility before the fact rather than after. The whole question of feasibility is an explicit concern of the planning process, and the definition step is an important beginning in establishing that determination.

2. *Establish goals and objectives.* Commit to writing the series of goals or objectives that should be satisfied by the business venture. This represents the applied process of goal setting. As noted earlier, there may be a wide range of goals or objectives to be fulfilled through the business operation, some of which are more important than others. It is necessary at this stage to clearly recognize the variety of goals or objectives that may be desired by the different participants or influential forces in the business. There may be other individuals or groups, in addition to the business principals themselves, who are interested in the outcome of the business operation. For example, investors, other owners, employees, customers, and suppliers all may have goal expectations that could influence the way the business is run.

One reason for business failure frequently listed by experts in this field is "incompatible objectives," either between the principals themselves or within the total set of pluralistic influences that may be relevant to or impinge on any given venture. The process of goal setting and the sets of factors or constraints that influence this activity were discussed at length in Chapter 2.

3. *Evaluate the idea, goals, and objectives.* This is a feasibility analysis activity, and its basic objective is to determine whether or not a specific idea makes sense, whether or not it can work, and whether or not it can fulfill the series of goals and objectives identified in the preceding step. Once the business idea and the goals and objectives have been defined in writing, they can be compared to determine where complements and gaps may exist. The business idea can then be evaluated in terms of its ability to satisfy the sets of objectives that have been identified as important.

The results of this analysis will help in determining the degree of satisfaction and/or dissatisfaction which will result once the business is established. Business ventures that do not satisfy objectives will give the principals and others involved in the operation very little satisfaction, thus causing them to lose their enthusiasm and reduce their support of the operation. Objectives that are vague may be unattainable and lead to frustrations. Either of these deficiencies will strongly contribute to the eventual failure of the operation.

4. *Project cash needs.* As the business idea becomes better defined and begins to take shape, written descriptions will provide a base for developing an implementation strategy. As this strategy emerges, it will indicate the cash investments associated with different sets of alternatives. These funding or investment requirements include the specification of needed capital equipment, various other initial cash needs, and the amount of working capital necessary, as determined through pro forma projections of income and cash flow.

Frequently, as a business develops over a period of time and increases in size and complexity, it will require additional injections of capital at different points in the future in order to support peak levels of activities. These peaks or needs for additional funds can be anticipated and must be provided for before the project is launched. If not, they may represent such critical problems in the future that the business operation comes to a halt or fails.

Financing proposals recognize the target goals of future cash needs and specifically identify the points in time when new injections of funds will be required. Early investors can thus be prepared for these future cash needs. When future cash needs are not anticipated and planned for, they generally lead to liquidity problems—a strong indicator of general incompetence of the business principals.

Bankers use the term *leverage* in reference to the multiple that debt represents of equity. A deal that is said to be leveraged three times (3×) has three dollars of debt for every dollar of equity, or is 75 percent debt-financed. A helpful rule of thumb is that many lenders would like to see one dollar of equity available for every dollar of debt, although they will frequently find a debt-to-equity ratio of two to one (2×) acceptable. Most lenders would be concerned about the stability of more highly leveraged businesses.

Again, a major objective of business planning is problem anticipation, and a major purpose of problem anticipation is problem avoidance where possible or, where avoidance is not possible, at least identifying the best solution available. The importance of projecting cash needs cannot be overemphasized. Insufficient financing or various capital deficiencies are the major cause of business failure. While it may be the most important cause of business failure, it is also one of the most avoidable. Anticipate the total funding required to successfully launch the business operation. If those funds are not available, then the business operation should not be started. It's that simple and that basic.

5. *Identify sources of funds.* Funds are potentially available to businesses from a wide variety of sources. The business developers must determine how much cash is available from their own funds and what additional funds can be obtained from various outside sources. They must determine the cost of these funds and then balance available funds against cash needs to see if sufficient funding is available to support the business idea through the start-up and development phase to where it begins to become internally self-sufficient.

Again, if there is insufficient funding to get through this start-up period, it is sheer stupidity to proceed with the development of the idea in the unrealistic hope that somehow needed funds will materialize at points in the future when they are required. Otherwise sensible individuals sometimes begin to develop a belief in a fairy godmother at this point. Appendix B contains a brief discussion of various sources of funds that may be available to a new or growing business.

6. *Write a business development plan.* A completed business plan is a summary and evaluation of the business idea. It is the written result of the planning process. It shows the probability of success, the principals' ability to make it work, the sources and uses of funds and projected income flows and cash needs. The proposal or plan contains all these items in a form that can be evaluated by the business principals themselves and by outside agencies such as loan officers or venture capital investors who may also be interested in the project. In addition, the plan serves as a primary means for communicating both the goals of the operation and the strategies for their achievement to subordinates and others who will be involved in the actual operation of the business. Finally, the document is most valuable to the business developers themselves, because it helps establish whether or not the whole concept is feasible.

A business plan may be the only tangible aspect of a new business in its early stages of development. Often the business plan is used to guide initial activities and is then updated as the business begins to develop and unfold. This is an emergent process.

As has been noted earlier, the planning process starts out with a series of abstracted assumptions which are then replaced with facts as quickly as the facts can be determined. This enables the plan to be modified in response to different aspects of reality as they are actually encountered.

In the case of a start-up business, the process of preparing a business plan also provides an opportunity to test the motivation, commitment, and technical expertise of other prospective team members. Ask each prospective member of the team to write up a plan for the business activity that will be his or her operational responsibility. There is perhaps no faster or cheaper way to determine which potential members of the management team do not have the necessary commitment to the business or level of technical expertise to be owners and key sparkplugs for the developing business. If the individual with the initial business idea is going to bring others into the development process, particularly in ownership positions, it is important to make sure they are contributing something of value to the process. If they do not, they are simply being given something for nothing, which is likely to result in bad feelings and serious arguments as the business unfolds.

A good plan can be prepared in 15 to 30 pages of text, excluding tables and charts. The style of the plan should be adapted to the background of the intended users and readers. Again, the preparation of a well-organized and properly documented business plan will accomplish two important objectives: first, the mental exercise required to commit a conceptual notion to paper and the writing of a plan for its actual accomplishment often highlight critical operational aspects that have been overlooked or neglected, and second, both internal and external communication are facilitated.

SUMMARY

Careful preparation of a business plan represents a unique opportunity to think through all facets of a new business, to examine the consequences of different marketing, production, and financing strategies, and to determine what human and financial resources are required to launch and develop the operation. The planning process should be used as an opportunity to experiment with different strategies, to test different combinations of ideas and different operating styles, and to determine what makes most sense for the specific individuals involved in the venture. All of this can be done on paper without the expenses of trial-and-error operation.

The principals should prepare a plan that they can discuss in their own words and that is based on their own understanding, but which also makes sense to an objective observer. The planning format developed here is a guideline to accomplishing these goals for most purposes. Common sense should be used in applying the guidelines to specific business situations. For example, a plan for a service business would not need to include a section on manufacturing or product development. On the other hand, there may be other activities or aspects of the business that are not even indicated here, but which would be highly relevant for that specific deal. In short, the suggestions offered here are a framework; they are not a straitjacket. They are tools, and like any tool, they must be used properly to be effective.

The best way to approach the business planning process is to take the framework presented here as an outline and consider the different topics, sketch out the critical answers to the questions raised, then develop the research necessary to substantiate opinions. Be detailed, specific, and, most important, concise. Make sure the information included is adequate and relevant. Business plans that are viable, useful, and impressive to others as well as helpful to the business principals themselves are so not because of their size, weight, or bulk, but because they provide a logical, critical evaluation and outline of the business and its proposed development.

The business planning process is evolutionary. As the framework of the plan is established and different parts of the plan are developed, previously ignored aspects of the situation come to the surface. Information generated from one part of the plan will reveal the need for more information on another part of the plan or answer questions that may have been left open in another section of the plan.

Do not load the plan to make it come out as a defense for a predetermined course of action. Let the process be as objective as it can possibly be made so that it is, at least for initial purposes, truly a feasibility analysis. It is simply pointless to proceed with a plan that is doomed to failure.

Finally, after the plan has been completed, subject it to the review of a number of objective outsiders. An attorney will help make sure that the content of the written plan is not misleading and does not suggest incorrect or illegal assumptions. A banker will be able to give an objective opinion as to whether or not the deal makes sense financially. Others who may be able to provide very helpful comments and criticisms include successful entrepreneurs, corporate executives, business consultants, CPAs, and any others who may have expertise relevant to the specific purposes.

No matter how good the principals may be, there will be issues which they overlook and discussions of certain aspects of the business which are inadequate or less than clear. A good reviewer can quickly point out these deficiencies as well as provide the benefit of an outside objective evaluation of the plan. A good reviewer can act as a sounding board to help in the development of alternative solutions to some of the questions that investors are likely to ask. Solve problems before they occur. The business will be healthier, and you will be happier.

Chapter 4:

Elements of the Planning Process

A plan serving both the internal purposes of the business principals and the external purposes of their bankers, advisors, consultants, and investors should include certain major elements. This chapter describes the eight important components of the plan and shows how these planning units fit together into a coherent, logically structured, sequential business development plan.

The business planning format recommended here comprises the following important components:

1. Definition of the business.
2. Market research and analysis.
3. Development plan.
4. Manufacturing plan.
5. Distribution and service plan.
6. Organizational plan.
7. Development schedule.
8. Financial plan.

In addition, the principals should develop a contingency plan. They must not only be concerned with assumptions about what may reasonably occur in the future but also develop a worst-case plan—a plan that is based on the occurrence of less than desirable circumstances in the future. This contingency planning adds an important dimension to feasibility analysis. The underlying question with which contingency planning deals is whether or not the venture will succeed even if everything doesn't work out the way it is hoped. Also, the contingency analysis may pinpoint the extra amount of funding or financing required to launch the business under unfavorable circumstances.

One important lesson that has been gleaned from an analysis of a great many different business situations is that the development of any business always seems to take much longer than is ever anticipated by anyone. Countless small problems crop up which introduce delays and cost the new business more money than generally expected. Contingency planning seeks to identify or anticipate some of the consequences that may result from these delays. It may not be possible to specifically identify the various problems that might arise, but it certainly is possible to identify the types of problems or the types of additional needs the business will encounter if some combination of these problems occurs and delays the development of the business for a certain amount of time.

Contingency planning is discussed at the beginning of this chapter because it represents a conceptual attitude which must be maintained in thinking through the implications for each of the other planning components.

Each of the eight major components of the planning process will be briefly described in this chapter. These components represent the conceptual framework of the plan. In a very real sense, they are interdependent: they contribute to each other, each provides additional questions which must be answered in other sections, and they all contribute to the development of the final plan itself. The creation of the actual plan, to be discussed later is a natural and logical extension of the conceptual activities suggested here. The planning process is not necessarily a simple sequence of moving from one step to the next, but rather involves simultaneous problem solving in each of these eight different major areas.

DEFINING THE BUSINESS

Just as the first section of the written business plan provides a general introduction to the whole project, so the planning process should start with a definition of the business. The items to be considered here are the nature of the company and its products or services, the nature of the industry and the opportunities available that can be exploited by the particular product or service that will be offered, and the reasons for the creation of the company and for entering a specific market or addressing a specific target group within the market. The background data on the industry and its growth serve as a reference for future projections and their justification. Once this general information has been prepared, a closer inspection should be made of the industry, the company, and its products or services.

The investigation of the industry should focus on its current status and prospects, new products and development, emerging new markets and customers, new requirements, new companies entering the industry, and any national or economic trends and factors that could affect the proposed business's viability, either positively or negatively. Along with this, the market potential and any peculiarities of the customers or the technology should be explicitly considered.

It is important to be specific about the exact nature of the business the company is in or intends to enter, the general products or services that will be offered, and principal customers. If the organization has been in business, prepare a brief sketch of its history, stating when it was incorporated, the types of products produced in the past and present or being developed, involvement of the principals, and, if the business has been operating over a period of years, its growth and performance. If the business has experienced losses in earlier years, it is important to explain exactly why these losses occurred. It is not necessary to apologize for loss operations, but it is necessary to understand the causes.

Virtually all businesses offer some products or services. They should be described here in detail, including their application, primary end users, and potential secondary applications. Any unique features of the product or service should be emphasized, including the particular need that it will fill, how it relates to existing products or services performing a similar function, and whether or not there are any proprietary advantages such as patent protection, trade secrets, or any other factors that provide an inherent competitive advantage in the marketplace.

Most business principals are quick to talk about special advantages their product or service has over the competition. Thus they will usually emphasize opportunities for expansion or development of related products or services and show how these opportunities will be taken advantage of. However, it is also important here to include a discussion of any product disadvantages, such as the possibilities of rapid obsolescence because of technological or styling changes or marketing fads. This will show that the principals have considered some of the inherent limitations of the venture, as well as its obvious advantages, and are not blithely floating along on a balloon of optimism.

MARKET RESEARCH AND ANALYSIS

The market survey or study is one of the most critical parts of the whole planning process. It establishes the base for the feasibility analysis discussed earlier. A market survey identifies target customers, the size of the potential demand, and the competition. Additionally, it should indicate the current size of the market, its conditions and trends, and the market share of the competition. Finally, it should include a comparison of the company's products or services with those of major competitors. A matrix format will facilitate this type of comparison.

Market research and analysis is perhaps the most difficult aspect of the business planning activity. However, all subsequent sections of the plan depend on the sales estimates developed from this work. Market research and analysis helps establish the optimum size of the operation, the estimated market share of the business, the marketing plan (including pricing strategies, sales tactics, service and warranty policies, and advertising and promotion), and, of course, the amount of debt or equity that will be required in order to make it all work.

There is a tremendous amount of market information available even for innovative, new concepts. Taking the time to accumulate and assess these data is critical to the business's future. Unfortunately, this aspect of planning is the one that most prospective business principals are unfamiliar with, and so it frequently does not receive the attention that it deserves.

In considering the potential customer base, it is important to be very specific. Clearly identify the target market. A market grid (see Figure 4-1) may be used to show the various market segments that are potential customers. Though not discussed in detail here, market gridding is a very useful way to evaluate and compare a variety of market segments and then organize this information in such a way that it is possible to establish and rank these different segments.

The market study will help in identifying potential customer interest and various demographic factors that will be used to evaluate the potential market size. Once the customer segments are

Figure 4-1. Market grid.

Characteristics		Upper Class	Upper Middle Class	Middle Class	Upper Lower Class
Cost	Low			✓	
	High	✓	✓		✓
Durability		✓	✓	✓	
Quality		✓	✓	✓	
Style		✓	✓		✓
Convenience		✓	✓		
Status			✓		✓

identified, market size and trends can be extrapolated from census and other demographic data. Discussions with potential distributors, dealers, sales representatives, and customers can be particularly useful in establishing both market size and trend parameters.

The market can be described in units and dollars. Price sensitivity testing—trying out different prices on actual target customers—can be used to project demand curves, which then provide critical information for market planning decisions such as pricing strategies. Again, major factors influencing the market growth, such as industry trends, socio-economic trends, government policy, or population shifts, should be identified so that the impact of each on the various target market segments can be properly evaluated. For the final, written plan, it is important to indicate the source of all data and the methods used to make projections.

In considering the relative strength of the competition, it is necessary to specifically identify the pertinent companies and then obtain the necessary data to evaluate their products. A matrix or grid (see Figure 4-2) can be used here as well to compare competing products or services on the basis of price, performance, service warranties, and other pertinent features. This matrix can then be studied to pinpoint combined strengths on the one hand and gaps or weaknesses on the other hand in the existing market structure.

Figure 4-2. Competition matrix.

Product Characteristics		A	B	C	D
Cost	Low	✓			
	High		✓	✓	✓
Durability			✓	✓	
Quality			✓	✓	✓
Style			✓		✓
Convenience		✓			
Status			✓		✓
Comfort				✓	

The companies themselves should also be studied in terms of their stability, sales distribution, and production capabilities.

It is particularly important to identify the price leader, the quality leader, and the innovation leader and to determine whether firms are entering or leaving the market and why. There are plenty of data available, particularly on the size and strength of leaders in various categories of industries.

Finally, it is helpful to identify three or four key competitors and indicate specifically why the new business will be able to compete effectively with each of these organizations. The underlying question to be addressed is how the new business will be able to do a better job than the existing competition. It is not always necessary to identify areas of organizational weakness on the part of the competition. A growing market due to population shifts, for example, may provide ample opportunity for new businesses in an area where existing firms have done a good job and continue to be stable.

In estimating the market share in sales, it is necessary to determine first the percent of the total market the new business will be able to capture. This determination is made on one side by reckoning with the capacity of the new firm, and on the other side by reckoning with the number of customers in the target market and the number, size, quality, and availability of firms competing for their attention. Within this market, it is important to identify major customers and determine the extent to which they are willing to make commitments to the new business.

Moving from the percent of the market that the new business expects to be able to obtain, both as it is commencing operations and over time, it is then possible to establish a projected share of market, which becomes the basis for the financial projections, especially the sales projections. For example, the growth of the new business's sales and its estimated market share could be related to the growth of the industry and customers and the strengths and weaknesses of competitors. When these data are compiled and presented in tabular form, they provide a clear indication of the sources of figures used in the plan, such as sales projections.

The new business must look to the future as well as the present, so a methodology should be developed that will enable the business to stay tuned to changes in the marketplace. Plans and procedures should be established for an ongoing market evaluation. Changes in the marketplace can occur very quickly, and any organization that is not tuned to such changes can quickly be left behind. Finally, it is critical to identify problems or negative factors and hazards affecting the entire industry or specifically facing the new firm. These should be reviewed frankly and completely and evaluated in terms of their aggregate impact on the new business operation.

The Marketing Plan

Flowing right from the market analysis is the information needed to create a marketing plan. The market analysis provides an insight into the nature of the marketplace. The marketing plan uses that information as a guide in developing strategies for success in the marketplace. It contains the overall marketing strategy, including a general marketing philosophy reflecting the attitudes of the business, and specific strategy decisions based on that philosophy.

In developing this plan, it is essential to focus first on the needs and wants of potential customers and then on the design of strategies for the business that will satisfy those needs and wants. That is, the marketing plan should not be a program designed to get rid of whatever the organization may want to produce, but rather should be aimed at producing (within the capability constraints of the firm) what potential customers want, then focusing on ways of informing the target customers that the firm has the capability of satisfying their needs, and, finally, making those products or services reasonably available to the target customers. Marketing strategy zeros in on the characteristics of the target market, especially on the behavior patterns of these target groups. This requires market segmentation, or the study of various market segments. There are three key components for effective market segmentation:

1. Specificity—there must be ways to identify exactly who is in the target market, by age, occupation, race, geographic location, marital status, education, or any other dimension that may be relevant.
2. Sufficiency—there must be enough people in the target market to make it worthwhile to bother with.
3. Accessibility—there not only must be enough people in the target market, but the marketer must be able to reach them as well.

The whole purpose of market segmentation is to enable the marketer to focus his efforts on one or more distinct classes of customers in order to achieve a strong market position in the particular market segments that he chooses to serve. There are several specific dimensions or bases for segmentation:

- Geographic—serving customers living in a specific area. There may be regional differences as a result of local cultural values and attitudes, climate, industry density, or any of a variety of other factors. Specific variables include region or city size, density of area, type of industry, natural resources, and climate.
- Demographic—referring to the vital and measurable distinctions of the population. There are a variety of ways of differentiating between individuals, including by age, sex, marital status, family size, income, occupation, and education.
- Psychographic—concerned with behavior or personality types. Even individuals within the same demographic characteristics may behave very differently. Specific variables include life style, personality, attitudes, and benefits sought.

- Sociocultural—group or anthropological characteristics, including religion, race, nationality, social class, and family life cycle.
- User behavior—including the rate of usage of the product and brand loyalty status.

Once the market segmentation has begun to produce target customer profiles, channels of distribution can be identified which are appropriate to satisfy the target group's needs. This involves the standard marketing considerations of product, price, place, and time—that is, the right product at the right price available at the right place at the right time. As a further way of responding to individual target group needs, the marketing concept involves a consideration of the product, not just as a specific item, but as the agglomeration of product plus related services, such as warranties, credit, delivery, service, and installation, that make it appropriate for specific target groups. All these considerations are part of the activity known as product positioning, which refers to the total design of the product package to optimally satisfy the needs of various market segments. This includes, of course, advertising and selling strategies.

Last but not least, the extra element that helps some marketing strategies be more effective than others is creativity. Conventions in any industry or area of activity tend to be restrictive. Just because something has always been done in a certain way, there's no reason why that should continue. So the effort must be made to find a better way. Specifically, for the marketing strategy, a search should be made for innovative approaches that can be appropriately applied. A good example of this type of innovation is the increasing use of leasing in an area where previously certain products have been available only through purchase.

Pricing

Price sensitivity tests determine to what extent target segment customers are sensitive to variations in price—that is, to what extent price variations will influence demand. Once acquired, these observations can be compared against the competition's price structure. Another important price sensitivity consideration is whether the customer's perception of appropriate price is influenced by any other marketing dimension, such as place or time. It may be important to know, for instance, whether customers are likely to want the product immediately or are willing to wait a little while and order it. In many cases, customers may be willing to pay more for immediate availability.

Along with the price/demand considerations must go a concern for margin. There are typically a variety of intermediaries in any marketing channel. Frequently, small manufacturers forget about the fact that these intermediaries need to make a profit too. In calculating the margin, it is not the margin on the final selling price which they should see as their gross profit; instead, they must look at margins as the percentages of the final sale price which are allocated to each of the members of the marketing channel. This constitutes the total price allocation.

To calculate the allocation of margin, it is necessary to identify the members of the marketing channel and the percentage of the final or total selling price each of the marketing channel members will receive. A typical breakdown would include each of the following as a percentage of the final selling price:

> Manufacturing cost.
> Manufacturing gross profit.
> Wholesaler cost.
> Wholesaler gross profit.
> Retailer cost.
> Retailer gross profit.
> Final retail selling price.

Sales Tactics

In considering price and identifying marketing channel members, sales tactics or strategies begin to evolve. It must be determined whether the product is to be aggressively or passively marketed and through which channels. Manufacturers' reps, for example, are a good choice for many businesses. Small manufacturers simply cannot afford to have a sales force out selling one or two products. Instead, through an arrangement with a manufacturers' rep, they can have their product included as part of a more general offering already marketed to an existing customer base. Simply stating in the plan that a salesman will be paid a commission on sales is not necessarily sufficient to induce anyone to sell the product and is certainly not a well-thought-out distribution strategy.

In formulating a sales strategy, channel members should be contacted to find out how receptive they would be to the products in question. To assure that relative margins are being maintained, the contemplated products should be compared against other or similar products the channel members may be currently carrying. A sales tactics strategy may involve a staging process whereby the organization moves from distribution through manufacturers' reps to distribution through dealerships to distribution through a regional sales force and perhaps ultimately to distribution through company-owned retail facilities. This can be planned over time, and various volume targets can be established that will indicate the feasibility for each level of operation.

Service and Warranties

In order for virtually any product to gain market acceptance, its potential customers are going to have to be reasonably assured that it will work, both when it is purchased and in the future. Thus, it must be determined what kind of promises should be made with respect to the product and what kind of support is appropriate.

It is very possible that these support issues can become a marketing or competitive advantage. If it is a tradition in the industry that a one-year warranty is provided with a product, then a new competitor in this industry should at least match the convention of the industry. On the other hand, offering a warranty may have important implications for the business. A warranty may carry a need to maintain a support force, and if so, that support force will also carry a labor cost. The costs associated with supporting the product will be a function of the reliability factor for the product. This can be determined if the product has been in use long enough to find out how it is going to hold up.

The warranty plan must describe the kind and terms of any warranty to be offered and whether service will be handled by company salesmen, agencies, dealers, distributors, or through factory returns. It is important to indicate the proposed charges for service calls and whether service will be profitable or at a breakeven or even a loss operation. The key here is to compare proposed service and warranty policies and practices with those of principal competitors.

Advertising and Promotion

Advertising is a double-edged sword. It is essential on the one hand, and uses up resources on the other. A balance must be established between what the organization can afford and what the organization requires. The key is to determine what kind of advertising or promotional activities will yield the maximum benefits for the dollars invested.

For any new organization, professional advice from a marketing or advertising agency is a practical necessity. Even though the new business will be paying heavily for this kind of assistance, in all probability it will be infinitely cheaper than experimenting with a variety of techniques and efforts which, at worst, may turn out to be completely ineffective.

It is not sufficient to merely have the product available for sale; it is not sufficient to merely have a distribution network established. The customers must be aware that the product is available, that it will satisfy their needs. They must know how they can get the product and how they can benefit from using it. Participation in trade shows, advertising in trade magazines, direct mail campaigns, and preparation of product sheets are all techniques that are available to market to technically oriented customers. Direct mail or mass media advertising campaigns are also appropriate for selling to retail customers. In the aggregate, all these techniques must be parts of a coherent advertising and promotion plan.

Finally, a good marketing strategy and implementation plan must be *reviewed quarterly* and adjusted or revised on this quarterly basis. There are two important reasons for this review on a regular basis. One is to make sure that the plan is proceeding as expected; the other is to provide an opportunity to evaluate the performance of each member of the management team. If there is no reward or penalty associated with failing to meet the timetable detailed in the marketing plan, that timetable will be disregarded.

THE DEVELOPMENT PLAN

This section may also be called the design and development plan or product development plan. Its purpose is to identify in specific detail a research and development program, establish requirements and a schedule for each phase of development, and identify the costs associated with each activity, either for a product being developed or for a totally new item.

To establish the development plan, it is necessary to identify the exact status of the product. Any additional work that needs to be done, such as testing, designing, modeling, prototype development, or any other activity of this nature, must be completely described. The nature and extent of the work to be done and the costs that will be associated with these activities should be discussed. The fact that any of this kind of work needs to be done means that the product is not yet available for sale, and thus raises the question of when it will be available for sale.

The design and development schedule must be realistic, because it will establish the beginning points for still other activities within the organization. PERT, CPM, and other planning, forecasting, and scheduling tools are appropriate here. In general, a planning sequence must be established which clearly shows what activities impose constraints on what successive activities. Such a schedule is not only an important planning and scheduling tool, but it is an important tracking control tool as well.

The development schedule should be laid out schematically as a large chart and nailed up on the wall in conspicuous view of all involved. It will be a constant reminder of the need to track the whole series of activities occurring simultaneously, any one of which may represent a constraint on the development of further stages of the development plan.

For example, it is not wise to develop a marketing force before the products are available for sale. Also, the development schedule that will be established must identify the specific tasks that need to be done in order to get the product ready for the marketplace. It should clearly identify what must be done, how it will be done, and who will do it. It should acknowledge the difficulties and the risks that are involved. It may be possible that the new product won't work. This becomes particularly critical when products of new technology are being developed.

Specific decision points should be established to help determine whether or not the whole project should be continued or whether developments at that stage are strong indicators of further infeasibility. If the latter is the case, it is important to acknowledge it as early as possible in order to minimize the investment that is being made.

The degree of risk in any area is a direct function of the degree of unknown. A brand-new innovation, because it is in an unknown area, carries an extremely high risk. Once a product is established, it is immediately necessary to begin planning for product improvement and follow-on new products. Thus, the business environment for virtually any industry or type of business is characterized by technological and social change as well as the quick entry into the marketplace of competition in areas where business success seems to be developing. Existing organizations must stay tuned to these pressures for change and must continually be developing strategies to cope with them. Anticipating the need for new product development and establishing a schedule and budget for carrying it out means that the organization is controlling the situation rather than being controlled by it.

THE MANUFACTURING PLAN

Once the product potential has been clearly established and the target segments and marketing activities identified, it is then necessary to focus on the process of manufacturing or creating the product or the service. This includes decision making about a whole host of factors: manufacturing facilities, location, size, cost of buying or renting, equipment needs, equipment costs, subcontracting component costs, and consideration of the labor force, both full time and part time, that will be required to produce the company's product or service. Included here should be considerations of inventory control, purchasing, production control, and a variety of make-or-buy decisions. For example, many businesses can start out as essentially assembly operations, gradually adding component manufacturing capability insofar as economies of scale and availability of capital make this possible.

Geography may be an important consideration in identifying a potential location. It is important, first of all, to determine the requirements for such factors as labor availability, prevailing wage rates, whether or not labor unionization is a concern, proximity to customers or suppliers, access to transportation, utilities, and any other factorial requirements. Then, a reasonable evaluation can be made of different locations in terms of how well each of the locales will meet the requirements.

Additional concerns in inspecting local areas should be state and local taxes and laws, including zoning laws, and any factors that could be inhibiting or derogatory to the business. All too often the process happens backward. A business begins to develop in someone's garage or cellar; as it grows beyond this initial incubation, it may be located in the local community area, or a building may be found to be available without a consideration of any of the other factors. All the factors must be considered, and, in addition, serious thought must be given to any specialized financial incentives available from the municipality or the state to attract new businesses to locate in that area. Industrial revenue bonds, special labor training programs, and tax deferments are frequently available to encourage new business to locate in a developing industrial part of a community or state which is concerned with economic development and job creation.

As noted, the selection of facilities can have important strategic implications. It is important to make a very careful assessment of location needs before efforts are made to choose the space. Defining geographic needs *after* available space has been identified may have the objective, or at least the effect, of rationalizing a decision that is already made, rather than providing the basis for optimizing such decision making. Among the considerations that are relevant to this decision making are whether or not the business requires new space or can use pre-existing space and, if it uses pre-existing space, whether serious modifications have to be made.

The initial needs for space should be compared to future needs as the business growth is projected over time. Certain ventures may have very high fixed requirements which provide them with a substantial range of business growth flexibility. Other ventures may require minimal start-up facilities that can be changed or expanded as the business grows and develops without any particular cost to the business. Least-cost, minimum-term facilities are generally important when the business is just getting started, since they maintain maximum flexibility with regard to new needs for space, the type of space, accessibility, or other locational considerations that may evolve as the business grows and develops. In some businesses there may be a direct correlation between location and advertising, because the exposure of the business through the location of its facility may have some value. In these instances, appropriate facility costs must be seen as a combination of payment for both space and promotion.

There are some important strategic implications to the wide range of decisions which are made around most business operations. Particularly important here are make-or-buy decisions and decisions involving choices between manufacturing or subcontracting. As noted, there is not necessarily any reason for a lot of organizations to be manufacturing anything. For many fledgling businesses it may be most appropriate that they be assemblers rather than manufacturers—that is, that they let others do the actual fabricating and then purchase the component parts on a subcontracted basis.

This is a particularly effective way to minimize start-up costs and risk. Once the business reaches a sufficient volume, manufacturing capability can be developed on an incremental basis. It is very helpful to recognize that it is not necessarily important or, in a lot of cases, even wise to design a full-fledged production machine at the very outset of a venture.

For almost any type of operation, there are typically a variety of alternative strategies available. Each must be thoroughly evaluated to determine exactly why one should be chosen rather than the others. Such choices should be very thoroughly justified and carefully documented. Facts and figures should be used to support such decision making.

Additional strategic implications may focus on labor versus machine. Initially in some operations, it may be most desirable to have the production process be labor-intensive with general-purpose machinery and, as the business grows, to gradually add more and more specialized labor-saving equipment to eventually automate the production/assembly process to the maximum extent possible. The important components of this decision-making process include: labor force requirements, the composition of the force, incentive payments, costs and other requirements such as union activity or any other particular demands which must be responded to, which are then offset against costs of specialized machinery and the relative economies of scale which may be available through its use.

These costs can and should be calculated. Making intuitive decisions in these matters is simply irresponsible. Another strategic consideration emerging from the marketing strategy concerns the maintenance of inventory levels, both within the organization and within distributorships or out in the field. If the organization is going to maintain a lot of inventory itself, then the space requirements as well as the dollar requirements tied up in the inventory must be identified. There are specific costs attached to each of these alternatives. Final costs, which are associated with the alternative selected, must be clearly identified, because they will be included in the financial projections.

One aspect of the feasibility analysis that should be recognized in these considerations is that the choice of the least-cost alternative is not necessarily the answer. For a small fledgling firm, the development of a full-scale manufacturing facility may not be an option at all, even though it may represent the most efficient choice. The organization may simply not have access to sufficient capital to build a new facility and equip it with a full range of

manufacturing machinery. Instead, the new venture may be forced
to adopt a subcontracting style of operation, even though this is
less economical (and profitable) than owning the full range of factors of production.

In addition to the availability of capital, the strategic implications of risk minimization must be considered here as well. If the
idea turns out to be a failure and the firm has created a special-
purpose manufacturing facility, then the resale value of that facility may be extremely limited or nonexistent, and so the recovery of
the capital invested in the facility and machinery may be impossible.

Lease-versus-buy decision making is often troublesome for
small firms. Frequently, it may seem clear from thumbnail-sketch
financial analysis that the economies are with the buy decision.
Leasing is simply more expensive. However, the other side of that
decision making must include a consideration of whether or not the
firm has the capital capacity to make the buy. In this context, capital capacity represents not only the total capital available to the
firm but also alternative uses of that capital, which are limited if it
makes a buy decision for this particular product versus other products. A frequently overlooked advantage of leasing is the flexibility
it provides for upgrading to larger or more sophisticated levels of
equipment. This issue is one of the real considerations in strategic
decision making.

At the conclusion of this phase of the analysis, subcontractors
should have been interviewed and the range of costs involved in
the manufacturing process, including costs of components, plant
costs, equipment costs, and labor costs, reasonably identified. Also,
some preliminary work should have been done to identify expected
costs at different levels of production over the next three to five
years. All these cost data will become an integral part of the financial plan and become important inputs for the final stages of feasibility analysis.

THE DISTRIBUTION AND SERVICE PLAN

The construction of a distribution and service plan raises the
question of strategy versus implementation. The marketing plan
involved the development of strategy; the distribution and service
plan involves the implementation of that strategy. In particular,
the distribution and service plan must identify the steps necessary

to bring the new product or service into the marketplace and to the customer. Costs of advertising and selling must be determined, market penetration and timing must be estimated, and pricing, sales, and service policies established.

The distribution and service plan will very specifically detail exactly what the company is going to do during the next six or twelve months, how it is going to do it, who is going to do it, the specific goals that can or should be developed, and the type of program required to achieve the goals. The plan should include some specific statements about when anticipated events are to take place—for example, when additional salesmen would be hired. It should include the assignment of specific responsibilities to specific individuals. Unless the responsibilities for carrying out the elements of the plan are clearly understood and assigned, there is a danger that the jobs will not be done or that planned actions will not be taken. If such individuals cannot be identified by name, they must at least be identified by function.

The distribution and service plan is tied to both the marketing plan and the manufacturing plan. It must evaluate the cross-implications of these activities and remain flexible. In addition, there must be a built-in re-evaluation procedure for measuring the company's progress against the plan. Among the activities must be included review and revision. A time-line continuum can be used to show the strategic points for changes in the distribution and service system to reflect the growth of the market, the development of target market segments, and the increased capacity and economies of scale that naturally accompany the various functions.

THE ORGANIZATIONAL PLAN

Creating an organizational structure means developing the management team and support personnel. It is extremely helpful to formalize this process in chart form (see Figure 4-3). The next step involves the exact duties and functions of each key person. Our example gives two such lists only. These duties must be described and related to resumes of each person's background. Even if management knows what it is going to do, the appropriate steps must still be taken in order to achieve the desired objectives, and the various responsibilities must be clearly assigned to make sure that they will be accomplished or, if they're not accomplished, who

Figure 4-3. Organization chart.

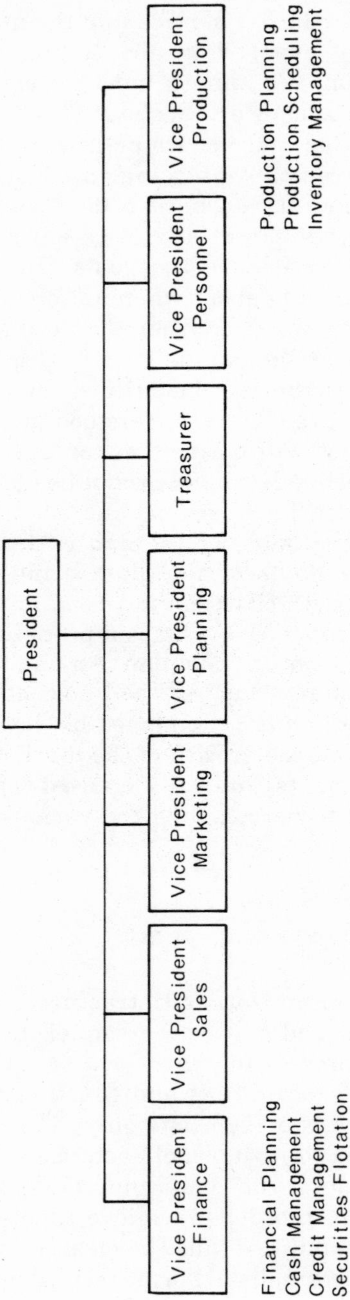

President

Vice President Finance

Financial Planning
Cash Management
Credit Management
Securities Flotation

Vice President Sales

Vice President Marketing

Vice President Planning

Treasurer

Vice President Personnel

Vice President Production

Production Planning
Production Scheduling
Inventory Management

will be held responsible. The organizational plan very specifically identifies who is going to do what.

Defining job responsibilities and requirements for the key management roles in the company and matching them with the personalities and prior working experiences of specific individuals is a particularly critical area for integration. The total needs of the organization must be identified, and the individuals within the organization who will be performing the different required functions must be specified as early as possible. Particular strengths and weaknesses of different individuals must be recognized, especially the contribution they are making to the organization and, where they exist, how deficiencies will be provided for.

Sometimes it becomes quite apparent through this form of analysis that some individuals do not really make a contribution to the organization at all. If that is the case, then it is important to decide why they are being included. It may not be possible to fill all the different management functions with a full-time person at the start of the organization's operations. If that is so, then it is necessary to decide how these tasks can be either divided up among existing personnel or distributed to outside consultants or other part-time individuals to assure that all important functions are being performed.

The key management personnel represent the real essence of any fledgling organization. The organizational plan that emerges should describe the exact duties and responsibilities of each of the key members of the management team. For each of these key persons, a resume must be prepared summarizing the career highlights. These resumes provide additional backup information to support the organizational plan and should stress the training, experience, and accomplishments of each manager in performing functions similar to the roles they will assume in the new venture. It is important here to clearly identify the particular strengths and contributions each individual will make to the organization. Again, it may become clear through this analysis that some individuals are not making a particularly relevant contribution to the organization at all. If so, their inclusion in the management team should be seriously re-evaluated.

Management compensation and ownership considerations represent another area of strategic decision making. Fledgling ventures usually cannot afford to pay their owner/developers. Beginning organizations that attempt to build substantial management/ownership compensation into their initial financing proposals will find this to be a primary reason why such requests are rejected by financing agencies. The rationale for the rejection is the financing agencies' view that the principals of the organization too must be prepared to make an investment and must not make unrealistic demands on the new organization. Some sacrifices generally must be made. Accordingly, the salary that is to be paid to each person should be clearly stated, and it should be compared to the salary that was received by each individual during his last full-time job. Also, a stock ownership plan for key personnel should be developed, including any performance-dependent stock options or bonus plans that are contemplated. Again, this information is particularly relevant to potential financiers of the organization, who want to assure that the owners or principals are making important investments in the new venture (even though that investment may be in the form of energy rather than actual capital) and that the venture is not being robbed of essential development capital during its critical stages of infancy and development.

A carefully structured board of directors can be a valuable asset for any business, particularly for a new venture. Individuals should be selected for the specific skills, support, and advice they can contribute to the organization. Directors help establish the general policy of the organization and should be looked to to provide needed conceptual expertise. They should be selected on the basis of their ability to fulfill these functions. The business must establish a philosophy as to the size and composition of the board, and the organizational plan should specifically consider each member's background and assess what that individual can contribute to the company.

Supporting professional services are another critical area. For start-up businesses, outside professional advisors are essential, even though, over time, such expertise may be incorporated as internal staff. Most fledgling ventures cannot afford the level or type and quality of expertise that is required for their effective development. One-time expert advice may be required initially within an organization for purposes such as establishing patent protection, stock offerings, initial organizational design, engineering questions, and a variety of other potential problems that the organization may not re-encounter ever or at least for some time into the future.

The need for professional advertising and marketing assistance has already been noted, but is very specifically reinforced here again. Most new, and a great many existing, firms simply do not place sufficient emphasis on the value of this type of advice. And, because benefits from expenditures for these particular types of services are not as obvious as they may be for other activities, their use may be forgone or severely constrained. The benefits that could result from some initial investment in this specialized knowledge and expertise are considerable.

Another group of expert advisors are professional bankers, both commercial bankers and venture bankers. The careful selection of these banking relationships may have a substantial impact on the business's flexibility and ability to grow in the future. Arranging for bankers to invest their funds is only one aspect of their participation. Having the benefit of their advice on a variety of current or potential operating issues, as well as their willingness to invest still more funds as the business grows, may be far more valuable than the initial financing that seems so important at the outset.

A good professional outside public accounting firm is required in order to provide certified audits of the organization's activity on an annual basis. Such certified audits are a practical necessity for any organization anticipating growth and seeking outside financing. Legal advice is a practical necessity for any developing organization and should be sought out for both immediate problem solving and ongoing advice as well.

Well-known support service organizations not only provide significant direct professional assistance but can also add to the credibility of the venture. In addition, properly selected professional organizations can help the new business establish good contacts in the business community, identify potential investors, and help in securing needed financing.

THE DEVELOPMENT SCHEDULE

The identification of the series of activities that are required to turn the idea into an operating reality and the amount of time projected for the accomplishment of each stage are the essential components in creating a development schedule. Techniques such as PERT or CPM can help define in tabular form the series of events which are necessary and must be accomplished during various future time periods.

As noted earlier, certain activities become absolute conditions for further development. For example, the construction of the product prototype must precede its field testing. Both prototype construction and field testing in turn determine when the business can prepare to manufacture or assemble the product, and thus determine expected dates of completion and delivery of the product.

The development schedule will indicate how the company is planning to change internally in response to projected growth rates by indicating the expected effects of the growth of manufacturing, financial, and personnel requirements. It will indicate the relative points in time when these effects will be felt and how each will be dealt with. All these factors can be captured in a concise time sequence chart, and topics needing further discussion or consideration can be identified.

In general, the development schedule will represent a summary of the various dates and targets that have been established in the other sections of the plan. As it is developed and refined, it should be shown on a large-scale chart and posted where it can be reviewed by all those immediately involved in the planning process. In this way, the schedule will be a constant reminder of critical aspects, collaborative or coordinating sequences, and the point where developments in one area constrain, seriously inhibit, or otherwise affect the development of another phase of the operation.

The development schedule can be a time-line continuum, PERT, CPM, or other chart. By reducing the strategic implications of all the planning components to dates or specific time frames and organizing this information on a single page, the critical points of the whole planning cycle can be effectively highlighted and integrated.

THE FINANCIAL PLAN

The financial plan represents the quantitative evaluation and summary of the various planning activities, including the development schedule of the business. If the preceding steps of the planning process have been completed, the financial plan can be constructed in a straightforward manner.

A financial plan serves several important functions. It provides an opportunity for a highly objective feasibility evaluation. It translates the marketing research data into sales projections. It incorporates the operations and organizational plans into expense categories. Consistent with the time frame structures, it shows stages in the future where new expenses will be incurred or new opportunities for growth and expansion will occur. It shows the cash needs of the business over time. It indicates possibility and feasibility. Through breakeven analysis, it provides an opportunity for evaluating a variety of alternatives. It provides a basis for an evaluation of the investment opportunity and communicates expectations of the business's performance to others, especially prospective financing agencies. In summary, its purpose is to indicate the business's potential and financial viability.

The financial plan covers the following items:

Capital investment requirements.
Breakeven analysis.
Profit and loss forecasts.
Pro forma cash flow analysis.
Pro forma balance sheets.
Historical records.

The capital investment requirements section indicates the front-end capital assets needed for the establishment of the business. It should include a specific list of equipment and other long-term assets that will be required by the new business. This will not only indicate that the capital requirements for the operation have been carefully considered, but also provide a list of collateral that a prospective financier will undoubtedly utilize as security.

The breakeven analysis provides a way of determining the level of sales and production that will cover costs. In the decision-making stage of the venture formation, none of the costs are fixed, so breakeven becomes a powerful tool for analyzing alternatives. Once these decisions are established, it is then useful for both management and investors to know what the breakeven point is, and whether it will be easy or difficult to attain. Considerations such as percent share of the total market required for breakeven can be introduced as a way of evaluating the reasonableness of the breakeven point. Generally, the smaller the percentage of the total available target market segment required for breakeven, the better, because it is only at operating levels above breakeven that the business will make any money. Therefore, if there is substantial market potential above the breakeven point, this suggests that there is also additional opportunity available to the business beyond a breakeven operation. Breakeven charts may be developed for a range of choices or decisions. They are especially valuable for identifying decision alternatives in contingency or worst-case planning.

Profit and loss forecasts, or pro forma income statements, reflect the potential profitability of the business operation. Carefully detailed, these pro forma estimates can illustrate the consequences of various decisions made regarding the construction of business. As noted, market research and analysis activities establish the basis for sales forecasts. These provide the income projections for the pro forma statements. Operations or production costs, levels of production, and inventory requirements have been established by the manufacturing plan, along with material, labor, service, and manufacturing overhead requirements.

A separation of the fixed and variable portions of these costs is desirable, and the effect of sales volume on inventory, equipment acquisitions, and manufacturing costs should be taken into account. Economies of scale can be indicated where relevant. Sales expenses should include costs of selling and distribution, storage, discounts, advertising and promotion, and any other variable costs that are tied directly to sales. General and administrative expenses should include management salaries, secretarial costs, and legal and accounting expenses. Manufacturing or operating overhead includes rent, utilities, fringe benefits, telephones, and any other costs that are directly related to the manufacturing operation.

Projections should be prepared on a monthly basis either for the first year or through the end of the quarter in which the business reaches its breakeven, whichever comes later. For some businesses this may take as long as three to five years. Many businesses will reach their breakeven in less than a year. Capital-intensive ventures or ventures in an industry where market penetration is difficult may well require relatively long periods before they reach their breakeven point. The only potential difficulty with such long start-up cycles is that the working capital requirements or the development costs may not be fully anticipated. However, the profit and loss projections, if properly constructed, will anticipate such problems.

If the earnings projections are to be truly useful, they must represent management's realistic and best estimates of probable operating results. Sales or operational cost projections that are either too conservative or too optimistic have little value as aids to policy formulation and decision making.

As noted in earlier chapters, a variety of assumptions must be made during the planning process. It is essential that these assumptions are explicitly stated. This is particularly critical in projecting costs and sales data. It is important both in reviewing projections and in evaluating them to accurately determine the specific assumptions that went into the creation of the numbers used in the projections. Generally, these assumptions will be included as an attachment to the financial projections and are referenced to the financial projections by line item numbers or a footnoting system. Factory and cost data are readily available for many different types of businesses and, especially for a new business, provide an extremely useful guideline as to both investment levels and relative expense percentage proportions. Finally, part of the statement of assumptions should include an assessment of the relative risks or "softness" of any of the numbers used in the projections.

For many new businesses, the pro forma cash flow analysis is more important than the forecasts of profits, because it details the amount and timing of expected cash inflows and outflows. Particularly during the start-up phase of a business, the level of profits will usually not be sufficient to cover operating costs, and, more generally, cash inflows may not necessarily match outflows on a short-term basis. The cash flow forecast will indicate these situations and enable management to plan for the cash needed to finance these deficiencies. An assessment of the accumulated initial negative cash flows will indicate clearly the required level of working capital. Determining the required level of working capital for a new venture is frequently seen as a difficult if not mysterious process by individuals putting together new business operations, but in fact, initial working capital requirements can be derived directly from the cash flow analysis.

The cash flow analysis also acts as a primary feasibility determinant, both in contributing to the assessment of the aggregate cash needed for financing the business and in specifying the growth opportunities of the business. For example, it may well be necessary to depress or restrict the rate of growth because of inherent cash flow constraints. In addition, the cash flow forecast will highlight the need for and timing of additional financing and indicate peak requirements for working capital at different periods throughout each annual period, thus indicating the different types of financing that may be required for the different needs the business will encounter.

If the business is in a seasonal or cyclical industry, or an industry where suppliers require a new firm to pay cash (which is typical for many initially), or if an inventory build-up must occur before the product can be sold and produce revenues, the cash flow forecast is critical in determining the additional cash that may be required to maintain the continued solvency of the business.

Another important factor that can be explored through the cash flow analysis is the impact of the credit the organization provides to its customers. Many new ventures automatically will provide accounts-receivable financing to their customers, without fully considering whether or not it is essential and whether or not they can afford it. This alone is a primary cause for illiquidity, especially for a firm that is growing rapidly.

As with P&L projections, cash flow projections should be made on a monthly basis for the first year of operation or until the business reaches its breakeven point, whichever takes longer, and quarterly for the second and third years.

Pro forma balance sheets are used to detail the assets required to support the projected levels of operation. In detailing the liability section of the balance sheet, an indication can be made of the various sources of financing used for the business. If trade credit is made an explicit part of the cash flow projections, then it must appear as accounts receivable or accounts payable on the balance sheet. Decisions regarding short-term debt, long-term debt, and equity financing will be reflected on the balance sheet as well.

Over time, the projected balance sheets will reflect the addition of retained profits, retained earnings, and declining balances of loans as they are repaid. Pro forma balance sheets prepared on a quarterly basis over a three-year period will indicate quickly how the financial composition of the business changes over time and provide a basis for ratio analysis and liquidity testing needed to assure that relationships such as debt to equity, working capital, current ratios, and inventory turnover are within acceptable limits.

Historical records should be prepared if the business planning process is being undertaken by an existing business. It may be that the business is seeking expansion capital or other types of outside financing; if so, balance sheets and income statements of a current operating period and the past two operating periods will be required in addition to the projection. Outside financing agencies will prefer, and perhaps require, that such historical documents be audited and certified. In the absence of certification, such statements should be corroborated by copies of the organization's income tax filings. Any other pertinent financial data may be included as an appendix in the final written plan.

In summary, the financial plan is primarily composed of a series of financial projections. These projections, including earnings and cash flow, should be completed for at least three years, and longer if market penetration will take longer. Assumptions should be clearly indicated. The cash flow statement is extremely important, since it reflects estimates and projections on the amounts of financing needed, when it will be needed, and the generation of income as the company matures. Profit and loss forecasts indicate the profitability of the operations as they are proposed. Pro forma balance sheets indicate changes in the financial structure of the operation as it goes through various development stages and provide an opportunity to assess the financial viability of the business at future points in its development.

Collectively, the financial projections form the basis for a control system which the business can utilize once operations have commenced. They provide the targets and the decision-making assumptions that indicate viability of operation. If these targets cannot be met or if the assumptions prove unrealistic, then the feasibility of the entire operating plan must be reassessed. An important purpose of the financial plan is to reveal such infeasibility implications and to show possible incongruence between different components of the total business system.

SUMMARY

A business plan involves a number of components necessary to determine whether or not a new business concept makes sense and, if it does make sense, what is required to establish it and help it progress through the development stages until it becomes a viable and profitable operation. In addition to the basic steps of the planning process, contingency plans are necessary to anticipate what may have to be done if things do not work out as expected or hoped. Contingency planning is not only an important aspect of feasiblity analysis but essential in determining the extra amount of financing or funding that may be required to develop the business if events take longer than anticipated, market development does not occur as rapidly as projected, or costs are higher than anticipated.

It is important to recognize the need for continuous planning, assessment, review, and revision at each stage of the business's development. Both product lines and individual products or services should generally be looked at as in a continual development stage, and both carry the same implications for additional needed funds to take full advantage of emerging opportunities. For any of these opportunities, the full range of planning activities outlined in this chapter should be brought into play, with the understanding that working the venture through on paper not only is much cheaper and quicker than trying it out in practice but also provides for immeasurably more flexibility since multiple alternatives can be simultaneously pursued. In reality, such simultaneous testing is rarely possible, because in application alternatives tend to become mutually exclusive.

People embarking on a new venture typically begrudge the time, energy, and money that may be required to go through the planning process at the depth recommended here. They are anxious to start actually doing things and sick and tired of merely thinking about the venture. On the other hand, experienced practitioners know that this is not only a valuable exercise for the internal planning needs of the business but probably the only way they are going to get outside investors to provide the financing inevitably required to commence a new venture.

Chapter 5:
The Mechanics
of Planning

The discussion up to this point has focused on the philosophical and conceptual implications of business planning. The next two chapters will deal with the mechanics of actually constructing a business plan for any type of venture.

A good plan consists of two parts: a written description of the business idea and the financial data and other projections which quantify the implications of the written components of the plan. This chapter is an introduction to the process of actually constructing a plan; Chapter 6 outlines the format and the requirements for developing the written portion of the plan; and Chapter 7 treats the financial section of the plan.

Together, the results of Chapters 6 and 7 will represent a coherent, integrated plan that serves the combined purposes of both feasibility analysis and financing solicitation. In addition, the completed plan becomes the plan of action and a control tool once the business is in operation. Here again, the advice is simple. Try the business idea out on paper. If the idea doesn't make sense or won't work, forget it. If the concept does make sense, evaluate all alternatives and pick out those that will best satisfy the objectives of the operation. Then, if everything makes sense, do it.

PLAN CONSTRUCTION

If the analytical process outlined in Chapter 4 has been thoroughly followed, much of the background work and the data collection, as well as a probing, searching evaluation of the idea it-self, will have been completed. The relationship between the planning process and the functional planning format to be followed in creating an actual business plan is outlined in Figure 5-1.

Constructing the actual business plan involves first assembling the accumulated data and information into a logical form. A well-developed business plan is a small book ranging from 20 to 100 or more pages, and should be treated as such. It should have a cover or a binder to protect it. It should be typed. Different sections or segments of the plan should be differentiated, say, as chapters. There should be a table of contents for quick reference and appendixes containing relevant backup material.

Business plans are to be *used*. They are tools to facilitate business development, formation, initiation, and success. The format and structure of the business plan presented here are designed to facilitate its use. Excerpts from the business plan of the Battleworks Furniture Company are included in Chapters 6 and 7 to show the application of the planning process. The toal plan for this hypothetical company is presented in Appendix A to show how a completed working plan actually looks.

The planning framework developed here is user-oriented rather than developer-oriented. It does not necessarily represent the sequence by which a useful plan is actually constructed. In reality, the planning process is not particularly sequential at all, but rather involves the accumulation and analysis, more or less concurrent, of various data in a number of different areas. The resulting information is organized sequentially later in the process. The reasons for this approach are that it is difficult to anticipate interrelationships until at least a base of data and understandings have been established and that information revealed in one part of the plan may require that different earlier sections of the plan be seriously re-evaluated and perhaps remodeled.

The format that is presented here has been tested and proven in many situations. It is the result of in-depth analysis of literally thousands of plans and an amalgamation of opinions of lenders, consultants, teachers, and entrepreneurs of what they find useful in a realistic, workable plan.

Although the business plan format outlined here is appropriate for the majority of business purposes, different types of businesses would ordinarily emphasize different segments or portions of the plan. It is up to the users to decide which sections of the plan are most relevant for their particular purposes and emphasize

Figure 5-1. Relationship between the planning process and the business plan.

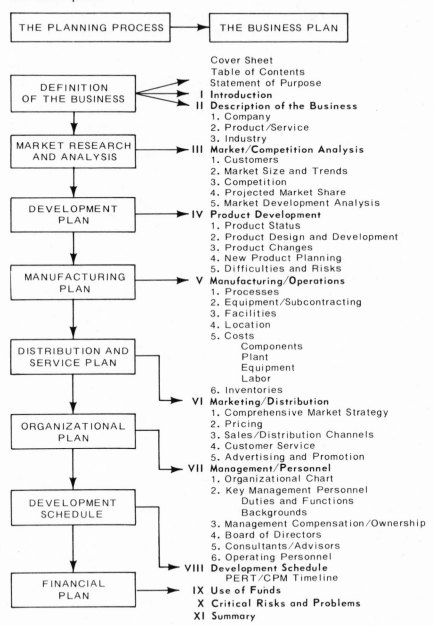

them accordingly. Also different individuals will have different gaps in their knowledge, which again will lead to emphasis on different problem areas in the planning process.

Even recognizing the differences between businesses, most ventures would need to include practically all the segments of the plan suggested in the outline here in order to fully serve their business planning needs. This leads back to the basic purpose of the business plan. The business plan is a free-standing statement of how a particular business is to operate and why that process makes sense. It is a stand-alone document that should be fully self-contained. If the business plan is going to be used to solicit financing, for example, the owners or the principals cannot staple themselves to the cover of the plan to explain its shortcomings. It simply is impossible to say, "What I meant was. . . ." Instead, the plan must convey clearly and explicitly what the principals intended to say. It must include all the information, in sufficient depth, that a reader of average intelligence and average knowledge would require in order to understand what the principals intend to do in their business and why it will be successful.

This is just as true if the plan is to be used only for internal purposes as it would be if the plan is to solicit outside support, particularly financing from others. For internal purposes, the plan can communicate to others within the organization, and it will remind the principals at some point in the future what they really intended to have happen. It will remind them of the assumptions made in the planning process that made the plan appear to be feasible, and finally, it will provide a benchmark against which to measure the actual performance of the business once it is in operation.

It is important to keep these objectives in mind, to be specific about the full set of objectives as the plan is in its early formative stages. More information is better than less. Specificity is infinitely more valuable than vagueness. Creating a good plan is an evolutionary process. It starts out with a hypothetical concept, and as the concept approaches reality, assumptions are replaced by facts. Projections and other operating premises are constantly modified in view of new information that turns up through the research and development process. Reducing the emerging ideas to writing forces clarity. The more these ideas can be clarified early in the process, the better will be the quality of the plan that emerges and of the business operation once the plan is put into effect.

Given this objective of clarity, the first step in creating a business plan is to make the purposes of that plan very precise, to spell out the objectives very specifically. These objectives will provide the focal points that make the information accumulated in the plan relevant and meaningful. A good plan collects and displays information in a logical and rational manner. It creates an analytical base from which to evaluate and verify assumptions and create realistic projections.

ADVICE TO USERS

It is very important that the business principals create the business plan themselves. Going through the planning process has an enormous educational value. A wide variety of alternatives must be considered, and decision making occurs at various points, each of which may substantially affect the direction of the business. Accordingly, it is critical that this planning function not be delegated to someone else within the organization or handed over to outside professionals. This is not to say that outside professionals cannot be extremely valuable to the planning process in providing a variety of necessary sophisticated tasks and services. However, the majority of the work of developing the plan should be undertaken by the managing principals. They will have final responsibility for implementing the plan.

In order to effectively manage their business, the principals must understand all the alternatives and the full implications of their implementation. This is possible only if they have been thoroughly and intimately involved in all stages of the planning activity. To an outside investor, one of the most powerful danger signals of a new business is when the managing principals send an outside spokesman to speak on their behalf. If the managing principals cannot explain and defend all aspects of the business plan, then their ability to implement and carry through with that plan is subject to serious questioning. This is such a critical point that it simply cannot be overemphasized. The planning process must not be delegated or assigned to someone else, it must be performed by the managing principals themselves.

SUMMARY

A good business plan will clearly and thoroughly explain the total business system, then show how the quantification of assumptions and plans bears out the philosophy of operations. It will provide sufficient detail and data to support its conclusions. A good plan serves the three important functions of feasibility analysis, operational planning, and communication, both internally and externally.

The quality of the plan is tested in application. Therefore, all thinking in the planning/modeling process must be constantly subjected to the test of practicality: Will it work? Why will it work? How will it work? Answer these three questions and the success of the business operation will be guaranteed to the greatest extent possible.

Chapter 6:
Description
of the Business

The first section of a formal, written business plan is a description of all the important aspects of the business operation. It develops a model of the total operation on paper before any activity commences. Through this process, vague generalities that exist in the minds of the business principals can be taken out into the light of day, carefully examined to see if they can withstand confrontation with reality, and then developed into a schedule of events that must occur in order to turn these ideas into a functioning organization with the best chances possible for success.

The plan will serve three important functions: feasibility analysis, operations guide, and communication. The plan will have readers. The principals themselves will use the plan as an operational guide; employees and subordinates will follow relevant sections in performing their own work; and outsiders, especially financing intermediaries, will want to understand both how and why the business will succeed. These purposes determine the level of detail and the form of the plan.

It is necessary to reinforce the advice that the plan must be viewed as a stand-alone document. The proponents cannot staple themselves to the cover to explain what they really meant; the plan must do that by itself. In addition, when the proponents themselves try to figure out what they originally intended six or nine months previously, they will need to have the original assumptions clearly and explicitly stated in order to understand the specific ways in which the reality of actual operations has deviated from the future anticipated in the plan.

Finally, of course, users must modify the format and other suggestions offered here to serve their own specific needs. The suggestions are a guide. They are management tools to facilitate the construction of the plan and to improve decision making throughout the planning and implementation process. To be most effective, the use of the recommendations made here must be metered by good judgment, careful thought, and much old-fashioned common sense.

THE FORMAT

The plan will have a cover sheet. The first item following that will be the statement of purpose, after which will appear a table of contents:

Introduction
Description of the Business
Market and Competition Analysis
Products(s)/Service(s)
Manufacturing/Operations
Location
Marketing Plan
Development/Future Change Strategies
Management Team
Operating Personnel
Venture Development Schedule
Proposed Uses of Funds Requested
Critical Risks and Problems
Summary

The Cover Sheet

The cover sheet identifies the plan and indicates its target and/or purpose. It will identify the business described in the document, the location and telephone number of the business or where the principals can be reached, and the individual(s) who prepared the business plan. If the business plan is to be used as a financing proposal, this specific purpose would be so stated on the cover sheet.

If the plan is being submitted to more than one source, a different cover sheet should be used for each. If it is being used as a prospectus for consideration by investors, there are some disclaimers which must appear on the cover sheet. Specifically, if the plan is to be circulated to more than ten potential investors, it falls under the SEC regulations and the assistance of an attorney should be secured to assure proper treatment.

The Statement of Purpose

The statement of purpose is provided to tell the reader exactly the purposes of the plan and the expectations that are placed on the reader. It may come before or after the table of contents, but often appears before it because it represents the primary communication between the authors of the plan and the reader.

This section is frequently omitted from the business plan, much to the detriment of the document. The reader needs to know at the very outset why he is being asked to read the plan and what he should keep in mind as he evaluates the venture.

If the reader is being asked to consider the plan as a potential investment, the amount of the investment or loan and the nature of the proposed relationship should be clearly stated. The reader will then have a much better understanding of what to look for as the rest of the plan is studied. If the plan is to be used as an internal planning document, it will state this and show the specific objectives the plan is seeking to achieve.

Because the statement of purpose must be complete and concise, it is often one of the most difficult areas of the entire planning process, in spite of the fact that it typically does not occupy more than a paragraph or two at the most. It is the intense specificity required by the statement of purpose which makes it so difficult to write. It forces a very close inspection of all the operating assumptions by the principals before they can begin to convey their ideas to others. The statement of purpose should provide the following information:

Who is asking for the money.
How much money is being requested.
What the money is intended for.
How the funds will benefit the business.
Why the loan or investment makes sense.
How the funds will be repaid.

If the business is not seeking a loan, the plan should still support and justify the use of whatever funds are involved. The statement of purpose cannot be completed until cash and capital needs are established on the basis of in-depth financial projections.

Here are two statements of purpose for the Battleworks Furniture Company. The first is the financing proposal, and the second is for internal use.

Statement of Purpose

The Battleworks Furniture Company, Inc., is seeking a loan of $63,000 for eight years to purchase equipment and inventory, prepare operating space as needed, maintain necessary cash reserves, and provide adequate working capital to successfully launch a vertically integrated, custom, butcher-block furniture manufacturing and retail operation. This loan, together with an equity cash investment of $8,000, will be sufficient to finance the transition through the development phases so that the business can operate as a viable profitable enterprise.

or:

Statement of Purpose

This business plan has been developed by the Battleworks Furniture Company, Inc., as an operating guide to the development of a vertically integrated, custom, butcher-block furniture manufacturing and retail operation. The aggregate investment of $71,000 being provided from private sources is sufficient to purchase equipment and inventory, prepare operating space as needed, maintain necessary cash reserves, and provide adequate working capital to successfully launch this business. This document is for internal planning and operations purposes only, and is not to be released outside the operation.

Table of Contents
The table of contents, as in any normal document, indicates the format of the plan. Roughed out at first, it can serve as an outline for constructing the balance of the plan. As the plan is nearing completion, the table of contents can then be finished off with page numbers and other relevant information. The sample table of contents shown here is the format recommended for virtually any business plan. This sample, with minor changes, should become the table of contents as well as the guide for creating the actual business plan.

Sample Table of Contents

Statement of Purpose

The Introduction

This section should be included particularly in a business plan that is soliciting an investment from a venture capital investor. It may not be as essential in business plans for other purposes, as it provides some specific technical detail of a level and type that is simply not relevant for the majority of business situations.

For the more complex business plans oriented toward venture capital investors, the introduction will summarize and highlight the whole proposal. It should be cogent and concise, describe the precise nature of the business, the participants, and why the plan will work.

The introduction should be confined to two pages. It should be written after the plan is done and provide a true summary of the highlights of the plan. It is intended as a brief way to convey the important aspects of the proposed business to intended investors. Its communication value for potential investors makes this perhaps the most critical section of the entire plan. It is in fact a marketing tool for the financing of the venture.

As a minimum, the introduction should contain a discussion of the business operation and principals, when it was formed or will be formed, what it will do, what is special or unique about the product, service, or technology, and what aspects of the backgrounds of the principals make them especially well qualified to successfully pursue this kind of opportunity. If it is an existing business, a brief analysis of its financial history should be included. A discussion of the market opportunity should be provided, including the size and growth rate of the market, the percentage of the market that the business intends to capture, a brief statement about industrywide growth trends, intentions for the development and modification of the product line in order to enter new markets in the future, and comments about other future plans of the business.

The products and technology should be discussed in sufficient detail to help a reasonably intelligent reader understand the situation. Included in this discussion should be an acknowledgment of proprietary technology and trade secrets or unique skills within the management team that provide a competitive edge within the marketplace. However, it is not necessary to have something unique in order to be successful. Many times new businesses are successful simply because they are more efficient, do a more effective job of providing ongoing standardized goods and services than the competition, or are serving an emerging target market segment in an otherwise conventional manner.

One venture capital guidebook suggests that experienced venture investors seek answers to the following ten basic questions* when evaluating a new company.

1. *Is the company in an area of emerging technology?* Does the technology have a solid base for growth as measured by the research and development efforts put into the technology, both by this and other companies? If the company thinks its technology is way ahead, is it too far ahead? Where is everybody else? Why? Do I, the reader, understand the technology and its potential growth? If it can't be explained to me, whatever my background, I am suspicious. If it can't be explained to me, how can it be explained to customers, directors, and other investors?

2. *Is there a market for the technology or product?* Basically, is there a need demonstrated already, or will it create a new market? New market speculation entails the highest risk but the greatest rewards. Does management understand the market and how to exploit it? What is the competition?

3. *Why didn't an established company decide to exploit and market the product?* The entrepreneur may tell me his old company didn't understand him, stifling his inventiveness. This can often be true; it may also be true that the parent company made a market evaluation and determined that the product was not worth exploiting further. On the other hand, maybe the parent company thought it was a good idea, but just couldn't invest resources in it.

4. *Is there a natural product line or follow-on technology?* In other words, does the new concept or product or technology have the potential for a long-range career? Is the management flexible and adaptive to change?

5. *Does management have corporate experience?* The key people, particularly the decision makers, should have experience either as officers or directors of a profit-making corporation in a technology area. There is always the exception to the rule, but the chief officials should have been around the corporate track so they know what to expect and how to plan.

* Adapted from *Venture Capital: A Guidebook for New Enterprises,* 2d ed., The Management Institute, School of Management, Boston College, Chestnut Hill, Mass., January 1973; prepared as a public document under a grant from the New England Regional Commission.

6. *What are management's goals?* Only to make money? This type of leadership will go over the side quickly. Its goals may be in conflict with corporate and stockholder goals. The entrepreneur may sell off the corporation when he has reached his own financial objectives. The best entrepreneurs are people who like to run things, organize them and grow them, as well as have financial incentives.

7. *Does management have a ten-year objective and a five-year operating plan?* These may change with time, but they should always be clearly stated at the outset.

8. *Does management understand and have capabilities for all phases of its operations* from research through production and marketing, as well as for support functions (comptroller, accounting, legal, and so forth)? The missing manager whom the company is going to hire tomorrow can always be the weak link in the chain. The full span of experience and authority should be visible at the outset.

9. *Does management understand the nature and use of money?* This is extremely important, regardless of how good the idea or the management is. Money is the fuel that stokes the fire.

10. *Does management have a competent recognized leader and decision maker?* Group decision making may be fine in the textbooks, but it doesn't work very well in the small emerging organization that has to make decisions fast if it is to survive. Above all, the decision maker should be a good manager.

Clearly, much of the information desired by the venture capital investor is very useful to other types of investors or lenders and, for many different types of businesses, to the management principals themselves. These questions should be given serious thought by anyone developing a business plan for any purpose and responded to where relevant in the appropriate places within the plan itself.

Description of the Business

This is a general introduction to the business idea, the status of the venture, the product or service, the personnel, the operation, why the plan will work, and any other information needed to provide a conceptual understanding of the whole business deal. If the previously described two-page introductory summary is provided, this section will repeat some of that information, but in more detail.

This section will establish the framework for the rest of the plan. It provides the reader with sufficient information to understand the more detailed discussion in the succeeding sections. It serves the two purposes of providing an introduction to the plan and establishing some background information.

There is a corny adage that is very helpful in putting together a business plan: Tell them what you're going to tell them, tell them, and tell them what you told them. You are going to tell them what you're going to tell them in the statement of purpose and in the introductory portion of the description of the business. You are going to tell them in the main body of the plan, and you are going to tell them what you told them in the summary section of the plan.

The business description should provide any reader with sufficient information to understand the objectives of this particular project and to be able to place it into meaningful context with other activities. There are some points that will need to be included in this discussion:

The nature of the product or service.
How it will be made and produced.
How it will be sold.
Who will buy it.
The status of the industry.
The nature and composition of the company itself.

This section is of particular importance to the business principals themselves. It requires a precise statement of exactly what the business will do, what it will sell, make, broker, or provide, exactly how it will do it, the form, nature, and structure of the organization that will be required in order to achieve these purposes, the products or the services themselves, and the nature of the industry's structure. The business principals will have to understand all these facets in order to write about them intelligently, and the process of gaining an understanding will help them in refining their own ideas about the business venture.

This section becomes a major statement of operating policy and will actually guide the business through its early stages of formation and development. *Specificity is critical,* because, unless the business venture is clearly conceptualized, early development activities will lack focus, scarce resources of time and money may be wasted, and the activities of the principals themselves may be aimless and diffused, all of which will mean that the new business will have a difficult time staying on the track, if indeed it can get on the track at all.

The objective here is to minimize risk and enhance success. Time spent in eliminating confusion in these early planning stages will result in better-quality decision making in the future. Knowing exactly what the business will do and how it will operate enables the principals to plan more effectively. Once all the objectives to be fulfilled through the developing business are made clear (and it must be re-emphasized that profit is only one; others may be equally or even more important), then operations can be designed which will serve these purposes in as near-optimal manner as possible. The entire planning process is based on the perceptions, understanding, and attitudes developed about the business at this point. The purpose of this section, again, is to establish these foundations in writing as clearly and specifically as possible.

It is usually helpful to break this initial section into three general parts: the company, the products or services, and the industry. The description of the company should include what it is, how it will operate, and why and how it will be successful. The particular strengths of the company, especially management strengths, should be stressed.

The discussion of the products or services should begin by describing what they are, whether there are proprietary advantages, patents, or trademarks involved, and any other particular competitive advantages. Any special skills or abilities needed to manufacture, service, or market the product should be noted.

The nature of the product or service will be an important determinant of the structure of the organization. Comments should be made on the type of opportunity represented by the product or the service and its application, both to primary end users and to secondary users. While unique features or differences between what is currently on the market and what the new business will offer should certainly be stressed, it should again be noted that uniqueness is not a requirement for a new business venture and may even be a hindrance. The vast majority of new businesses provide nonunique products or services to an existing market, but either offer better quality or service or lower price than the competition or move into an expanding marketplace or a developing or new market segment.

Because much opportunity for new businesses comes about through change, anticipating the impact of change on the future of the business is important at this point as well. The potential of the business to serve new or potentially emerging market segments in the future should be seriously considered, and follow-on or new products or services should be anticipated and described.

In discussing the industry, it is important to note its current status, future prospects, new products or developments, new markets or customers, new requirements, and new companies. Demographic, social, or economic trends or factors that could negatively or positively affect this trade should be included. A great deal of information is available describing various industry segments, the structure of the industry, and trends within the industry's market, including future viability and potential as well as the nature, size, and structure of the competition within the industry.

In the example presented in Appendix A, the Battleworks Furniture Company was deliberately seeking an industry which was truly nonoligopolistic. This makes sense for a new small firm, because, if the market is dominated by large buyers or sellers, then all the odds are against a new firm entering the marketplace. It is important to consider any threshold or entry-level requirements into the industry. If the industry is characterized by capital intensity, then a new firm, in order to be competitive, will simply have to have the requisite level of investment, which, by definition, may be extremely high. If the industry is characterized by ease of entry, then the new firm must be concerned with the emergence of other new competitors as well. Careful documentation of all sources of information and other references used is essential, not only in this section, but throughout the rest of the plan as well.

For a sample description-of-the-business section, see Appendix A.

Market and Competition Analysis

A good market and competition analysis provides the first stage of feasibility testing for any idea, whether it is an expansion of an existing venture, a takeover, or the development of a brand-new business. It is worth investing time in this analysis, because it is one of the primary tools for determining whether the business will work. The purpose of the analysis is to find out if there are sufficient people in the market, to identify the nature of the competition, and to locate possible gaps in the market into which the new business could fit. Some of the data that will be collected for this section will appropriately become part of an appendix. The following items should be included in the discussion:

Customers.
Market size and trends.
Competition.
Projected market share.
Market development analysis.

Typically, demographic data and other primary and secondary information are combined here to provide a full picture of the opportunity available to the business and to determine the specific dimensions of that opportunity. The result of the analysis will be the identification of the specific target market segments that the business will seek to serve.

Market segmentation is the process of dividing a vast potential market into smaller groups or segments, each of which is internally similar with respect to some characteristic that is relevant to the purchase or usage of the product or product categories. A market segmentation strategy is based on designing a specific marketing mix to satisfy the needs and wants of one or more distinct segments selected as target markets. If a company is to effectively practice a policy of market segmentation, it must be able to identify, measure, and conduct research on significant subgroups within its total potential market.

The various categories used as bases for segmenting markets include geographic, demographic, psychographic, sociocultural, and user behavior variables. The point is to inspect each market segment to make sure that there are a sufficient number of people with the same characteristics to make it profitable for the marketer to develop a policy of market segmentation for that group, and to make sure that the segment is accessible, that the marketer will be able to reach the market segment efficiently through appropriate media with a minimum of waste coverage.

For some products, consumers differ in their consumption preference according to the geographic regions in which they live. Demographic segmentation includes objective characteristics, such as age, income, occupation, sex, and education. Psychographic segmentation examines the intrinsic characteristics of individuals, such as personalities, buying motives, lifestyles, and attitudes and interests. Individual psychological differences are important bases for segmentation, since people within the same demographic group can differ widely in their consumption behavior. Sociological (group) and anthropological (cultural) variables, such as social class membership, reference group membership, cultural and subcultural memberships, and stage in the family life cycle, indicate different bases for consumption behavior, depending on the different sets of forces and influences that each of those bases may carry. User behavior segmentation includes the rate of usage of the product category and the degree of brand loyalty which is exhibited by the consumer.

This is a research section. In most cases, it will involve secondary research—gathering available information such as census data, technical product information, and a wide variety of market data—rather than the accumulation of primary data through unique new research. Primary information may be accumulated through market surveys, product testing reports, research conducted by outside consultants, or any other specific studies that have been done on behalf of the particular business or product or service.

It should be noted that an enormous quantity of information exists on almost any subject. This information is generally available without great expenditures of time and effort, yet the vast majority of business organizations do not avail themselves of this valuable data base. For example, secondary data, particularly demographic research or census figures, may be supported by a so-called car-window analysis of the market area the business tends to exploit. A car-window analysis means that someone simply gets in a car and drives around the relevant neighborhoods and views the competition, other stores in the neighborhood, and the nature of the community itself, all as a basis for forming some subjective opinions which confirm or reinforce expectations derived from the secondary data.

In addition to indicating the size of the market, this section must include an analysis of the competition—the companies, their products, their prices, and the share of the market they currently have. It is only through a very frank assessment of the competition's strengths and weaknesses that the new business can truly decide whether or not it will be able to capture a slice of whatever market opportunity may be available. Intuitively believing that the new product is "better" and therefore will be more attractive to the target market segments is simply not sufficient. The dimensions of "better" must be clearly identified, along with the strategy of conveying this information to the existing or potential market segments.

The identification of the competition can be done through industry reports for sophisticated or wide-area operations or, for firms with a local orientation, on a much simpler basis through a Yellow Pages survey. As noted, in a local area one helpful technique is a car-window survey, that is, simply driving around the neighborhood or local market area and identifying competitors. As the type of business increases in sophistication, techniques for evaluating the competition must also increase in sophistication. For large firms there is an enormous supply of public information available, including stockholder reports, SEC filings, and other public documents. Again, the vast majority of business firms do not avail themselves of the information and consequently compromise their planning capability.

Many of the sources of market and competition data have been described in earlier discussions on marketing. The market-and-competition-analysis section brings together all this information to provide a meaningful basis for decision making. An important aspect of this portion of the plan is that it provides an objective basis for feasibility analysis. The critical questions of market sufficiency and accessibility must be answered. If there are not enough potential customers or the business will not have reasonable access to them, then it is unlikely that the business will be able to survive, let alone grow and flourish.

Here is how the Battleworks Furniture Company presented its market and competition analysis.

Market and Competition Analysis

An in-depth analysis of the furniture industry competition structure and market segments in the target Standard Metropolitan Statistical Area has indicated the existence of an undersatisfied target market of sufficient size to warrant exploitation by the Battleworks Furniture Company. As noted earlier, the existing market delivery structure offers either quality finished products at high prices, which automatically exclude certain market segments that cannot or do not want to pay this amount, or alternatively offers lower-quality products, finished and unfinished, at lower prices, a combination which provides a poor compromise.

Once the gap in the existing delivery structure was identified, intensive market research was undertaken to identify the specific market segment of individuals who would be potential customers. These individuals can be described as young, educated professionals, who are married, have children, and are either suburban or city dwellers. As indicators of market sufficiency, within the target SMSA there are 1,136,474 individuals employed who are 16 years old and over. Of this total, 416,732, or over one-third (36.6 percent), can be classified as white-collar workers (not including the 260,400 workers who are clerical and related types). Using education as a second indicator of market potential, of the 1,529,168 persons 25 years old and over within the SMSA, 181,358 have completed one to three years of college, and 240,937 have completed four years or more of college, for a total of 422,295, or 27.6 percent of the total. In using income as a barometer of market sufficiency, of the 661,650 families in the target SMSA, 306,045, or 46.25 percent, earn over $12,000, and 199,139, or 30 percent of the total, earn $15,000 or more. Finally, using age as a determining characteristic, of the 2,753,700 total individuals living in the SMSA, 420,677, or 15.28 percent, are between 20 and 44 years of age.

COMPETITION.   In assessing the nature of the competition in the target SMSA, two separate views must be taken. The first view would be a consideration of all of the stores marketing furniture. For example, there are over 350 furniture stores listed in the Yellow Pages for the city alone, not including a variety of additional stores scattered throughout the suburbs. Of this total, however, only 14 are felt to be direct competitors, and of these 14, the following five are felt to be the closest in terms of type of furniture offered, style of operation, price, and potential customers: The Ardvark, Union Square Furniture, Spiffys, Smith's Furniture Emporium, and Joe's Store. Of these five, the first two stores offer the same high-quality contemporary furniture as Battleworks, have convenient and accessible locations, and advertise competitively; however, their prices are considerably higher than those that would be charged by Battleworks for the same type and quality goods. The other three stores are similarly priced and equally accessible but have furniture of lower quality. The corresponding lower-quality image is reflected in their storefronts, signs, and general marketing approaches utilized. Battleworks steps into the gap between these competitors, offering quality at a reasonable price.

A market study was conducted of retail firms within the target SMSA selling furniture similar to that proposed by Battleworks and to a market segment similar to that addressed by Battleworks. The data shown were selected as representative of the volume of specific items in these stores. They do not indicate the total volume of these stores, nor do they suggest that Battleworks, though selling similar items, will necessarily achieve these volumes. These data are included to support the unit sales volumes used to project reasonable sales levels for Battleworks.

Competition Analysis

Store	Item	# Sold per Month	Price	Battleworks Price, Similar or Better Quality
A	3' x 5' Dining Table	20	$75	$75
	3' x 6' Bookcase	30	$80–92	$75
	Desk Pedestal—Single	10	$55	$75
B	Platform Bed—Queen	13	$358–400	$150–250
	39" Child Bed	10	$120–135	$100
	3' x 5' Dining Table	8	$150	$100
C	Bed—Queen Plain	6	$245–290	$150–250
D	Bed—Queen	10	$300–320	$150–250
	Oak Coffee Table	8	$250	$125
	3' x 5' Butcher-block Table	5	$225	$125
	3' x 6' Bookcase	10	$110	$75

Product(s)/Service(s)

This section should clearly and concisely describe the product or services that will be provided. It follows the market and competition analysis conceptually and in fact, as the products provided by the new venture should respond to needs or gaps identified in the preceding section. A useful rule of thumb for businesses with complex or unique products is to provide a one-page summary of the functional specifications of each product in the overall product spectrum. This discussion should be definitive, but be careful not to get lost in too much detail. The following points should be discussed:

Product status.
Product design and development.
Product channels.
New product planning.
Difficulties and risks.

It is important to identify exactly what is going to be sold, its state of development, what it does, how it works, any special problems likely to be encountered in its creation or the delivery to the customer, and the kind of customer field support system that will be required in order to adequately provide service to the customer, including follow-up or guarantees that may be necessary. It is frequently helpful to talk about a family of products or services, a group of closely interrelated and highly supportive items or activities which together provide potential customers with a broad range of choices or enable them to satisfy multiple needs at one time. Given this concept of a family of products or services, it is possible to work from a single or limited selection or offering to some specific target segments and then gradually expand the range of offerings. This amounts to a staged developmental activity.

Such a product development guideline will make it clear how various products will fit together and reinforce and complement each other, thus increasing customer appeal. A lack of this kind of coordination frequently causes confusion on the part of the customer. It may introduce competition between product lines, thus causing redundancy, which is expensive in terms of marketing and product inventory as well as support capability, or it may lead to totally unrelated products or services which greatly magnify marketing problems. If very different target market segments must be appealed to in order to sell unrelated products or services in the product line, then the selling process becomes enormously more expensive.

Specific difficulties and risks which may be encountered in the marketplace must be acknowledged so that their negative impact can be anticipated and corrective strategies can be established in advance. This is an application of the proactive problem-solving approach described earlier.

For a detailed product description section, see Appendix A.

The Manufacturing or Operations Plan
The purpose of this section is to describe exactly how the business is going to operate. The answers can be provided by flowcharts, timetables, time-line continuums, and a variety of other techniques and devices. The objective is to make explicit the flow of materials through a plant or any other activities required to deliver the product or service to the customer.

As in the case of the marketing plan, the more detailed the

manufacturing or operations plan can be made, the more useful it will be for guiding the operation itself, communicating the specifics of the operation to others within the firm, and establishing the credibility of the organization to those outside the firm. If the principals truly understand what it is they are trying to do, then it is a relatively easy and straightforward task to create an operations plan in sufficient detail for it to be truly useful.

The following points should be discussed:

Processes.
Equipment/subcontracting.
Facilities.
Location.
Costs of components, plant, equipment , and labor.
Inventories.

The way to deal with these issues is to develop a concept of the business in the mind's eye, to see it as an operating entity. Then imagine a customer trying to do business with the company. It is essential to identify exactly what activities must be performed and how they all fit together. Then it can be determined if space is adequate for these purposes and personnel adequate to serve the needs.

A well-thought-out, carefully documented plan of operation will point out shortcomings in the business before it is ever started. It will point out special needs relative to a particular location which could require a particular style of operation. Finally, it will help to anticipate a wide variety of problems and provide an opportunity to determine how they can best be resolved.

Production and manufacturing strategy should be developed after the product prototypes are available. Specialists such as cost accountants and manufacturing engineers may be required to help develop this strategy. The underlying concern will be to develop a system which will produce, test, and deliver the products or the services at target costs while making sure that they meet all specifications.

For a production operation, the alternatives to be considered might include building or buying a manufacturing plant or farming out production of subsystems, leaving only final assembly and testing to the company's own production staff. Alternatives such as purchasing versus leasing a plant, facilities, or equipment, renting equipment, or jobbing must be carefully evaluated in terms of costs and benefits. The exact strategies adopted will be influenced by required inventory levels, available financing, availability of labor force, as well as various operating and production considerations.

Innovative but practical alternatives that provide significant cost advantages over competitors may be worked out. However, it would be fallacious and presumptuous for the new owners to assume that they are simply smarter than the competition and therefore will be able to do a better job. Instead, it is necessary to be very specific about the way this better job will be done.

Some very sophisticated production planning techniques have long been used by large organizations. These can very appropriately be applied in new small organizations and sometimes provide insights leading to those innovative strategies which are essential for cost competition. At the same time, it must be recognized that the new firm, by virtue of the fact that it is new, will need to learn, and these initial learning costs should not be discouraging or surprising. Most ventures require a trial-and-error period to thrash out operational problems and determine the most efficient way of performing certain activities within the specific constraints of the organization. This testing process is just as important as planned product R&D programs.

A sample manufacturing and operations plan can be found in Appendix A.

Location
Choosing a location is a strategic decision for virtually any kind of operation. It has both marketing and manufacturing/operations implications. If the business is a retail operation, then customer accessibility becomes a critical concern. If it is inconvenient or difficult for customers to get to the location, then sales will suffer accordingly. If it is a wholesale operation, access to transportation routes and corresponding cost efficiencies may be the most critical concerns.

Many times organization go about their location selection process backward. They look around and find out what is available and then pick a spot. A far more desirable alternative is to first very carefully consider the specific needs of the operation and then describe the ideal location. Relevant considerations include the amount of space needed, layout, type of construction, access, visibility, neighborhood, and surrounding businesses. Then, as these dimensions are clearly established, the business can begin a search for a location that satisfies these requirements as nearly as possible. Once the ideal or optimal specifications are made explicit, they can be modified in the face of reality with a clear understanding of what is being traded off.

While many businesses, consciously or by default, settle for a location that fails to meet some important requirements, it is not uncommon for a business to wind up with a location that considerably exceeds its requirements. If this occurs, the business simply will be spending more than is necessary. On the other hand, for many retail locations and even for some wholesale locations, there is a close correlation between location visibility and advertising. This relationship may provide the justification for paying a premium price for a given location because that higher price in fact represents a combination of rent and advertising and should be viewed accordingly. However, this must be made explicit. Again, the objective is to establish a framework for decision making, to move away from hunch decisions by making the decision process as logically structured and as coherent as possible. A sample description of location is included in Appendix A.

The Marketing and Distribution Plan

A good market and competition analysis and the product(s)/service(s) description lay the foundation for the marketing plan. If a thorough job has been done in these earlier sections and the business has clearly identified the target market, then the development of a marketing plan is a relatively straightforward process. Included will be a discussion of the following main points:

Comprehensive market strategy.
Pricing.
Sales/channels.
Customer services.
Advertising and promotion.

Marketing represents another major area of weakness for many businesses. The focus of these businesses typically is on product development, the assumption being that once the product is developed, it will be sold. This is the fallacy of the better-mousetrap logic. The better-mousetrap logic suggests that if you develop a better mousetrap, the world will beat a path to your door. This, of course, is not necessarily true. The world first needs to know not only that the better mousetrap is available and where and how it is available but, more importantly, exactly how the better mousetrap will better satisfy their needs. The market may not even know that it needs a mousetrap at all.

The problem for many businesses is that, because they are so thoroughly tuned to the functions and advantages of their product or service, they simply forget about the fact that others who are not as thoroughly involved may not have any understanding of the problems, needs, and potential in this specific area at all. The business may have to overcome a significant educational problem before it can attract customers. It may be necessary to first inform people that they have a need before they can be informed that the business has the means to satisfy that need. This is an important conceptual issue. In fact, it is the basis for developing the entire marketing strategy.

The marketing plan includes advertising strategies and an evaluation of different advertising media, and it develops an attitude and approach to the product or service that helps to reflect and govern the style of the operation itself. It describes exactly what needs to be done in order to move the product or deliver the service to the ultimate customer. Typically, target groups can be ranked in order of their relative accessibility, both in terms of convenience and in terms of costs. Then a series of plans or stages of attack can be developed, focusing on first the target group where the largest, most rapid sales can be made for the least cost and broadening out to additional target segments as the resources and capability of the firm permit.

The more specific the marketing plan can be made, the more helpful it will be and the more likely will be its success. A philosophical statement of a vague and generalized approach is not especially useful as a marketing plan. What is useful is the identification of the specific series of activities that must be undertaken in order to accomplish the objectives of the enterprise. Once the specific activities are identified, they can be assigned to different personnel or groups within the organization. It will be clear to each of these individuals or groups exactly what their tasks are and how they relate to others engaged in other parts of the activity. This is a further example of the systems approach to problem solving.

The specific information that should be provided in the marketing plan includes:

- The anticipated selling price to the ultimate customer for each product or service in the projected line.

- A brief price comparison with competitive products.
- A list of potential customers who have expressed an interest in the proposed products or services.
- The alternative channels of sales distribution of the anticipated field service organization, now and in the future.
- Special marketing strategies.

In summary, for most businesses the marketing plan is one of the keys in determining success or failure. For many businesses, however, it is an area that is ignored for a variety of reasons. Many businesses seem to feel that merely because they have a good product or service and are concentrating their activities on providing that product or service, they have adequately satisfied the marketing requirements. This may be the furthest from the truth, because products or services, no matter how good, are not good unless the target market is familiar with their availability and convinced that they are needed. The marketing plan includes not only advertising, but personnel, style of operation, location, and a variety of other factors, all of which have to do with the process of delivering the product to the customer. Each one of the factors in the marketing plan represents another aspect of strategic decision making, which considers the relationship of each facet of the business as an integrated component of the total operation.

A detailed sample marketing plan is found in Appendix A.

Development/Future Change Strategies

Logically following the manufacturing and/or operations plan, the discussion of the products or services and the developmental marketing plans are the future change strategies of the firm. For many organizations the focus of the initial planning activities is on simply getting the business started, on opening the doors and getting the customers to flow in. However, once that is achieved, planning activities must immediately be focused on how the operation will be maintained.

One important consequence of the present state of the external environment for most businesses is dramatically shortened product life cycles. It is not sufficient to be competitive in the marketplace today. Plans must be made for what the business will do tomorrow when many customers have purchased the product, when the competition comes along and introduces similar products, and when new technology comes along and renders the existing offerings obsolete. In the present day of change and acceleration of technology, it is rare for a firm to remain competitive even with a totally proprietary or a patented product unless it has a carefully designed and utilized change strategy.

It is particularly difficult for a small firm to engage in the type of research and development necessary to maintain competitive advantage because of the sheer costs involved. The magnitude of that investment relative to the sales base, as compared with much larger organizations, is frequently forbidding. Even given these limitations, it is perhaps even more critical that the small firm very consciously and actively pursue new alternatives, because its ability to withstand a competitive onslaught is limited as well.

The purpose of this section is twofold: first, to make sure that there is a logical progression or futurity to the business operation, second, to indicate to others that the organization has actively considered the dangers of product obsolescence or competition and has figured out what to do for an encore.

Below is a sample discussion of future change strategies.

Future Change Strategies

Once Battleworks has successfully made the transition from a conceptual model to an operating reality and unknown quantities have been defined and other assumptions of the model tested and revised as needed, the organization proposes to expand in two directions.

The first will be the gradual development of commercial sales. The butcher-block style of furniture which is proposed to be the basic product line of Battleworks is attractive and durable and increasingly seen as appropriate for contemporary business firms, especially in reception areas, employee leisure areas, and other such commercial space that requires comfort, attractiveness, and durability in its furniture. Battleworks will be in a position to be completely competitive with other sources of supply, in terms of both price and quality, and as the organization develops, it will have the capacity to take on such sales.

The second dimension of projected expansion is the development of satellite storefronts. The creation of one or more satellite stores has the potential to increase sales volume dramatically. The satellite store will be a retail showroom operation employing one salesperson. It will have on display a selection of Battleworks furniture and sales literature.

Since the satellite store would be strictly a sales operation (all manufacturing would continue to be done at the primary Battleworks location), it would occupy relatively little space. Given a satellite store's modest space requirements, it can be in a high-traffic location affording maximum exposure without prohibitively high rent. The satellite store would have a selection of furniture representative of Battleworks' total product line, which would be complemented by large photographs and other such sales aids. A competent salesperson would be able to satisfy most customers' needs and, in the few instances where it would be necessary, customers could always be referred to the primary store location.

Such an operation could contribute significantly to Battleworks' sales and profits. Aside from the materials costs and the salary of one salesperson, most of the organization's normal operating costs will continue to be carried by the primary location. The satellite store could thus contribute significant income while incurring only a low level of direct cost.

Both of these strategies would be put into operation only if the development of the business itself warrants this and the additional projected required funding is available.

Management Team

There are two important purposes to this section. First, it identifies the range of skills required to properly run the business. Second, it shows how the particular members of the proposed management team will provide that full range of skills. The following should be included in the discussion:

Organization chart.
Key management personnel—duties, functions, and backgrounds.
Management compensation/ownership.
Board of directors.
Consultants/advisors.

The underlying question deals with who is going to run this organization and why they are qualified to do so. Frequently, the prime actors are the principals starting the business. It is important to indicate the contribution made by each in order to show their relevance to the operation. People should not be included in the team merely because of convenience or because they happen to be hanging around or because they happen to be someone's brother-in-law, but only if they can be expected to make a meaningful contribution to the total operation.

It is important to indicate that operational tasks have been made explicit and clearly distributed, even though, particularly for a start-up venture, the demand in any single category may be small. It is still critical at this early stage to project these time demands ahead and to determine whether or not there is sufficient management personnel available to handle the management needs that go along with the business's growth.

In developing organizations, management tasks are typically assigned on a rather casual basis, in particular, in terms of the principals' subjective preferences for different activities. It is important to identify the different needs or management functions that must be performed and then determine whether or not adequate management talent exists on the business development team to provide for those needs. Through a systematic analysis and functional assignment of duties it may be revealed that other people are required in order to round out the management team either now or in the future.

A time-line progression may be useful here, as in other sections of the plan, to show what additional members will be added to the management team as the business develops and that there is a development strategy for creating this enriched management hierarchy in response to increasing demands within the different operational divisions of the business firm. For example, the management plan may provide for the creation of separate departments for marketing and production in larger organizations, even though at earlier stages of development combining the two may be the most efficient way of handling the activities.

A one-paragraph sketch should be provided for each of the key people, describing their background and talents. This would also indicate present or proposed distribution of ownership and the reasons for this allocation. Generally, in-depth resumes would be provided in an appendix to the plan as backup documentation.

Here is how Battleworks described its management.

Management Team

The firm will be under the management of Mr. John M. Silver, President of the Battleworks Furniture Company, Inc. Mr. Silver is extremely well qualified to manage such an operation, having undergraduate training in engineering and personal interests that have led him to experiment with the application of advanced engineering technology to the centuries-old craft of furniture building in wood. This includes such methods as the application of ultrasonic technology in combination with new forms of bonding materials to produce structures stronger and less expensive than previously possible. Various articles of furniture have been produced by Mr. Silver using such technology, and given to friends as presents.

Mr. Silver gained management experience while in the Navy where he attained the rank of lieutenant and had responsibility for over 300 men. His duty in the Navy made excellent use of his engineering training, particularly when he was assigned major responsibility on the USS Delong. While in the Navy, Mr. Silver had further opportunity to utilize his woodworking skills, manufacturing various articles of furniture for his friends and colleagues in the well-equipped woodworking shops available where he served. He has since received his MBA from the East Podunk Graduate School of Business.

The combination of experiences gained, supported by manufacturing operations responsibility at Johns-Manville, qualified him for a position on the faculty of the College of Engineering of the State University. Among other responsibilities, he assisted in the successful presentation of a proposal to the Engineering Council for Professional Development for accreditation. The State University is the first and only institution to be accredited in manufacturing engineering. The concept of manufacturing as an engineering discipline is relatively new, and the accreditation by the Council is a reflection of its belief that the solutions to many manufacturing problems are through the application of skilled engineering.

Mr. Silver, as part of his MBA studies, performed a major, in-depth study of the furniture industry as research for his Master's Thesis. Through this research, complemented by his personal interest in small-scale furniture manufacturing and retail operations, he has gained extensive knowledge of the operation of the industry, the nature of the competition, problems to avoid, and requirements for successful entry into the industry.

Mr. Silver, as principal of the firm, has arranged for professional outside support to assist him during his planning implementation phase and to provide a source of continuing advice and counsel once the business has been established. Arrangements are currently under way to secure the services of a major CPA firm, and Smith, Fargell and Wasp, a Podunk-based law firm, provide legal counsel.

Mr. Silver will be performing all the management team functions initially. As the business develops, he anticipates the need to develop a production manager while retaining the sales and marketing responsi-

ORGANIZATION CHART
BATTLEWORKS FURNITURE COMPANY, INC.

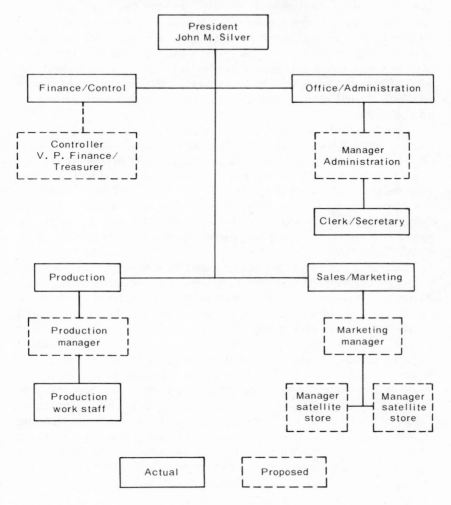

bilities himself. This one additional individual will be the only anticipated addition to the management team throughout the time period covered by this plan, although the need for additional personnel at future points in the development of the business is identified and shown on the accompanying organization chart.

Operating Personnel

Personnel choices are especially critical in a small business, because these organizations, almost by definition, typically lack the capability of burying mistakes. Personnel choices certainly are important in larger firms, because they seriously affect the efficiency of the organization. An incorrect or bad choice in personnel not only results in the loss of productivity of that individual but also affects the productivity of others in the organization. There can be a serious morale cost to having the incorrect people involved in the business.

Being explicit about the personnel needs, particularly indicating a true understanding of the skills, aptitudes, and capabilities that are required, will be enormously helpful. As in the earlier sections, the more explicit these requirements can be made, the easier will be the job of fulfilling them, or, if they can't be fulfilled, at least the organization will know to what extent compromises are being made. After this profile has been established, it is a matter of searching out and hiring the correct people for the tasks which need to be performed.

Once the combination of skills and talents required is defined, it can be determined whether or not individuals with the requisite skills are available or if they must be trained. If people need to be trained for the operation, additional costs will be incurred and start-up time will be prolonged.

Labor pool data are available for just about any geographic or skill area from the state and/or federal Department of Labor. There is little need to speculate about whether or not available skills will be found in the area. That information may generally be obtained with a high degree of accuracy. In addition, there frequently are state or federally sponsored programs for training specific individuals for a given business. Thus, if the skills required by the business happen not to be represented in the local labor pool, it is very possible that a state or federal agency will be willing and able to train workers. In any event, a clear specification of required skills and capabilities is essential.

Information concerning prevailing wage rates at various skill levels can be obtained from the same sources. Therefore, once the skill levels required are identified and the number of individuals needed in each skill area is specified, labor costs can be projected with a high degree of accuracy.

In determining labor costs it is essential to include the full range of items that may become involved, particularly less obvious forms of compensation such as various benefits, health insurance plans, vacation days, and other time given off with compensation. Typically, these other costs represent a full third of the primary wage cost. For a labor-intensive operation they are therefore by definition an important cost category. In many organizations these costs are not accurately forecast or budgeted, much to the detriment of the actual viability of the operation. Anticipation of personnel needs and specificity of requirements can avoid some major problems once the business is in actual operation. Here's a sample description of operating personnel, taken from the Battleworks Furniture Company's business plan.

Operating Personnel

The initial workforce of the firm consists of two skilled craftsmen, who will perform the majority of the manufacturing operation. This staff will be expanded only as needed. Mr. Silver will directly supervise this operating staff and be responsible for all of the sales activity. The initial employees will have woodworking experience and be familiar with the style of operation necessary in a small semicustom fabrication shop. There is a sufficient supply of such talent in the area so that hiring appropriately experienced people will not represent a difficulty. As noted, additional craftsmen can be added if and when required by the volume of work.

In addition to the production workforce, one clerk/secretary will be hired. This person will be responsible for the required correspondence, billing activities, bookkeeping, and other normal office activities. It is expected that one person will be sufficient to perform these functions, at least initially. At such point in time as the work load requires an additional person, one will be hired. Market wages and normal benefits will be standard for all staff personnel.

Venture Development Schedule

It is important to establish in outline form the time required for each of the activities and the sequence of events that are required to complete all the steps of the business development process. This is, by definition, a plan of activity, and the more precise it can be made, the more effective and useful it will be.

Ideally, this section of the plan will be greatly blown up and nailed to the wall to be used as a chart of events or a time line of activities. Planning techniques that are helpful here are PERT, CPM, and others, depending on the complexity of the process and the interrelatedness of the different activities. For a relatively simple and straightforward process, a time line may be sufficient.

Activities tend to be sequential—that is, activity A must be accomplished before activity B can commence. Accordingly, it is necessary to identify the programmatic constraints within the start-up process. The venture development schedule may occupy only a single page of the whole plan, yet it may be the most critical page in the plan. It is an explicit chronology of activities that must occur, stating the order in which they must occur and their interrelationships.

A sample venture development schedule follows.

Battleworks Furniture Company, Inc.
Venture Development Schedule

Month

Activity	1	2	3	4	5	6	7	8	9	10	11	12

Complete Planning Process   ⊢————————————————————————➤

Arrange Financing   ⊢———⊣

Locate and Secure Facilities   ⊢———⊣

Purchase Equipment   ⊢———⊣

Hire Workforce   ⊢———⊣

Commence Operations   ⊢————————————————➤

   Purchase Wood Inventory   ⊢——⊣

   Commence Marketing   ⊢——————————————➤

FUTURE

   Develop Satellite Stores   ———➤

   Hire Management Personnel   ———➤

—— initial concentrated effort
---- ongoing maintenance

Proposed Uses of Funds Requested
The majority of new businesses require some outside financing. Existing businesses that are contemplating a substantial in-

crease in operational activities also typically need additional funds, which ordinarily would be provided by others than the business principals themselves. However, even if outside funding is not contemplated or required, it is necessary to show the nature and extent of the financing that will be required by the venture. Even if the only funding needed is being provided by the operating principals themselves, it is still important to be explicit about when and how these funds are to be utilized in order to assure that there will be enough available. Also, a reasonable budget must be established that indicates how funds will be used once the development process is under way.

If the plan is aimed at outside investors, this discussion will summarize the rationale for the investment being requested. The purpose is to convince investors that the funding that is requested is necessary, that it is critical to the success of the venture, that it is not excessive, and that there is a logical and reasonable return inherent in the use of those funds. After all, if there isn't, why should anyone invest in the business at all?

This section calls for more than a simple listing of purposes; it should provide a detailed explanation of how the funds made available to the business will be put to profitable use. It should be kept brief, yet as explicit as possible.

Here's how Battleworks presented its proposal:

Proposed Uses of Funds Requested

Tools and equipment	$17,000
Legal and organization	600
Hardwoods inventory	6,000
Plywoods inventory	4,000
Semifinished inventory	1,200
Other inventory	5,000
Supplies and office materials	1,000
Working capital	28,200
Contingency	8,000
TOTAL	$71,000

The tools and the equipment are the mainstay of the production operation. The equipment listed is necessary to have a complete shop. Included are high-quality, special-purpose items which together will represent the optimum combination of quality equipment required for a full range of production activities, providing for a maximum amount of automation in the process and a minimum of hand-oriented operations.

Items were specifically selected to assure that this shop will be well balanced in order to assure smooth efficient operation of the manufacturing process. The list provided was derived from extensive planning discussions with J. F. Munroe Company, distributor of woodworking machinery. It is supported by a listing of the equipment used by the Podunk Partition Company (see Appendix IV), a fine modern custom furniture shop which has the reputation of being one of the best-equipped, best-run shops in the area.

It should be noted that while the equipment is listed at retail, it is expected that many of the items can be purchased at a discount or even second-hand. This cannot be accomplished, however, until funds are available for actual negotiations to finalize an on-the-spot cash deal.

Wood inventories, representing a major portion of the investment, are in quantities sufficient for initial levels of production and sufficient to secure reasonable quantity discounts, yet not so excessive as to tie up cash for inordinate periods of time or to represent serious storage problems. Working capital, a third major investment category, is sufficient to support the firm through its initial stages of development until it has passed its breakeven point. The contingency reserve is for conditions outside the purview of the plan as it is presently envisioned. The funds shown are conservative and yet adequate to cover the full range of costs that will be encountered in commencing and developing this business.

Critical Risks and Problems

It is important to look not only at the bright side of the picture but also at the negative side, to anticipate potential limitations and decide in advance what will be done when those problems arise. This is consistent with the proactive approach to problem solving. Optimism is great, but not when it is based on foolish idealism.

A careful job here indicates that the principals did their best to anticipate the potential limitations or problems of the situation. It will not only be extremely helpful to the principals themselves by reducing potential risks, but will enhance the credibility of the plan to others who view it. A typical (and correct) investor response to just about any proposal is to automatically look for the problem areas, or the potential limitations of the venture. If the proponents of the deal can show that these problems have been anticipated and that there are reasonable ways to overcome potential deficiencies or limitations, then the viability of the whole project is considerably enhanced not only to the outside investor, but more importantly to the owner/managers themselves who will have the responsibility for making the operation work once it is commenced. For example:

Critical Risks and Problems

The project shown here seems to be feasible as described. The factors that could be serious feasibility constraints are essentially the untested variables at this point. Of concern here should be the following:

1. The ability of Mr. Silver to organize and operate a business of this type.
2. The actual extent of production economies available through the process described.
3. The rate of business acceptance (it may not be accepted at all).
4. The introduction of competition of exactly the same type, directed at exactly the same market segments.
5. Technological difficulties in production.

These variables can actually be tested only in application. However, the limited initial investments in the business, the staged development philosophy, and the fact that there is sound evidence in support of the underlying assumptions substantially mitigate the risk of failure.

The Summary
The summary should wrap up in a concise, succinct fashion the discussion of all the preceding sections of the plan. In essence, it should state that "the business will succeed because. . . ." The arguments and answers have already been developed. The summary will review them again in a concise and abbreviated form.

The summary is perhaps the most likely point a reader would turn to for an overview of the total discussion. It provides a quick opportunity for any interested party to obtain an immediate understanding of the purposes and methodology of the business operation. Thus it should be a highly condensed review of the operation, summarizing the key strengths and unique features of the basic product or service concept, its implementation through the business plan as described, and the benefits to management, key employees, investors, and customers. Keeping these goals in mind will be helpful in providing the needed focus and discipline to make the summary efficient, concise, and effective.

Summary

The Battleworks Furniture Company, Inc., will be a manufacturing and retail operation producing contemporary furniture made from wood, utilizing advanced production techniques. The planned manufacture of unassembled products for inventory offers the capability of providing an infinite range of finishes with a minimum of inventory. Short production cycle time will enable the company to respond immediately to changes in market demand without having to sacrifice large inventories that could suddenly become obsolete. Vertical integration brings economies of operation by eliminating shipping, handling, and middleman costs.

The product pricing strategy fills an existing gap in the target SMSA. The marketing strategy has identified individuals who are affected by the existence of this void, and they will be reached in a direct manner. The marketing plan represents a low-cost, highly effective way of accomplishing these marketing purposes.

The expertise and experience of the President in engineering, production, and business administration assure that the business will be run effectively and efficiently. Conservative income projections demonstrate that the firm will operate at a profit, even under less than favorable conditions. The corresponding cash flow analysis demonstrates that the financial structure proposed will be adequate to satisfy the working capital needs of the business, purchase the required equipment, and service any potential debt.

All these factors combine to clearly show that the firm will be a viable, profitable enterprise.

Chapter 7:
Financial Data

The first section of the plan, described in the preceding chapter, is a written description of the total business operation. It contains the sets of assumptions, ideas, and operating strategies required to make this operation a viable and profitable business. The financial forecasts, or financial data section of the plan, is the other half of this picture. It is the objective quantification of the more subjective discussion described in the earlier portions.

The financial data provide, in a rational and logical fashion, the justification for arguments, a demonstration of the feasibility of the project, an evaluation of alternatives, and a consideration of the finite limitations which may be represented by different levels of investment. For many business plan reviewers, the financial section is the portion of the total plan that is most revealing.

The organization of financial data recommended here is deliberately designed to provide a rational and logical flow of information. It is a systematic development of the idea, its explication and support. The components of the financial projections are interrelated and interdependent. Assumptions made in one section must be carried through into others. The results revealed through one set of analyses provide input for other analytical reviews.

The mechanics of financial forecasting are not especially sophisticated, and will be described here in general terms. More detailed, sophisticated treatment of these techniques can be found in any good text on financial management. The point is that the techniques and processes suggested here are those that can be applied without extensive background or training, so lack of knowledge or skill in this area should not discourage any users from this dimension of the total planning process. It is essential that the operating principals create the projections themselves, because it is through the examination of the various assumptions that go into the projections that a number of elementary and critical operating decisions will be made. Understanding the bases for these decisions and the impact of alternative sets of assumptions will help in determining the potential for success or failure of the organization, or better, the extent of success the operation will be able to attain.

The financial data section is the explication of the financial strategy, and thus should include annual pro forma financial statements for a three- to five-year period. It is desirable to show the first year by month, since this is when new businesses invariably experience financial control trouble. In fact, it generally is a good idea to project by month until such time as the organization reaches its breakeven point, which may well extend beyond the one-year period. The period of time involved will vary dramatically for different types and sizes of businesses.

Once prepared, the forecasts should be reviewed by a CPA or some other professional who has experience working with managers in the specific type of operation. As a financial analyst, the professional may spot some deficiencies of reasoning that could represent potential trouble areas. As an outsider, this professional brings objectivity, which is critical in the evaluation of the new business. As a specialist in the field, he will have experience with similar operations and so should be particularly tuned to problems endemic to ventures of that kind.

The financial strategy will portray the financial resources and assets required to get the operation started, the generation of cash, and the earnings flow, including return on investment. It is through this process that the consequences of selecting various alternatives will be most visible.

Showing the financial consequences of major alternatives can be extremely helpful. First, such alternative forecasts can illustrate the impact of alternative strategies. These forecasts can then be quickly compared in order to provide a justification or rationale for the strategy selected. Similar to other sets of constraints limiting optimized decision making within the organization, some alternatives may simply be excluded because their financial requirements exceed the available resources of the new business.

The question of how much money is needed in order to start the venture is frequently troublesome to the principals who are involved. Some seem to think that the more financing they can generate, the more successful they have been. Others think that the less they raise, the more successful they have been. Both are wrong. The business which raises more money than it needs is either selling off more ownership in the company than necessary or incurring greater debt obligations than necessary. The principals who raise insufficient funds are in a potentially precarious situation, since they will have underestimated or understated their requirements and may then have to return hat in hand to their lenders or investors at a critical stage of business growth. When this occurs, these lenders are not going to be happy to see the principals reappear with this obvious acknowledgment of their own inefficiency.

The correct amount of financing requested is determined by an analysis of how much money the business will require, in terms of both capital investment and working capital investment. The determination of both is a straightforward process. It may be that the development process will require additional injections of capital in the future. Business growth frequently carries with it additional capital or working capital demands. This is bad only if these additional needs are not anticipated, in which case they are likely to carry with them problems of business illiquidity. Accordingly, out of the cash planning activities should emerge target dates when new injections of capital may be required by the business to sustain growth, provide new equipment, or whatever. The target dates can be tied to performance levels. Initial financing sources can then recognize that their initial investments implicitly include an acknowledgment of the future financing requirements of the business as well. Under this strategy, the circumstances defining needed new funds are predetermined and their arrival, instead of signaling a disaster in the business, is actually an indication of success.

The following discussion will be in the same format as the preceding chapter. Each section of the business plan will be discussed briefly, and most of them will be illustrated by an example from the Battleworks Furniture Company.

THE FORMAT

The plan will present the company's financial data in accordance with this outline:

Sources and Applications of Funds
Capital Equipment List
Pro Forma Balance Sheet
Breakeven Analysis
Pro Forma Income Forecasts
  Three-Year Summary
  Detail by Month, 1st Year
  Detail by Quarter, 2nd and 3rd Years
  Notes of Explanation
Pro Forma Cash Flow Analysis
  Three-Year Summary
  Detail by Month, 1st Year
  Detail by Quarter, 2nd and 3rd Years
  Notes of Explanation
Pro Forma Balance Sheets
  By Quarter, 1st Year
  Annual, 2nd and 3rd Years
Existing Business (Takeover/Expansion)
  Historical Operating Data
  Deviation Analysis
Supporting Documents

Sources and Applications of Funds

This is a one-page outline description of the major purposes of various categories of funds requested, the amounts of those funds, and where they will come from. This is particularly important where funds are provided from other than the personal resources of the principals themselves. These additional funds are generally raised through some sort of combination of external debt and/or equity.

It is essential to be very specific about both what the funds will be used for and exactly where they will come from. In most cases, these funds will be needed for the commencement of the venture. If funds are likely to be needed at additional points in the future, this should be so indicated.

This section, which should stand alone on one page, is, for all practical purposes, a formal statement of the funding needed by the business operation.

The following outline is taken from the business plan of the Battleworks Furniture Company.

Sources and Applications of Funds

APPLICATIONS

Tools and equipment	$17,000
Legal and organization	600
Hardwoods inventory	6,000
Plywoods inventory	4,000
Pre-finished inventory	1,200
Other inventory	5,000
Supplies and office materials	1,000
Working capital	28,200
Contingency	8,000
	$71,000

SOURCES

Equity funds available	$ 8,000
Requested loan	63,000
	$71,000

SECURITY

Equipment, chattel, and store inventory
Signature: John M. Silver

Capital Equipment List

An important segment of investment in virtually every business is concerned with capital equipment. This will include the various fixed assets that are required to start the business operation and to keep it going. Normally, this equipment will be referred to as production equipment, but it may include other equipment that is necessary for any other purposes of the business.

The capital equipment list should be very specific, identifying not only items but brands and models as well. Best-estimate dollar value should be used. Where possible, leasing should be considered as a viable alternative to purchasing. Used properly, leasing can increase flexibility and reduce the early commitment of limited capital resources to fixed assets. The total value of this list is a part of the sources-and-applications-of-funds statement.

The following example is taken from the business plan of the Battleworks Furniture Company.

Capital Equipment List
Equipment Selection

Major Equipment and Normal Accessories	Model	List Price
Rockwell Delta 9″ Circular Saw	34–647	$ 360
Rockwell Delta Uniplane	22–300	590
Rockwell Delta Shaper	43–301	800
Rockwell Delta Unidrill	15–107	575
Rockwell Delta 12″ Radial Saw	33–489	575
Rockwell Delta Combination Sander	31–715	520
Rockwell Delta Overarm Router	43–502	800
SCM Joiner	F–4	1,705
SCM Surfacer	S–63	3,230
SCM 24″ Band Saw	C–600	1,130
Samco Stroke Sander	LL–2500	1,700
Newton Twin Spindle Horizontal Borer	B–100	500
Sand-Rite Contour Sander	DD–63	260
Workrite High-Frequency Electronic Welder	4000	1,040
Rockwell Delta 28-Gallon Vacuum Cleaner	49–255	55
Rockwell Delta 6″ Tool Grinder	23–636	170
		$14,010

Minor Shop Equipment		
Assorted power hand tools		$ 650
Hand tools, clamps, etc.		300
Jig, fixtures, patterns, etc.		500
		$ 1,450

Other Equipment		
Sewing machine and accessories		$ 500
Conductivity meter		100
		$ 600

	Subtotal	$16,060
Transportation (some equipment is F.O.B. factory)		940
		$17,000

Pro Forma Balance Sheet

Balance sheets recommended are of two types, and so are included in two sections. In this section, a pro forma balance sheet should be prepared as of the day the business commences, or as of the day the business plan is put into effect. This will illustrate the distribution of assets and liabilities throughout the organization and thus will provide an opportunity for testing the financial soundness of the business operation.

The pro forma balance sheet should indicate the variety of in-

---

Pro Forma Balance Sheet
as of Commencement of Business

Assets

Current Assets		
Cash	$27,150	
Inventory	15,700	
Rent Deposit & First Month's Rent	2,000	
Prepaid Insurance	1,800	
Prepaid Marketing	1,150	
Utilities Deposit	200	
Total Current Assets	$48,000	
Fixed Assets		
Leasehold Improvements	$ 6,000	
Tools and Equipment	17,000	
Total Fixed Assets	$23,000	
TOTAL ASSETS		$71,000

Liabilities & Net Worth

Current Liabilities		
Current Portion of Long-term Debt	$ 2,885	
Long-term Liabilities		
Long-term Debt	60,115	
Total Liabilities	$63,000	
Shareholders Equity	$ 8,000	
TOTAL LIABILITIES & NET WORTH		$71,000

vestments that have been made or will be made in equipment, inventory, and any other assets that may be needed, including prepaid deposits on facilities and utilities. It will also indicate the sources of those funds, tying these investments back to the sources and applications statement and indicating their distribution as personal investment (stockholder equity), subordinated convertible debentures (quasi-equity), long-term debt, and current liabilities (short-term debt and accounts payable). See the sample pro forma balance sheet shown on the previous page.

Pro forma balance sheets prepared for future periods in the business operation, which will give an indication of the ongoing viability of the total business operation, should be included in a later section of the financial data part of the plan, and accordingly are discussed later in this chapter.

Breakeven Analysis

Very simply stated, breakeven is that point in the business where sales and revenues exactly equal all expenses. The business neither makes a profit nor incurs a loss; it breaks even. Breakeven analysis is a powerful management tool, not only as a critical component of planning, but also as an essential part of implementation, follow-up, and control. This is such an important part of the planning and management process that it is described in some detail in the next chapter. The brief explanations and examples offered in this section are intended to illustrate only how breakeven fits in as a component of the financial data section of the business plan.

The major functions for which breakeven analysis is particularly relevant are planning, decision making, pricing, and expense control.

Planning. As a planning tool, breakeven analysis provides a direct way of identifying feasibility parameters or constraints. There will be some levels of activity below which it will not be economically feasible for the business to operate. On the other side, breakeven requirements may be so high that it may not be possible to reach them. For example, the breakeven point, when translated into the number of customers required to achieve that level of sales, may represent all or even more than all of the available market—clearly an unrealistic objective. On the other hand, the breakeven analysis may show that only a tiny percentage of the market is required to recover costs, in which case it may make sense to expand the scope of the operation. Efforts must be made to probe the planning framework from as many angles as possible. Breakeven analysis provides a reasonably objective tool for achieving this by forcing the planning assumptions into a single framework for effective comparison.

Decision making. As a decision-making tool, breakeven analysis simply continues with the logic developed for planning. The objective is to systematically evaluate alternatives, to establish the feasibility constraints, both upper and lower, of the various alternatives available to the organization, and to evaluate different combinations of alternatives. Breakeven analysis considers three variables—sales level, gross profit (net of sales minus variable costs), and fixed expenses—and each of these can be systematically manipulated in combination with the others to determine the optimum mix possible.

Pricing. Pricing decisions are critical in any organization. Classical economics suggests that demand is likely to be inversely correlated with price, and this is certainly true in application for a great many products and services. Breakeven analysis can be used as an important component of demand analysis. To develop an appropriate pricing strategy, a balance must be achieved between volume, gross profit, and net profit. In other words, maximizing sales is not necessarily going to maximize net profit. Unless there are other objectives, such as developing the business organization, the maximization of net profits is the desirable objective. Breakeven analysis can provide a direct and rapid assessment of the impact of various pricing alternatives on the bottom-line results of the operation.

Control. Control is measuring performance against budget. Although the budget benchmarks should not be inflexible, a systematic process must be established to evaluate the desirability of deviations from the budget. Breakeven analysis provides an integrative evaluative technique to illustrate the impact of various activities upon the total business operation, just as it helps evaluate the choices between alternatives in planning and decision making.

As noted, these four important dimensions of management are closely interrelated and interdependent, and any discussion of one must consider the others. Given its crucial role in planning, decision making, pricing, and control, breakeven analysis must be an integral part of the total business operation, both for new and for established businesses. In other words, it should be looked at as an ongoing management activity.

For the initial purposes of the plan, breakeven analysis will indicate the viability of the basic sets of assumptions underlying the financial projections. Breakeven analysis can provide a flexible set of revenue and expense projections under assumed conditions, thus providing the basis for evaluating alternative management strategies. It provides a way to systematically evaluate information concerning volume, selling price, expenses, and product mix relationships in an integrated manner.

As noted, through the application of breakeven analysis, budgeting expenses can be more closely controlled. Furthermore, breakeven analysis permits a more realistic determination of selling price, since it can be used to illustrate the effects of alternative pricing strategies. Decisions relating to planned expansion or to other capital outlays can be carefully considered when studied within the framework of a breakeven analysis. Finally, the graphic presentation of breakeven analysis provides an easy-to-read reporting device for summarizing data obtained in various income statements or illustrating the effects of alternative proposals involving capital expenditures.

To a great extent, the limitations of breakeven analysis are related to the difficulties encountered in obtaining reliable estimates of revenues and expenses, the assumptions made in carrying out the analysis, and competitive conditions in which the firm may operate. Breakeven analysis assumes that expenses are known. It further assumes that they can be divided into fixed and variable expenses. This is arbitrary, however, because expenses within the organization are not necessarily accumulated in these categories. Fixed expenses sometimes do not remain fixed, and variable expenses sometimes do not vary in the same proportion to sales as depicted on the breakeven analysis. The final danger here is that the assumptions made in constructing the breakeven analysis may result in the oversimplification of a complex situation. Changes in list price, product mix, commissions, distribution channels, and so forth can invalidate assumptions quickly. For example, as a product mix is changed, the breakeven point may move depending on the increase or decrease in sales of wider-margin items or lower-margin items as a percentage of total sales.

Finally, it is also recognized that two types of breakeven are critical to the new emerging firm: the conventional form of breakeven analysis just described and the cash breakeven analysis. For a variety of reasons the flows of cash into and out of the organization will not necessarily conform to the actual accounting records of sales and expenses. It is the cumulative operating cash deficit that the new business will incur from the time it starts operation until it reaches breakeven which will determine the working capital requirements for the operation.

The pro forma statements and cash flow analysis will provide a direct approach to the derivation of the breakeven point at a given point in time. However, the dollar amount represented by this point can also be calculated from the standard breakeven operating formulas. As noted earlier, profitability may be irrelevant if the critical issue of liquidity is ignored. In other words, while engaging in profitable operations, the firm may run out of cash.

Simply stated, breakeven refers to the level of sales necessary to cover all fixed and variable expenses. If a firm's costs were all variable, the problem of breakeven would never arise, because sales would automatically cover the costs of goods sold as long as each item or service is priced at cost or above. By having some fixed as well as variable costs or expenses, the firm suffers losses up to a given volume. The purpose of the breakeven analysis, then, is to identify that point where the contribution margin (sales minus variable costs) or excess of selling price over variable costs exactly equals the fixed expenses.

Calculating the breakeven point can be simple (for a one-product business) or complex (for a multi-line business), but whatever the complexity, the basic technique is the same. The basic breakeven formula is:

$$S = FC + VC$$

where S = breakeven level of sales in dollars
FC = fixed costs in dollars
VC = variable costs in dollars

Fixed costs are those costs which remain constant no matter what the sales volume. In other words, they are costs which must be met even if the business makes no sales at all. Included here would be overhead, such as rent, office, administrative salaries, and so forth, and the less direct but still fixed costs of depreciation and interest. Variable costs are those costs associated with sales, including cost of goods sold, variable labor costs, and sales commissions. These are costs that vary or change directly with output. By definition, variable costs are zero when no output it produced. At that time, fixed costs are the only costs which will be incurred. It will be clear in examining these costs that in some instances, their allocation to fixed or variable categories will be arbitrary. The test is one of reasonableness and good judgment.

Breakeven is based on the relationship of these fixed and variable expenses to sales.

$$B/E = F \div \frac{(S - V)}{100}$$

where F = total fixed costs in dollars
S = total sales as 100%
V = total variable cost as a percentage of sales

Alternatively, since $S - V$ = the contribution margin:

$$B/E = F \div \frac{CM}{100}$$

where CM = contribution margin as a percent of sales

If instead of calculating a dollar breakeven it is desired to determine how many units the business must sell to break even, simply divide the breakeven in dollars by the unit price to get the number of units to be sold.

Breakeven Analysis

Fixed costs	=	$55,824 (per annum)
		($4,652 per month)
Variable costs	=	55% (.55)
Contribution margin	=	45% (.45)

thus:

$$B/E = FC \div \frac{CM}{100}$$

$$B/E = \$55,824 \div .45$$
$$B/E = \$124,053$$
$$B/E \text{ per month} = \$10,338$$

Customers Needed Per Month at Breakeven

Assumptions:

Average unit selling price	=	$175
Average customer repeat sales	=	2 × per annum
Average revenue per customer per month	=	$29.16
Average number of customers needed per month	=	$\frac{\$10,338}{\$29.16} = 354.53$

The breakeven analysis of the Battleworks Furniture Company is shown here as an example.

Another way to determine breakeven is to use a breakeven chart. The visual display of the internal relationships may be found to be more revealing than the quantitative analysis. Many people find such visual charts more useful than the more accurate quantitative method described previously. The relationship between the elements holds relatively constant, and any close decision will probably be made on grounds more comprehensive than just these calculations anyway. It is well to remember that the breakeven figures are not the single final criterion. Whether or not the conclusions make sense must remain uppermost.

A breakeven chart may be constructed on a dollar, per-unit, or other basis. The Battleworks example shown is on a per-unit basis. In the diagram, fixed costs (FC) of $55,824 are represented by a horizontal line. Sales (TR) are figured at $175.00 per unit. Variable costs (VC) are $96.25 per unit rising from the fixed costs level to indicate total costs (TC). It is further assumed that each

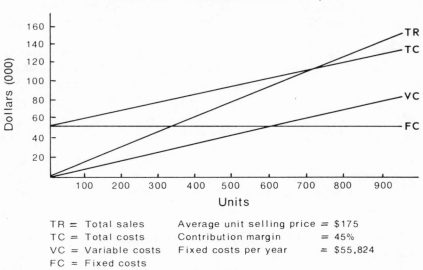

BREAKEVEN CHART
BATTLEWORKS FURNITURE COMPANY, INC.

TR = Total sales   Average unit selling price = $175
TC = Total costs   Contribution margin   = 45%
VC = Variable costs   Fixed costs per year   = $55,824
FC = Fixed costs

unit produced is sold. Since the rate of ascent of the sales income line (TR) is greater than that of the total costs line (TC), the two lines will eventually cross. The breakeven point is where they coincide—in the example, 709 units. Thus total sales equal total costs at approximately $124,000.

It should be kept in mind that this is a linear chart based on a constant selling price. However, it is possible to change the assumptions and yet quickly use the chart to advantage. For example, the effect of price changes can be estimated fairly closely by varying the slope of the income line. Similarly, by altering the slope of the variable costs line, the impact of cost changes can be estimated. Collection problems should also be remembered here. Cash flow does not necessarily correspond with income flow. If there are important differences between sales and cash flow, it may be important to construct a breakeven chart for each. Finally, it may be desirable to construct a variety of breakeven charts to consider the impact of changing assumptions concerning price, margin, and fixed costs. Used properly, a breakeven analysis in either the quantitative or linear form will prove to be a valuable management decision tool.

Pro Forma Income Forecasts

Income statements, also known as profit and loss statements, are the traditional measures of business profitability. If projected into the future, they provide a picture of the viability of the planning process.

It is important here to make a distinction between viability and feasibility, because a plan that may be viable in terms of its profitability may be infeasible because of its cash flow. The possible differences between these two will be considered in the next section.

This section will include the following:

Three-year summary.
Detail by month, first year.
Detail by quarter, second and third years.
Notes of explanation.

Just as the general function of the financial projections is to show the quantification of the business planning assumptions, within the financial projections framework it is the responsibility of the income forecasts to show the profit and loss implications of those assumptions. One of the important purposes of the profit and loss projections is to show the expected growth of sales and the corresponding increase in expenses and to enable management to review the results of that process over time. The period of time under review will vary according to the more specific purposes of the plan. If the plan is being used as a solicitation for venture capital, potential investors may require forecasts for a five-year period. Since the quality of the forecasts degrades proportionally to the time period involved, a five-year forecast may not be particularly relevant for many other purposes. Instead, a three-year period is generally considered adequate for most planning purposes, with the understanding that the forecasts will be constantly revised as the validity of the planning assumptions are tested by real operations and replaced by facts.

The second important value of these projections that must be realized is that they are a control tool as well as a feasibility analysis tool. The forecasts that are created here become the actual budget the operation can expect to follow as it commences or pursues its operations. Keeping this second objective in mind will be helpful in determining the level of detail that is desirable in creating the forecasts. A useful rule of thumb is that the more specific the forecasting can be the more useful the projections are likely to be in the future and, interestingly enough, the more accurate they are likely to be as well. The reason for this is that the gross assumptions that are made must be refined in order to provide more specific detail. Testing the actual components or subcomponents of the gross expense assumptions and specific line item expenditures will force a more critical review and a more detailed set of assumptions to support the projections.

All of this leads to a third important consideration concerning the forecasting process. All assumptions used in the process must be clearly stated in the plan. There are two important reasons for this. First, it will forestall readers' questions about the basis of the projections, thereby improving the credibility of the forecasts. Second, it will enable the creators of the plan to recall the specific assumptions that went into creating the forecasts. Once the business has gone into an operational phase, the forecasts are to be used as a budget. Many times business principals are left wondering where in the world the numbers came from that they themselves created six or nine months or a year earlier.

The first component section of the profit and loss or income projections is a summary of the annual totals. This provides any

observer with a very rapid review of the viability implications of
the forecasts and provides immediate insight into the sets of assumptions that have been used and the trend of those assumptions
over time. The three or five years covered by the forecasts can be
immediately compared in terms of each line item.

This summary page is followed by projections providing the
backup detail for the period under consideration. Generally, these
projections should be prepared on a monthly basis for the first year
or until such time as the business reaches breakeven. This will
give an opportunity to assess the impact of the operation through
relatively short time intervals. This becomes especially critical
when the forecasts are used as a budget control tool for the early
stages of operation. The feasibility constraints require the fulfillment of the assumptions, so it is especially critical to be able to determine, as early in the process as possible, where reality is deviating from those assumptions and either bring expense deviations
under control or, if they cannot be controlled, to recast the projections and redetermine the feasibility constraints. It may turn out
that the venture will not work. If so, it is important to determine
that as early as possible. More typically, it may turn out that some
of the assumptions are wrong and the basic strategy needs to be
changed. This, too, must be determined as early as possible so as to
minimize any periods of loss or depressed profits.

The forecast format suggested here is a standard accounting
format and should be varied according to the specific needs of the
business. Manufacturing organizations, for example, require a
somewhat different cost-of-goods-sold section than a retail or service business. The point is to use the format that provides the level
of detail sufficient for the purpose of the plan. The planning format
recommended is a guideline, not a straitjacket. It should be modified to serve the particular purposes of any specific venture. For
periods following the attainment of the breakeven point, operations should be projected on a quarterly basis again, because the
quality and usefulness of forecasts tend to degrade as a function of
the time span. For these periods, quarterly projections provide the
level of detail sufficient to analyze the viability of the operating
decisions being made for the venture. These decisions, while they
certainly have immediate impact, will have an ongoing influence
into the future as well. The forecasts provide the opportunity of assessing the impact of these decisions throughout the time period
under consideration.

It may be advisable to establish a series of forecasts. This has been suggested earlier as a form of contingency planning to determine what might happen to the business if things do not turn out as well as predicted. It is also an extremely useful way to test the potential impact of a range of various alternatives. Assumptions may be changed, and the impact of those changes can be shown for the forecast periods. This form of contingency analysis and decision-alternative analysis, even though somewhat time-consuming, is likely to pay dividends in the form of improved understanding many times over the time investment involved.

Pro forma income statements for the Battleworks Furniture Company are shown in Appendix A.

Pro Forma Cash Flow Analysis

The cash flow analysis is the alter-dimension of the P&L or income projection. It is the most critical of all of the analytical and decision-making tools available for the business planning process. The pro forma cash flow analysis will determine the actual flows of cash within the operation and the cash flowing into and out of the business. A simple-minded definition of cash flow is "cash in minus cash out." The objective, of course, is to have the result be a positive number.

Initially, in virtually every operation, the cash flow will be negative and so must be financed from some outside source, whether it is from the resources of the business principals themselves or from some outside lender of investor. These initial negative cash flows during the start-up phase represent the need for initial working capital. Cumulative negative cash flows, or the sum of the negative subtotals up to the point where the business reaches its cash breakeven point, represent the total working capital that will be required to finance the business.

In addition, some cash balance must be maintained as well. It is not desirable for the business to have a zero cash balance at any point in time. Some additional amount may be factored into the system by including the extra cushions in the cash balance initially or by adding a cash balance onto the high point of the cumulative negative cash flow. Either way, a realistic cash balance must be retained. A useful rule of thumb is to maintain a cash balance equal to one to three weeks of sales in order to protect against an interruption in the business activity (a flood, fire, or blizzard, for example). This suggests that an adequate cash balance would be 2 percent to 6 percent of gross annual sales.

A third component of working capital is a contingency reserve—funds that are available in the event that projections do not materialize as expected. A slower rate of growth, for instance, will result in a longer period before the cash breakeven is reached and therefore requires a greater investment in initial cumulative negative cash flows (working capital). The cash flow analysis also carries implications for cash management. Specifically, it bears on the type of capital investments to be made, loans or other financing needed, and a policy concerning dividends or withdrawals to the principals.

The cash flow can be determined by extrapolating the data that have been prepared in the breakeven and income analyses. The additional assumptions that must be formulated relate to the actual flows of cash with regard to the receipt of sales revenues and the payments of expenses. In constructing a pro forma cash flow analysis, the ultimate test is one of reasonableness and practicality. Some of the questions that may be relevant here are:

- What are the actual flows of cash into and out of the business?
- Is it realistic to expect all customers to pay cash?
- Does the business have a credit policy?
- If the credit policy is net 30 days, is it realistic to expect that all customers will pay in 30 days? More realistically and more typically, customers on a 30-day basis will pay in 45 or 60 days, and in a declining economy, customers may stretch that to 90 days. What is the impact of this delayed receipt of sales revenues on the flow of cash within the business?
- Are there any other sources of cash or flows of cash within the business? Typically, cash comes from sales, new investments, sale of capital assets, or a delayed payment of payables. In most business operations, however, the cash inflows to be primarily concerned about are those from sales. Sales ultimately represent the relevant sources of funds in any business operation.

The other dimension of the cash flow anaysis is the cash outflows. Again, realistically, what can the venture expect? Will it truly be able to utilize trade credit in its initial phase of operation? Probably not. Most new ventures will be on a C.O.D. basis until such time as they have established a track record. They must create some confidence on the part of their suppliers. It may be necessary to pay for shipments of goods in advance or at least C.O.D.

Again, a practical assessment of these implications will clearly indicate the impact of the actual operation on the financial structure of the business. A degree of pessimism is extremely useful here. Reasonable expectations for cash inflows should be decreased. Reasonable expectations for cash outflows should be slightly increased. It is impossible to run a business on figments of imagination. They do not collateralize well and they are not prized by creditors as payments.

Apart from the application of good sense and pragmatism, there are no secrets to cash flow forecasting. There is, however, a format which is especially useful. Some generally accepted formats begin with an opening cash balance, add to it cash receipts, subtract cash disbursements, and result in a closing cash balance. This format obscures the impact of any given period of operation and therefore is undesirable from an operational point of view. The format recommended here calls for estimating cash inflows and deducting cash outflows to determine net cash flow. The net cash flows per month are then totaled for a cumulative cash flow over time.

Format Sometimes Used	*Recommended Format*
Opening Cash Balance	Cash Inflows
+ Cash Receipts	− Cash Outflows
− Cash Disbursements	= Net Cash Flow
= Closing Cash Balance	+ Previous Period's Balance
	= Cumulative Cash Flow

If the recommended format is followed, the impact of any operational period can be separated from the rest of the forecast, and its net contribution, negative or positive, can be quickly determined along with the cumulative status of the operation. The format recommended here also does not introduce cash from sources outside the business operation. For example, an additional investment or the receipt of a loan would not be shown in the cash flow. The objective of the cash flow analysis, according to the view taken here, is to determine the impact of the actual operation on the financial structure of the venture. Therefore, the initial negative cash flows provide a correct indication of the necessary level of working capital.

An additional section that may be added to the projection itself is a reconciliation analysis, which includes the receipts and disbursements of cash from nonoperational sources as well. An example would be:

Opening cash balance + Cash receipts (sales, new investments, loan
                    proceeds)
                  − Cash disbursements (expenses, fixed asset
                    additions, loan payments, dividends)
                  = Net cash flow or closing cash balance

The forecast period recommended for the cash flow analysis is very similar to that suggested for the income projections. First, it is desirable to illustrate the development of the operation through the period in review. If a three-year period is being shown, then a summary of the three annual totals would be provided first. This would be followed by the backup detail for the total period, cash flows projected monthly for at least the first year or until such time as the cash flow becomes positive (reaches cash breakeven), and then quarterly throughout the duration of the period under review.

Notes of explanation are as important here as they are for the income projections. They will provide information necessary to evaluate the analysis. The notes will state, for example, reasons why cash flows (whether they are receipts or disbursements) will lag or accelerate. The more detail provided in the notes of explanation, the more useful will be the projections themselves, especially as the business moves into actual operations and the income and cash flow projections become budget control tools.

Pro Forma Balance Sheets

Many analysts, especially lenders, place a great premium on the information provided by a progression of balance sheets reflecting the changes in the financial structure of the business over time. Ratio analysis is considered by many to be a useful tool, and it certainly is for the majority of lenders. Pro forma balance sheets reflect the changing composition of the assets and financial structure of the business over time and therefore provide the information required for calculating the various ratios felt to be useful to that particular business. The calculation of these various ratios and their implications are shown in the next chapter. It is recommended by many analysts that pro forma balance sheets be constructed by quarter for the first year and annually thereafter. Some analysts prefer monthly pro forma balance sheets. However, such frequent balance sheet compilation is seldom a useful analytical exercise.

Existing Business (Takeover/Expansion)

The business deal contemplated may be an existing business situation where the principals are proposing to buy out some other business operation or expand their own existing business operation. If this is the case, there will be some additional information needs. Because these operations have been in existence (by definition), they will have a pattern of history of their past operations. The historical operating data are generally in the form of historical financial statements, preferably ones that have been certified by CPA firms. Typically, these should be provided for the past three years of operation. If certified statements are not available, then the operating data should be confirmed by corporate or other business tax returns for the same period of time.

The historical data can be made more relevant through a deviation analysis that compares the firm's operating data to some industry operating averages. Data on industry averages are available for virtually all types of business operations except totally innovative enterprises. Deviation analysis itself is a relatively straightforward process. The historical expenses are reported as relative percents of sales and, line item by line item, compared with the industry averages. Deviations or differences quickly become apparent and their causes can be analyzed. Negative deviations may be the result of management inefficiencies or peculiarities in the operating environment. These are both important factors to identify. In the first instance, they represent opportunities for management control and improved profitability; in the second instance, they represent additional constraints that must be factored into the pro forma forecasts and the feasibility analysis.

In all cases, the historical operating data, once they have been carefully considered through deviation analysis, should provide the basis for future projections of all expense categories. The historical sales trends provide the basis for future operating trends. In the absence of any significant changes, either in the operating environment or in the management of the enterprise, there should be no particular reason why the sales should increase, unless that has been the trend in the past. If sales increases are projected from a reasonably stable historical operating basis, then an explanation should be provided as to what additional impetus is being injected into the situation to provide the new momentum for change. People often assume that business operations will simply improve. In reality, they will improve only if systematic, determined efforts are made to effect changes for the better.

Supporting Documents

Any documentation that will lend support to statements made in the body of the business plan must be included in this section. Some of this information may be explicitly referred to in the plan, and some of it represents additional information required by a lay reader of ordinary intelligence but without specialized knowledge of the field.

While it is important to include all relevant information, it is also important to be discreet in the process. Too much information and too many supporting documents look like filler and so compromise the usefulness and credibility of the plan. Items which are included will vary according to the needs and stage of development of any particular business. Some of the items that may be relevant include the following:

- Resumes for the operating principals. This is a necessity.
- Quotes or estimates from jobbers/suppliers, contractors engaged for leasehold improvements, suppliers of raw materials or finished goods, and so on.
- Letters of intent or actual orders from prospective customers.
- Leases or buy/sell agreements.
- Census/demographic and other market data.
- Technical reports in a condensed version.
- Legal documents relevant to the business.

ATTRACTING VENTURE CAPITAL

As a way of summarizing this discussion of actually constructing the business plan, it may be useful to consider how a venture capital proposal is actually evaluated by a venture capitalist. The following list* is generally accepted as being representative of what a venture capitalist will look for in an investment proposal.

1. *The people involved.* It is virtually a unanimous consensus among venture capitalists that people are the most important aspect of a venture situation. A first-rate man with a second-rate idea is preferred to a second-rate man with a first-rate idea. The management team is the keystone of the new technically oriented business. Most venture capitalists feel that a major weakness on

*Venture Capital, pp. 33–35.

the part of the management team is grounds for the rejection of the proposal. The usual criterion for the management team appears to be "balance"—the presence of both technical and managerial skills in complementary proportions.

2. *The technology.* The investor's attitudes toward technology will range from considering only exciting new technological developments to anything that promises capital growth, technological or not. Another factor might be that the technology must have some promise for civilian (versus space and military) applications. Some investors may require that the technology have the possibility of attracting some government research and development contracts that would help support the firm in its early years.

For some investors, an exciting technology in itself seemed to provide sufficient reason to invest. This attitude has changed substantially during the last decade. At the present time, venture capital investors are less influenced by exciting technology than by actual demonstrations of commercial market viability.

3. *The product.* It is virtually impossible today to attract backing for an entrepreneur with nothing but an idea. In the research conducted, it was found that some investors felt the existence of a working prototype was sufficient, while others felt that the product should be essentially ready for manufacturing and marketing. A few investors stated that they would not even consider a proposal unless the first sale had already been made. Thus, even when talking about initial equity financing, it is frequently necessary that a substantial investment have already been made by the entrepreneur, if not in money, then at least in time and energy. The product should have a natural product line or follow-on product.

One area most investors in new companies carefully examine prior to investment is market growth. Naturally, this makes it more difficult to find financing for ventures which depend upon markets that do not yet exist or are not yet developed. Of course, of even greater importance than the size and growth characteristics of the market is the question of competition. If the entrepreneur proposes to sell lightbulbs in competition with General Electric or Sylvania, he had better have a very unique lightbulb. In short, the investor must look at the ground rules, the competition, the pricing structure, the distribution patterns, and the industry averages for the market the company proposes to enter.

4. *Size of investment.* While many investors do in fact have a minimum economic investment, the range is enormous. Several in-

vestors have put as little as $1,000 to $2,000 initial capital into tiny new companies. At the other end of the spectrum, one group asserted that it would not consider any investment under one million dollars. It is estimated that most initial capitalization of technology-based companies (perhaps as much as 75 percent) falls between $100,000 and $300,000.

5. *Procedures.* Venture capital investors have a strong sense of risk and usually employ methods designed to avoid unnecessary degrees of risk. Such practices normally center about the investigation of the proposal in depth so that some set of highly individual standards may be applied to the situation.

Typically, three levels of screening exist through which a proposal must pass before it is considered for investment: initial, secondary, and final screening.

Initial screening. Much of the initial screening is done on a highly informal basis. The reading of a proposal or a brief telephone conversation is usually sufficient to disqualify 80 to 90 percent of the possible ventures.

Secondary screening. The real scrutiny begins in the secondary screening. Some groups require the applicant to complete an extensive set of questionnaires which cover in detail such things as the technology, the product, the market, and fiscal and personal histories of the principals. This information is then verified and supplemented by conversations with the entrepreneur's legal counsel and auditors, suppliers, customers, dealers, competitors and competitors' customers, and present and former associates and employers of the principals. Perhaps 25 to 50 percent of the projects that are subjected to the secondary screening survive it.

Final screening. The usual reason given for the time delay (six to twelve weeks) encountered in the final screening is to conduct a "market survey." Such a survey may or may not actually occur. The actual reason for the delay seems to be to provide the venture capital group an opportunity to watch the management team perform under a variety of circumstances. The venture capital investors rely heavily on their contacts in business and technical areas in assessing the prospects of a technology, a market, or a group of entrepreneurs. In appraising the potential market, they may also enlist the aid of a professional consulting group to do a limited study.

In spite of all that has been said above, a great deal of irrationality runs through the investment policies of many individuals. Such things as personality conflict can cause the rejection of a very good venture. Similarly, if an investor likes the entrepreneur, he may overlook much that would ordinarily call for the rejection of a proposal.

While it is recognized that the vast majority of new businesses are not appropriate candidates for venture capital investors (although many would like to think they are), these items of importance to a venture capital investor are important to other types of investors and other lenders as well, and for a very good reason. They tend to be determinants of success. This should be of relevance even for the principals of a new business who do not require any outside financing at all but are able to provide all of the needed funds from their personal resources. The business must be viable. There must be a return on the time, energy, and money that is being invested.

The business planning process described here is first of all the framework for an in-depth, solid, rational, objective, pragmatic feasibility analysis. This objective has been stressed throughout this entire section. It is important to be honest, realistic, and practical, because, whether the funds belong to the principals themselves or to outside investors or lenders, the viability of the whole venture, its prospects for future success, are the underlying concern of the whole project.

A business plan assembled with the explicit objective of feasibility analysis firmly in mind as a primary goal is most likely to produce a viable operational guide, which is the second purpose of the entire plan. The third purpose of the plan is control, and the plan should be designed with that purpose in mind as well. In other words, the ultimate goal is not to convince some outside investors or lenders that they should part with their hard cash but, rather, to establish a sensible plan for taking advantage of a real opportunity. If the latter is achieved, the former will come about as a natural consequence.

Chapter 8:
The Mechanics
of Finances

There are a variety of financial management techniques that are useful to the business planning process and critical to the control activities that must follow the plan's implementation. The purpose of this chapter is to discuss some of the more important of these tools so that they can be understood and used by business principals who are themselves not necessarily sophisticated financial analysts.

The techniques of financial analysis, forecasting, and control are necessary skills for any manager in any organization. Even if there are specialists within the organization who prepare and evaluate the financial data, general management personnel must understand the implications of those data for decision-making activities. A financial or quantitative record of the business activities is critical in forecasting because, in the absence of extreme environmental or organizational changes, the future is going to be an extension of the past. In addition, such data have important control implications in that performance must be evaluated against expectations.

Financial analysis comprises three important techniques that are both planning and control tools: budget deviation analysis, ratio analysis, and breakeven analysis. Budget deviation analysis involves the monitoring of activities against the plan. Ratio analysis provides a way of comparing the projected and actual business activities with accepted institutional and industrial norms. Breakeven analysis is a critical decision-making tool in a variety of capacities.

Financial control and review is a very straightforward process, and yet one that is frequently ignored or denigrated within many organizations. Significant efforts have been expended in creating a budget, which represents an abstract model of behavior of the organization, and various activities have been quantified. As reality begins to unfold, it can and should be compared against these budget expectations in order to determine whether or not the operation is proceeding as planned. If it is not proceeding as planned, it must immediately be determined why not because, since the plan as established is by definition feasible, if reality is not consistent with the plan, then the operation may actually be infeasible. Any budget deviations must immediately be analyzed to determine their cause. If the causes are managerial, controls should be tightened. If the causes are environmental or beyond the control of the organization, then perhaps the entire plan should be re-evaluated to determine whether or not it will continue to be practical in application. The technique for performing this inspection is known as budget deviation analysis.

BUDGET DEVIATION ANALYSIS

Budget deviation analysis has two purposes. The first is comparing projected costs against industry averages. The second is comparing historical costs against the budgeted costs. For an ongoing business, the historical costs should first be compared against the industry averages in order to identify deviations from the norms. These deviations must then be inspected to determine whether they were due to ineffective managerial control or uncontrollable environmental factors. If they were controllable, plans should be made for their relief; if they were not, they should simply be incorporated into the new budget.

For a start-up situation, industry averages provide a starting point for the construction of the budget projections. In the absence of any historical data, it is perfectly reasonable to assume that a new venture should be in line with operating averages of other firms within the same industry. As real cost figures (for example, the actual rent figure for the proposed facility) are collected, they can replace the averages or be compared against the averages in order to determine whether or not they represent reasonable costs for the new venture.

An important objective of this aspect of deviation analysis is to consider where the business is deviating from the industry norms and, where differences occur, determine why. Differences are not necessarily bad, but they do point out areas warranting extra consideration. The norms indicate that other businesses in the same industry manage to control expenses within those limits and, by doing so, experience certain profit levels. If the specific business in question is negatively deviating from any of these industry norms, then, in the absence of economies in other areas of the business, the profitability will be reduced. It may be that nothing can be done about the areas of deviation, in which case they will represent extra costs that will merely have to be assumed by the organization. If this is true, then it should be at least recognized and incorporated into the planning activity. To the extent that these extra costs lower profits, they will increase the break-even point and thus increase the period of negative cash flow that will have to be financed.

The second aspect of deviation analysis is the control issue mentioned earlier. A feedback budget deviation analysis compares the actual operating data with the projected data on a period-by-period basis—generally month to month and year to date. This analysis is, in effect, an early warning system which will indicate quickly when and exactly where the venture is getting out of whack with the plan. It is important to recognize that the plan is valid for only a precise set of assumptions. To the extent that reality deviates from those assumptions, the plan will be distorted. It is important to be sensitive to these deviations and to be able to assess their impact as soon as they occur. The result of this analysis helps in determining whether operating strategy may have to be changed in order to make sure that the business operation is not jeopardized in any way.

The accounting system produces objective, quantified data, which should be in the same format as those projected. Budget deviation analysis merely involves a comparison of the actual performance figures with the budgeted figures and an inspection of the differences between the two, typically on a percentage as well as dollar basis in order to indicate the relative importance of a given deviation. This can all be recorded on a standardized form, such as the one shown in Figure 8-1 (monthly budget deviation analysis) or Figure 8-2 (year-to-date budget deviation analysis). The format is exactly the same for the two forms; the difference is that the data are cumulative for the operating period in question in Figure 8-2.

Generally, a one-year period is useful for review because as

Figure 8-1. Budget deviation analysis, profit or loss, monthly basis.

Month _____

	(A) Actual for Month	(B) Budget for Month	(C) Deviation (B − A)	(D) % Deviation (C/B x 100)
Sales				
Less: Cost of Goods				
Gross Profit on Sales				
Less: Operating Expenses				
Variable Expenses Sales Commissions Advertising Miscellaneous Var. Total Variable Expenses				
Fixed Expenses Utilities Salaries Payroll Taxes Benefits Office Supplies Insurance Maintenance Legal & Accounting Delivery Licenses Telephone . . . Miscellaneous Depreciation Interest Total Fixed Expenses				
Total Expenses				
Net Profit (Loss)				
Tax Expense				
Net Profit after Taxes				

Figure 8-2. Budget deviation analysis, profit or loss, year-to-date basis.

Year to Date _____

	(A) Actual Yr. to Date	(B) Budget Yr. to Date	(C) Deviation (B − A)	(D) % Deviation (C/B x 100)
Sales				
Less: Cost of Goods				
Gross Profit on Sales				
Less: Operating Expenses				
Variable Expenses				
Sales Commissions				
Advertising				
Miscellaneous Var.				
Total Variable Expenses				
Fixed Expenses				
Utilities				
Salaries				
Payroll Taxes				
Benefits				
Office Supplies				
Insurance				
Maintenance				
Legal & Accounting				
Delivery				
Licenses				
Telephone				
.				
.				
.				
Miscellaneous				
Depreciation				
Interest				
Total Fixed Expenses				
Total Expenses				
Net Profit (Loss)				
Tax Expenses				
Net Profit after Taxes				

Calculations: **(A)** Add current-month actual to last month's actual Year-to-Date
                 (B) Add current-month budget to last month's budget Year-to-Date

the period progresses, deviations resulting from accounting system fluctuations are leveled out. In other words, a particular expenditure may by chance be included in a given period although in fact it is more appropriately related to the next or preceding period. Over time, such mechanical allocation deviations will be quickly leveled out. Deviation analysis is possible for both P&L (Figures 8-1 and 8-2) and cash flow (Figures 8-3 and 8-4).

If expenses are accelerating significantly beyond the levels projected in the budget, the business must immediately determine why this is the case. The impact on the business is an automatic increase in the breakeven point. If sales are not similarly accelerating, even though they are proceeding at the projected levels, the business may be entering a deficit stage of operation, clearly an undesirable situation. If reported expense figures are significantly below those projected, they may represent an equally serious cause for concern rather than satisfaction. For example, necessary expenditures may not have been made and so hold negative consequences for the future. Any deviations over or under the budget must immediately be inspected to determine their implication on the total business operation.

The point is, the plan as projected will work according to the mechanics of the calculations involved. An operation that behaves exactly as the plan will achieve exactly the same results as those anticipated. However, because reality frequently deviates from predictions, such changes must be carefully monitored and the business strategy adjusted accordingly. If reality proves to be significantly different from the set of assumptions that provided the basis of the plan, then only a fool would continue to maintain confidence in the plan's ability to work.

An interesting aspect of budget deviation analysis is that it requires a remarkably small investment of time and energy to put the technique to fruitful use. Nonetheless, too many organizations, after investing massive quantities of time, money, and energy in a thorough planning effort, frequently place these plans on the shelf, once the organization is under way, and run the venture from the seat of their pants. That is much like buying a car to use to commute to work and then pushing it back and forth rather than using the engine. Plans are tools to be used, as has been emphasized throughout this text. Developing a plan merely to have it take up shelf space is totally without value to its creators and represents an abstract intellectual exercise.

Figure 8-3. Budget deviation analysis, cash flow, monthly basis.

Month_____

	(A) Actual for Month	(B) Budget For Month	(C) Deviation (B − A)	(D) % Deviation (C/B x 100)
Cash Receipts				
Sales Revenue				
Other Revenue				
Total Cash Receipts				
Cash Disbursements				
Variable Disbursements				
Cost of Materials				
Variable Labor				
Sales Commissions				
Advertising				
Miscellaneous Variable				
Total Variable Disbursements				
Fixed Disbursements				
Utilities				
Salaries				
Payroll Taxes				
Benefits				
Office Supplies				
Insurance				
Maintenance				
Legal & Accounting				
Delivery				
Licenses				
Telephone				
.				
.				
.				
Miscellaneous				
Loan Payments				
Mortgage Payments				
Equipment Purchases				
Total Fixed Disbursements				
Total Disbursements				
Net Cash Flow				
Add: Beginning Cash Balance				
Ending Cash Balance				

Figure 8-4. Budget deviation analysis, cash flow, year-to-date basis.

Year-to-Date _____

	(A) Actual Yr. to Date	(B) Budget Yr. to Date	(C) Deviation (B − A)	(D) % Deviation (C/B x 100)
Cash Receipts				
Sales Revenue				
Other Revenue				
Total Cash Receipts				
Cash Disbursements				
Variable Disbursements				
Cost of Materials				
Variable Labor				
Sales Commissions				
Advertising				
Miscellaneous Variable				
Total Variable Disbursements				
Fixed Disbursements				
Utilities				
Salaries				
Payroll Taxes				
Benefits				
Office Supplies				
Insurance				
Maintenance				
Legal & Accounting				
Delivery				
Licenses				
Telephone				
.				
.				
.				
.				
Miscellaneous				
Loan Payments				
Mortgage Payments				
Equipment Purchases				
Total Fixed Disbursements				
Total Disbursements				
Net Cash Flow				
Add: Beginning Cash Balance				
Ending Cash Balance				

Calculations: (A) Add current-month actual to last month's actual year-to-date analysis.
(B) Add current-month budget to last month's budget year-to-date analysis.

RATIO ANALYSIS

Ratio analysis is a useful tool to bankers and others evaluating the quality of loans, as well as to business consultants, planners, and business practitioners themselves. Ratio analysis involves a comparison of different categories of financial data, or financial variables, for a given business. Once derived, these ratios can then be compared with industry standards as one way of establishing the relative merits of a given business. With this in mind, ratio analysis has two important purposes. It is an important forecasting tool, especially in the establishment of pro forma balance sheets, and it is an important control tool useful in evaluating business performance.

In forecasting or establishing pro forma balance sheets, the industry averages can indicate areas of potential concern for the business. If the business situation being forecast differs significantly from the industry norms, it does not mean necessarily that there is anything wrong, but it does mean that the reasons for those deviations must be inspected. In that sense—and more importantly in the matter of control, as noted—budget deviation analysis can be an important indicator of troubled areas.

The process of analysis is relatively simple. First, identify deviations; then, examine the causes of the deviations. Again, deviations from the industry norms themselves are not necessarily bad, but the fact that they exist means that the business under consideration is doing something different from the average business in the industry. The important point about the industry norms is that they are compiled from businesses that are surviving, so if the business under consideration is significantly weaker in a given area, it may be an important symptom of infeasibility.

The different types of ratios can be divided roughly into five categories:

1. Liquidity ratios which measure the ability to meet maturing obligations.
2. Leverage ratios, which show the extent to which the firm has been financed by debt.
3. Activity ratios, which show the relationship between different operating components within the business.
4. Profitability ratios, which show how well the business is doing relative to various benchmarks.
5. A general catch-all category of ratios with a variety of

other purposes (for instance, trade association data are especially useful in defining critical operating relationships for specific businesses).

While the major types of ratios will be discussed here, they are not necessarily relevant for all businesses. As with other business planning and control tools, each business must select those which are appropriate for its particular circumstances. Ratios, as with other business guidelines, are tools; they are not straitjackets. Used as tools, they can greatly facilitate business planning and analysis. Used as straitjackets, they will stifle creativity and individuality and ignore the vagaries of fate and circumstance, which by definition make one business situation different from another.

Liquidity Ratios

1. *Quick ratio.* The quick ratio, or acid test, is an indication of the business's ability to meet its current liabilities on an immediate basis. It compares so-called quick assets (cash and near-cash items) with current liabilities. Near-cash items include very few additional assets other than cash. Typically, only marketable securities and accounts receivable would come into this category. Also included would be any other items within the organization that can be converted into cash virtually instantly without degrading their value particularly.

Marketable securities have a ready market by definition. They may be taken down to the bank or to the local brokerage house and sold for cash. This is not true of most other assets. Inventories, for example, if they were to be converted to cash instantly, would typically experience a serious loss in value. Other assets tend to experience an even more severe loss in value. Buyers have a tendency to recognize the emergency nature of the situation and respond to it by offering the lowest prices possible. A quick ratio of one to one is generally felt to be desirable. This relationship indicates that the current liabilities would be covered by the quick assets on a very immediate basis. The formula is:

$$\text{Quick ratio} = \frac{\text{Quick assets}}{\text{Current liabilities}} \qquad \text{Norm: 1:1}$$

2. *Current ratio.* The current ratio is a measure of the actual liquidity of the venture. It indicates the relationship between current liabilities and current assets. Since current assets by definition are those assets which will either be used or converted into

cash within one year and current liabilities are those which must be paid within one year, this liquidity ratio very simply is an indicator of the business's ability to meet its current obligations. A current ratio of two to one is felt to be desirable for many businesses. The formula is:

$$\text{Current ratio} = \frac{\text{Current assets}}{\text{Current liabilities}} \qquad \text{Norm: 2:1}$$

Leverage Ratios

Leverage ratios indicate the extent to which the firm has been financed by debt.

1. *Debt to worth.* Debt to worth is also frequently spoken of as leverage itself. It refers to the number of times the owners' capital has been leveraged by the use of debt within the organization. A highly leveraged deal involves a substantial use of debt and a limited use of equity.

The debt-to-worth ratio, then, is the relationship between the capital contributed by creditors and the capital contributed by the owners. Using leverage factors as an indicator of economic health suggests that the lower the ratio, the easier the financial pressures on the business and the greater the protection for the creditors. On the other hand, the higher the leverage ratio, the greater the potential return on the owners' investment. The risk with the higher leverage, however, is that if the business experiences a downturn it may not be able to meet its obligations. A debt-to-worth ratio of one to one is a reasonable norm, although two or three to one is not unusual. The fomula is:

$$\text{Debt to worth} = \frac{\text{Total debt}}{\text{Net worth}} \qquad \text{Norm: 1:1}$$

2. *Debt ratio.* A variation on the debt-to-worth ratio is the so-called debt ratio used by some bankers as a measure of collateralization. The debt ratio indicates the relationship between the total debt and the total assets and is calculated by dividing total debt by total assets. One to two is desirable from a banker's point of view, because that would indicate that the assets are twice as much as the debt, and if the business fails, it may be sufficient to repay the loan. The formula is:

$$\text{Debt to worth} = \frac{\text{Total debt}}{\text{Total assets}} \qquad \text{Norm: 1:2}$$

3. *Fixed assets to net worth.* This ratio indicates the relationship between investment in capital assets and the total amount

of the owners' capital in the business. It is sometimes seen as a measure of collateral availability or usage, and to some analysts it is an indicator of the relative availability of working capital. The lower the ratio, for example, the higher the potential for working capital usage, since it would indicate that a lower rather than higher amount of the total capital in the business is more or less locked in permanently in fixed assets and so is not available for other uses within the business. In addition, the more liquid the net worth, the greater the protection to creditors. The formula for this is:

$$\text{Fixed assets to net worth} = \frac{\text{Fixed assets}}{\text{Net worth}} \qquad \text{Norm: .75:1}$$

4. *Fixed charge coverage.* Fixed charge coverage is another indicator of the economic health of an organization. It indicates the degree of flexibility available to the organization, either to absorb an economic downturn or to significantly change its total business direction. Fixed charges are the regular commitments the organization is obligated to, such as installment loan payments, property taxes, lease payments, and any other regular payments the business would have to meet irrespective of its level of sales or profitability. The higher this ratio, the more desirable. The formula is:

$$\text{Fixed charge coverage} = \frac{\text{Profit} + \text{Fixed charges} + \text{Taxes}}{\text{Fixed charges}} \qquad \text{Norm: 4:1}$$

Activity Ratios

1. *Inventory turns.* This ratio, also known as inventory turnover or stock turns, refers to the number of times on the average (at least in theory) a given item of inventory would be replaced on the shelf during the course of a year. This is an important measure of activity for many businesses, since it helps in drawing up pro forma balance sheets and projecting original start-up investments by determining what the required inventory level for the business should be relative to sales, as compared to the industry averages. It is also a measure of relative efficiency or effectiveness in inventory management once the business is under way.

For example, inventory turns of four times (4×) would mean that on sales of $100,000 the average inventory required or maintained would be $25,000. If the inventory is less relative to sales, indicating a higher number of turns, then there is a very real possibility that the business will experience stock-outs or other deficiencies, which may result in disappointed customers and lost sales. On the other hand, if the base inventory is high relative to sales, it may indicate that the business is maintaining the wrong types of inventory or has too much of its funds invested in inventory, all of which could lead to inventory obsolescence and/or shrinkage and generally lower the return on capital.

The stock turn averages for different types of businesses will vary widely. Four times is frequently considered a norm, although in such businesses where product freshness is an important consideration inventory turns would be very high relative to sales—30×, for instance, for dairy products, 40× for fresh fruits and vegetables, and as low as 2× for jewelry stores and other such high-value, low-turnover items. The ratio will vary depending upon the method used for computation. The formula is:

$$\text{Inventory turnover} = \frac{\text{Sales}}{\text{Average inventory at cost}}$$

$$\text{or} \quad \frac{\text{Cost of goods sold}}{\text{Average inventory at cost}} \qquad \text{Norm: } 4\times$$

2. *Average collection period.* This ratio measures the average age of the accounts receivable. Its computation will sometimes lead to very shocking conclusions. Businesses that believe they are offering and maintaining terms, for example, of 30 days net, when calculating the average collection period, may discover that their receivables are 45 or 60 days old instead. This ratio measures both the relative liquidity of the receivables and suggests their relative safety. Generally speaking, the shorter the collection period, the more liquid the receivables and the safer the receivables—that is, the greater the likelihood that they will be paid. The longer the collection period, the more danger there is that the debtors may not pay. In some industries, a collection period of over 90 days is seen as extremely dangerous.

Calculating the average collection period from one operating period to the next will provide a quick indicator of trouble if the average collection period begins to get longer. This may suggest that the businesses or individuals owing money to the organization are having difficulty making their payments, or it may be symptomatic of some other trouble within the business or the industry.

Especially for many smaller retail businesses, accounts receivable may not be necessary at all. Instead, the business may offer the same charge capabilities to its customers by utilizing BankAmericard (Visa), Master Charge, or some other form of bank credit card, thus transferring the credit verification and collection activities to other organizations that have the professional staff capabilities to properly handle those functions. Of course, the most effective procedure is the regular utilization of an aging schedule, whereby each account is regularly evaluated to indicate its relative status. This will quickly show which accounts are becoming troubled and need special attention. The norm may be diluted where industry averages reported are a combination of cash and credit sales. The calculation is:

$$\text{Average collection period} = \frac{\text{Receivables}}{\text{Sales per day}} \qquad \text{Norm: 20 days}$$

where sales per day is simply annual sales divided by 365.

3. *Fixed asset turnover.* This ratio compares fixed assets to sales and is an indicator of capacity for use. A high figure will mean a high use. It is a relative indicator of the efficiency of the capital investments of the organization. A capital-intensive business, for example, would tend to have a lower ratio than a labor-intensive business. However, the extent to which labor and capital are substitutable in a given industry reduces the value of this indicator. A high ratio where the decision has been made to substitute labor for capital, for example, may be negatively reflected in lower profits. Thus any conclusions drawn must be further considered as part of the evaluation procedure. The formula is:

$$\text{Fixed asset turnover} = \frac{\text{Sales}}{\text{Fixed assets}} \qquad \text{Norm: } 1\times$$

4. *Total asset turnover.* This ratio is subject to the same interpretation as the fixed asset turnover, the difference being that current assets as well as fixed assets are included in the calculation. The implications are generally the same. In all cases, caution and discretion must be exercised in deriving conclusions from the calculations. The calculation here is:

$$\text{Total asset turnover} = \frac{\text{Sales}}{\text{Total assets}} \qquad \text{Norm: } 2\times$$

Profitability Ratios

1. *Profit.* When used alone, profit typically refers to the profit margin on sales. It may refer to the net profit before or after taxes, and the intended meaning must be specified. For smaller businesses, the proper industry profit averages may or may not include wages paid for the owners' time and trouble as an employee of the

business, which, of course, could make a substantial difference in
the amount of net profit shown.

Net profit is probably the single most regularly used ratio,
and the one which has almost universal application, the reason
being that business operations must at least break even or, in most
cases, show a profit in order to stay in business. If they are not
profitable, they by definition they will require some outside sub-
sidization. Certain businesses, however, known as tax shelters,
will utilize depreciation as a way of using up profits, and therefore
may in fact represent operations that are proceeding at an acceptable level even though they are reported as operating at a net loss.
Depreciation is one of a number of factors that can affect the reported profitability of any given operation, and so the notes to the
financial statement should be carefully studied to find out exactly
what is being included in the final calculations. For many businesses, a 5 to 15 percent net profit is acceptable. The formula is:

$$\text{Profit margin on sales} = \frac{\text{Net profit after taxes}}{\text{Sales}} \qquad \text{Norm: 5\%}$$

2. *Return on total assets.* The return on total assets is a measure of the return on investment in the business. After all, there
should be some return for the funds committed. This return can be
compared to alternative uses of the funds so as to determine
whether or not good use is being made of these assets. Generally
speaking, it is expected that funds invested in the business will
produce a higher rate of return, either in the present or over time,
than these same funds would earn if they were invested in a savings institution, simply because the risk factors are higher in a
business investment than in the savings institution.

The considerations represented by this ratio are critical in
much of management decision making, especially opportunity
analysis, where both the aggregate return and the marginal return
on investment are considered as an important decision rule. As a
measure of effectiveness, generally speaking, the higher the return, the better. The calculation is:

$$\text{Return on total assets} = \frac{\text{Net profit after taxes}}{\text{Total assets}} \qquad \text{Norm: 20\%}$$

3. *Return on net worth.* This ratio is the measure of the relative effectiveness of the owners' equity. There is a correlation between this ratio and the debt ratio or the debt-to-worth ratio, to the
extent that debt has been used effectively in accelerating or in-

creasing sales. On the other side, the excessive use of debt may carry with it high interest payments, which reduce profitability and so may lower the potential return on net worth. Generally speaking again, a higher ratio is an indication of more effective utilization of resources. The calculation is:

$$\text{Return on net worth} = \frac{\text{Net profit after taxes}}{\text{Net worth}} \qquad \text{Norm: 15\%}$$

Other Ratios

1. *Working capital.* Working capital may well be the most critical variable of all for young and developing organizations. Working capital is a relative indicator of liquidity and is measured by the difference between current assets and current liabilities. If a business does not have working capital, it is by definition illiquid and may well be on its way to being insolvent. A business may be conducting profitable operations and still experience a shrinking working capital position. The rule here is that working capital should always be positive. The formula is:

$$\text{Working capital} = \text{Current assets} - \text{Current liabilities}$$

2. *Net worth.* Net worth refers to the dollar value of the business that is owned by the owners. If there is no net worth or a negative net worth, the business is technically insolvent and so would experience extreme difficulty in obtaining further debt or credit. The formula is:

$$\text{Net worth} = \text{Total assets} - \text{Total liabilities}$$

3. *Sales growth per year.* This ratio is a comparison of the growth of sales over time and is a very helpful indicator of whether the business may be expanding and growing and, if so, at what rate. It must also be recognized, however, that the geometry involved in the calculations may indicate that business growth is slowing down when in fact it is proceeding at a perfectly desirable rate. A complete evaluation of sales growth would have to consider the geometric relationship as derived by the first formula indicated below or the absolute rate of growth as indicated by the second. The formulas are:

$$\text{Sales growth per year} = \frac{\text{Sales of current year}}{\text{Sales of previous year}}$$

$$\text{or} \quad \frac{\text{Sales of current year} - \text{Sales of previous year}}{\text{Sales of previous year}}$$

In concluding this discussion on ratio analysis, it is useful to reiterate that the ratios themselves are not particularly useful unless compared with something else; and unless compared with the *correct* something else, they may lead to dangerous, incorrect, or fallacious conclusions. There is a well-developed body of industry averages for practically any type of existing business. Only the ratios for the specific type of business under consideration are relevant, and so a great deal of care must be used to assure that the correct comparison base is being employed.

On the other hand, it is not wise to ignore the value of the ratios. Ratios in general, and especially the ones indicated here, are highly valued by bankers and financial analysts, because over time they have proven to be extremely valuable and accurate indicators of business viability. If the ratios for the business under consideration show significant negative deviations from the average ratios, this should be a cause for concern, and the reasons for these deviations should be identified as quickly as possible in order for the business to avoid taking a wrong avenue.

Of course, the final advice is to repeat that given earlier: the ratios are guides, or basic tools, and not straitjackets. It is perfectly reasonable to expect a specific business to deviate from the industry norms or averages. The point is, determine exactly why those deviations exist and whether they exist for acceptable reasons or indicate a hazard to the health of the organization. These are management decision-making tools and should be used for making management decisions.

Here is an example to illustrate how ratios might be used in business planning and analysis. Assume that a furniture store is anticipating sales of $400,000. In that industry, inventory traditionally turns four times. This immediately indicates that this business will require a base inventory of $100,000. In addition, it is very possible that $15,000 to $20,000 might be invested in preparing this company for business. That is, there are a variety of things in addition to inventory which must be purchased in order to commence operations, such as various items of equipment and leasehold improvements. In addition to the capital equipment and leasehold improvements, it is very possible that a business of this type would require initial working capital, perhaps at the level of $30,000, to fund the initial negative cash flow (operating deficits) of the start-up operation.

Totaling these figures suggests that such a business would require a $150,000 minimum investment in order to become established. Furthermore, in this particular industry a debt-to-worth ratio of two to one is not unusual. Very simply, then, dividing $150,000 by three immediately indicates that the prospective owner or owners must have the capability of putting up $50,000 in cash before they commence this venture. Considering that the typical furniture store averages around a 10 percent net profit, this business will have a net profit (before interest and taxes) of $40,000 on gross sales of $400,000 after the owner has received a salary for his trouble.

To evaluate the true value of the $40,000 in net profit, it is necessary to first consider interest payments on the $100,000 which has been borrowed for the debt portion of the capitalization. This will immediately require $12,000 of the net profit. In addition, if these funds have been borrowed on an installment basis for five years (which is not unusual), they would be carrying a need for an additional $20,000 a year in principal payments, which, together with the $12,000 in interest, means that $32,000 must be committed to debt service. Adding back the noncash expense of depreciation projected at $4,000 per year for five years to the net profit yields available cash of $44,000 which, minus the $32,000, leaves $12,000 available for new investment in the business operation to support further growth.

If the owner were a conservative person who would consider placing his money in a savings institution as a reasonable alternative to investing in the business operation, he might obtain a 6½ percent return on the $50,000 of his own funds, or $3,250. Now, subtracting that from the $12,000 net cash position would leave a net return of $8,750 available to the business. Further, assuming that the business has a business tax rate of 20 percent on the $12,000, $2,400 must be set aside for federal income tax, leaving $9,600 available within the business to use to finance growth. If all of that is plowed back into the business, the business could theoretically increase its sales by almost $40,000 a year, or it could fund a growth rate, in other words, of roughly 10 percent a year. This means that in the absence of any additional investment, it would be totally unrealistic to project a sales growth at a more rapid rate. If this figure is further adjusted to reflect for the rate of inflation, the business will wind up with the real projected growth rate of about zero—not thrilling, but totally realistic.

Utilizing this kind of analysis will help maintain a sense of reasonableness, which will enhance feasibility of the anlysis and planning process. Again, the ratios are helpful guidelines, and there are a variety of ways they can be used. They should be looked at as helpful indicators because that is exactly what they are— useful planning and forecasting tools.

BREAKEVEN ANALYSIS

Breakeven analysis is an integral part of the business planning system, a critical component of forecasting, and, in general, a powerful management decision-making tool. Very simply, breakeven is the point where the business neither makes a profit nor incurs a loss. It is the point where total costs exactly equal total revenues. Because the breakeven point is affected by changes in the fixed expenses and the variable costs, it can illustrate what the impact of various alternatives available to the business may be on the total sales that are required for the business to simply break even, and thus become an important decision-making tool.

Of course, the objective is not just to break even, but to make a profit. Nonetheless, understanding the balance point between expenses and revenues and the factors that affect or change that balance point is essential for both establishing targets or goals for the business and for evaluating the total operating assumptions.

A breakeven analysis provides a minimum sales objective, which can be expressed in a number of dollars, units of production or sales, or whatever else is relevant. If the breakeven point is known, it can be a definite target to be reached and exceeded by carefully reasoned steps. Many businesses have destroyed themselves by ignoring the need for breakeven analysis. It is essential to remember that increased sales do not necessarily mean increased profit. For example, if the selling price is reduced in order to stimulate sales, the breakeven point may be forced upward to such an extent that, practically speaking, the business could never achieve sufficient sales to break even.

Breakeven analysis is helpful in more than forecasting. It is a problem-solving tool. Breakeven analysis can be invaluable in determining whether to buy or lease, whether to expand into a new area, whether to build a new plant, and for a variety of other considerations. Breakeven analysis will not force a decision, of course, but it will provide additional insights into the effects of important business decisions on the bottom-line profits of the firm. Informed decisions have a better chance of being correct than random, seat-of-the-pants decisions.

Breakeven is a planning tool, a decision-making tool, a pricing tool, and an expense control tool. As a planning tool, breakeven analysis indicates the targets the business must achieve and provides a quick and direct way of evaluating the impact of the various alternatives on the business strategy. If the breakeven is unrealistically high and it is clear that the business will never be able to achieve those levels of sales because it would require an inordinately high percentage of the target market or the processing of more goods or services than it has the capacity to handle, then clearly that alternative should not be pursued. On the other hand, if the breakeven is extremely low, it may suggest that a more profitable strategy could be pursued or at least seriously considered.

These factors lead to the second function of breakeven. As a decision-making tool, breakeven helps in evaluating the various alternatives available to the business. Following these alternatives through a breakeven analysis is a far safer way of determining their impact on the business than actually experimenting with the real operation. A proactive anticipation of the negative impact of certain alternatives will automatically help eliminate those alternatives and thereby avoid their projected negative impact. Problem solving by avoidance is far preferable to any other alternative that may be available to a business.

Breakeven analysis is an important pricing tool showing the relationship between price, contribution, and volume. For example, it provides a direct and straightforward approach to considering a series of prices and their impact on the business. It is generally assumed that as price goes down, volume is likely to increase. As noted earlier, however, this is not necessarily desirable. The underlying focus must be on the relationship between contribution, or gross profit, and fixed costs. This is critical because, as the contribution or gross profit decreases relative to the fixed costs, the breakeven point will increase. It may increase to such a point that the sales figures required for breakeven are simply too high, thereby creating a totally unrealistic situation.

Finally, as an expense control tool, breakeven provides a way of evaluating the impact on the business of various expenses and provides an interesting and sometimes very different way to consider the need or relevance of a given expense on the total operation. If removing that expense could significantly lower the breakeven and lowering the breakeven increases the feasibility of the operation, then it is advisable to assess the importance or relevance of that particular expense to the total operation. If it is not essential and the business is feasible without it, it can be eliminated and profits improved. If it is essential and the business is not feasible without it, then the choice must be made not to pursue that course of action.

There is a simple and direct relationship between expenses, sales and profit. Profit can be increased typically by increasing sales or decreasing expenses. Accordingly, it is useful for any business to view expenses as profits which would otherwise be available to the owners and, on that basis, determine whether or not particular expenses are truly essential to the business operation. An ongoing breakeven analysis can be incorporated as part of the expense review and control process, which carefully observes the relationship between sales, gross profits, and expenses to maintain a floating sales objective.

Expenses have a tendency to increase in an almost invisible way in most operations. Accordingly, these operations may feel that they are improving or doing better, and yet find that their profits are in fact shrinking. The ongoing breakeven analysis will help indicate the impact of any such changes.

Calculating the Breakeven Point

Calculating the breakeven point can be simple for a one-product business or complex in a multi-line business. However, whatever the complexity, the basic techniques are the same. The two basic approaches that may be used are mathematical computations through the application of a breakeven formula and constructing a breakeven chart or graph. Both will be discussed.

Breakeven can be calculated either in dollars or units. The specific technique and approach to be used will depend on the situation and the kind of information required. For certain types of decision making, it is most useful to place breakeven on a time continuum that shows the impact on required volume of various changes the business anticipates due to growth over time.

Since breakeven refers to the level of sales necessary to cover all the fixed and variable expenses of an organization, the problem of breakeven would never arise if a firm's costs were all variable, because the sales would automatically cover the cost of goods sold as long as each item or service was priced at cost or above. By having some fixed as well as variable costs or expenses, the firm must suffer losses up to a given volume. The objective of breakeven analysis is to identify that point where the contribution margin, or the excess of selling price over variable costs, exactly equals the fixed expenses. The breakeven, then, is the point at which the business will make neither a profit nor a loss but merely break even.

As a going concern, any business will generate expenses over the course of a year. Those expenses will continue whether or not any products or services are sold, made, produced, or provided, and they remain fixed within a range. If the business expands sufficiently to require larger facilities and more administrators, then these costs would rise, but in the short run they are reasonably constant. Those costs which vary or change directly with output are variable expenses or costs. They are the costs which are associated with producing and/or selling a product or service and are frequently identified as the cost of goods sold. These variable costs will not accrue if the business is not actively engaged in selling or production activities. By definition, variable costs are zero when no output is being produced or no sales are being incurred. At that time fixed costs are the only costs which will be incurred. Examples of fixed costs are:

> Executive and office salaries.
> General office expenses.
> Insurance.
> Property taxes.
> Interest.
> Depreciation of plant and equipment.

Variable costs include:

> Cost of goods sold.
> Factory labor.
> Sales commissions.
> Raw materials used.
> Freight in and out.
> Variable factory expenses.
> Utilities other than fixed.
> Direct labor.
> Sales expenses.

The figures that go into breakeven analysis computations will be either estimates or the actual figures that have been incurred in the business operation. If they are actual figures, it is important that they be compared against the industry operating averages to help determine whether or not costs are too high or even really necessary. If these figures are estimates, again, the industry operating averages can be used as helpful benchmarks. In any event, it is important that the cost figures be as accurate and reasonable as they possibly can be made.

The breakeven point is a level of sales that exactly covers total costs:

$$S = FC + VC$$

where S = sales in dollars
$\quad FC$ = fixed costs in dollars
$\quad VC$ = variable costs in dollars

If a projected breakeven is desired, and therefore total variable costs are unknown, it is necessary to use a variation of the $S = FC + VC$ formula. If the contribution margin can be identified, the following formula can be used:

$$S = FC \div CM$$

where CM = contribution margin as a percent of sales divided by 100.

If instead of calculating a dollar breakeven a unit breakeven is desired, the breakeven derived in dollars may be divided by the unit price in order to arrive at the number of units which would need to be sold.

Still another variation on the formula that will produce exactly the same answer is:

$$B/E = F \div (S - V)$$

where F = total fixed costs in dollars
$\quad S$ = total sales as 100% $\div$ 100 (1)
$\quad V$ = total variable costs as a percent of sales

In this formula, $S - V$ equals the contribution margin CM.

An Example of Breakeven

Assume that an appliance dealer has sales of $1 million per year. Variable costs are $650,000, and fixed costs are $70,000.

$$B/E = \$70,000 \div (1 - .65) = \$70,000 \div .35$$
$$= \$200,000$$

In other words, the dealer needs $200,000 per year in sales to cover all the fixed expenses. At this point, the business will neither make a profit nor incur a loss but break even. The appliance industry has a high margin, whereas, for example, the grocery business has a low margin—15 percent as opposed to 35 percent. For the same fixed expenses, a grocer would need $70,000 $\div$ .15, or $467,000, in sales. The lower the contribution margin, the higher the sales must be to cover the same amount of fixed costs.

With this type of analysis it becomes relatively simple to evaluate the impact of discrete units of cost. Does the firm really need a Lear jet? Maybe, but each decision here can be evaluated in terms of the impact of that expense on the breakeven level of sales. The gross profit or mathematical approach to breakeven provides for a very rapid calculation of any such changes.

Breakeven for a multiple product line can be calculated for any given product mix by looking at the average contribution for the total product line. It can be calculated for the individual products as well. However, practically speaking, it would need to be calculated for every combination of alternatives. This may become infeasible simply because of the logistics involved. A useful alternative is the graphic representation. Representing a breakeven analysis pictorially or by way of diagram is a helpful tool in constructing forecasts, budgets, or projections and allows easy substitution of different combinations of numbers to obtain rough estimates of their effects on the business.

One helpful technique is to make worst-case, best-case, and most-probable-case assumptions, chart them, and then derive more accurate figures by applying numerical formulas as previously suggested. For example, this can be of special value in considering a capital investment where the need is for a quick picture of the relative merits of buying or leasing an item. Finally, to make maximum use of breakeven analysis, the results can be focused on expense categories rather than sales. Expense categories typically are subject to much greater control than sales. It is possible to reduce sales by merely deciding not to make commitments in those categories; on the other hand, increasing sales involves decisions of others that are not so directly controlled.

In creating the breakeven chart, typically dollars are plotted on the vertical axis and quantity is plotted on the horizontal axis. A breakeven chart constructed on a per-unit basis is shown in Figure 8-5. In the diagram, fixed costs of $70,000 are represented on the horizontal line (FC). Variable costs (VC) of $1.30 per unit rise from the origin, indicating the accumulation of costs as more units are sold. In reality, these costs are in addition to the fixed costs, so the VC line is raised from the origin to the fixed costs line (FC) and thus indicates total costs (TC). Sales (TR) are calculated at $2.00 per unit, with the assumption that each unit produced is sold. Since the rate of ascent of the sales income line is greater

Figure 8-5. Revenue/unit cost breakeven chart.

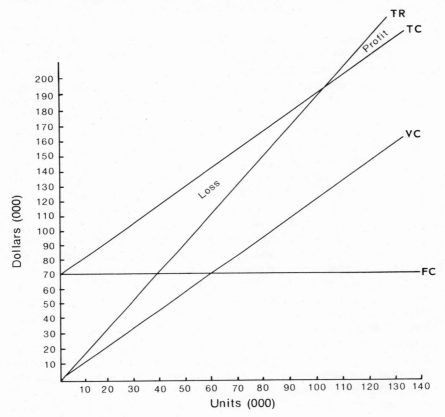

than that of the total costs, the two lines will eventually cross, the sales line rising from the origin and the variable costs line rising from the fixed costs line to indicate total costs. The breakeven point is where they cross—in the example, at 100,000 units, which corresponds to total sales and total costs of $200,000.

Certain conclusions can be reached from studying the breakeven chart. At zero sales, total costs equal fixed costs, or $70,000. As output increases from zero, total costs equal the total fixed costs, $70,000, plus the variable costs, $1.30 per unit. To determine the breakeven point, it is necessary to identify the point at which total costs are equal to total revenues. With a selling price of $2.00 per unit, total revenue is determined by multiplying the quantity sold by $2.00. At zero quantity, total revenue is zero. At 35,000 units, total revenue will equal $70,000, or be exactly equal to total fixed costs. However, as will be seen from examining the chart, the total variable costs have risen at that point as well, and at that point, total costs are $115,500 (FC of $70,000 + VC of $1.30 per unit or $45,500), resulting in a net loss at that point of $45,500.

The graph also indicates that the total revenue line (TR) crosses the total costs line (TC) at exactly 100,000 units and $200,000 in sales. Examination of the breakeven chart for levels of sales either above or below the breakeven point will provide an estimate of the profit or loss achieved at the various other levels of sales. For levels of sales above 100,000 units, total revenue exceeds total costs, meaning that the firm will earn a profit. For sales below 100,000 units, the firm will incur a loss, the amount of which can be derived by subtracting the total revenue from the total costs.

Some examples will indicate the utility of the breakeven chart. The impact of increasing fixed costs may be observed by moving the fixed costs line (FC) up on the grid, which would automatically move the total costs line (TC) up on the grid. This means that TC will intersect TR at a higher point, thus indicating a higher breakeven point. Another variation may be seen by changing the slope of the total costs line. If the total costs line becomes steeper, it again will intersect with the total revenue line at a higher point, thus indicating a higher breakeven. If the total costs line becomes shallower, indicating lower variable costs, then the breakeven will go down.

Some conclusions from the breakeven chart shown in Figure 8-5 are:

1. The breakeven point for this firm in its present income expense position is about $200,000 in sales. This was derived by reading the point where the total revenue (TR) and total costs (TC) lines cross.
2. Any amount of total revenue less than $200,000 puts the firm in the loss area of the chart. Above $200,000, the profits expand more widely with each increase in sales.
3. Total expenses do go up with a sales expansion, but not as rapidly as sales. This is because the fixed expenses are being covered in full after the breakeven point has been reached, and so all of the additional gross profit becomes net profit.

4. The higher the fixed expenses become, the further to the right will be the breakeven point.
5. Each $20,000 expansion in sales yields a greater percentage profit than the preceding $20,000 expansion, because less of the profit is required to cover fixed costs to the breakeven.

Creating a Breakeven Chart

The conventional breakeven chart assumes that over a relevant range, selling prices do not change, total fixed expenses remain constant, and variable expenses increase or decrease in direct proportion to sales. These, of course, are highly idealized assumptions and must be recognized as such. However, such assumptions are very apt to hold true over a relatively short-run term such as a year. Over longer periods of time, the functions may become curvilinear. Economies of scale are introduced which lower costs; variable expenses do not vary directly with sales; and fixed expenses, in fact, become semifixed.

Even recognizing these limitations, however, the breakeven chart is a quick and efficient method for determining breakeven and assessing the impact of changing price, contribution margin, and fixed expenses on the required sales levels for the operation to break even. A step-by-step explanation of how to create a conventional breakeven chart follows.

Step 1. Set up the graph. On the horizontal axis, mark off a scale for units sold, percent of capacity, direct labor hours, dollar sales volume, or any other measure of volume that may be relevant. Unit of sales may be most useful in a small single-product-line business, because it will illustrate the relationship between revenues and units. For multiple-product businesses, however, dollar sales volume may be most useful, because it will provide a consistent base of reference for all product lines, divisions, and departments. Mark off a scale of dollars on the vertical axis for revenue and cost items. Identify the point on the vertical axis which represents the amount of the fixed cost (a). Then, extend a line (FC) from that point parallel to the horizontal axis, representing the fact that at all levels of volume, fixed costs will remain constant. Figure 8-6 illustrates this step.

Step 2. Identify the point on the vertical axis which will represent total costs (b). Extend a dotted line from that point parallel to the horizontal axis. Identify the point (c) on the horizontal axis

Figure 8-6. Constructing a breakeven chart, step 1.

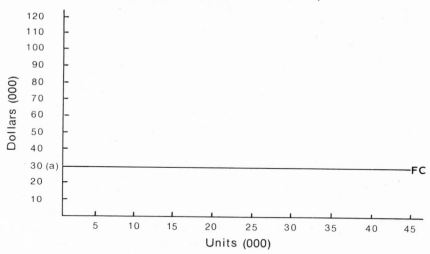

representing the volume at that level of cost. Extend a dotted line from point (c) parallel to the vertical axis. Construct a line (TC) from point (a) to the intersection of the two dotted lines just created representing total costs. The area between the line TC just created and the total fixed costs line represents the variable costs at different volumes of sales, and the area between the line TC and the horizontal axis represents the total costs incurred at different volumes of sales. Both the total and the variable costs, then, can be inspected at any level of volume simply by extending a line from the desired quantity on the horizontal axis parallel to the vertical axis and reading off the value on the vertical axis of the point of intersection with the line TC. This step is summarized in Figure 8-7.

Step 3. Identify a point (d) on the vertical axis representing the total revenue for the operating period in question. Extend a dotted line from that point parallel to the horizontal axis. Identify the corresponding volume for that level of revenue on the horizontal axis. Now, construct a line (TR) from the origin of the graph through the point just created by the intersection of the two dotted lines. TR represents the total sales revenue at any level of activity. The result of step 3 is illustrated by Figure 8-8.

It will be observed that the line TR crosses the line TC. The point of the intersection of those two lines represents the breakeven point for this business. The dollar sales volume required for breakeven may be read off the vertical axis; the unit volume

Figure 8-7. Constructing a breakeven chart, step 2.

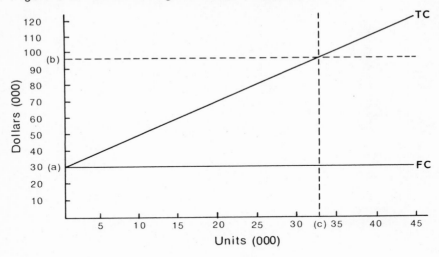

Figure 8-8. Constructing a breakeven chart, step 3.

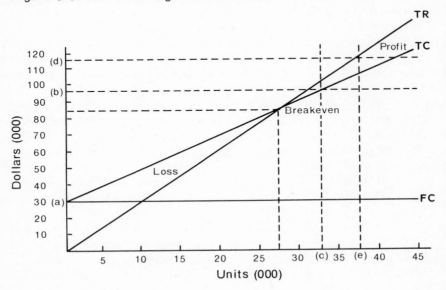

required for breakeven may be read off the horizontal axis. At any point to the left of the breakeven point where line TC is above line TR, the business will incur a loss, by definition, because the total costs exceed the total revenue. Similarly, at any point to the right of the breakeven point the business will incur a profit, because total revenues (TR) exceed total costs (TC).

Cash Breakeven Analysis

It is frequently helpful to calculate the cash breakeven point for a business as well as the profit and loss breakeven point. There are two important reasons for this. Some of the items contained in the P&L analysis are not cash items—depreciation, for example— and for a given period of time some sales may be in the form of receivables, and thus, the actual receipt will lag behind the technical date of the sale. The extent to which receivables lag behind payables will introduce potential cash flow problems for the firm.

The only adjustments required to change the P&L breakeven analysis to a cash flow breakeven analysis are to include only real cash items in the fixed expense category and to look at that as a fixed payment category. These changes, for example, typically add the principal portion of a loan or mortgage payment to the interest portion included on the P&L statement, and eliminate noncash expenses such as depreciation.

A cash breakeven analysis cannot fully represent cash flow. To accomplish this, a cash budget is required. The cash breakeven analysis can be useful as a picture of the flow of funds from operations, however. A firm could incur a level of fixed costs that would result in losses during periods of poor business but enlarged profits during upswings. If cash outlays are small, then even during a period of losses the firm might still be operating above the cash breakdown point, thus the risk of insolvency and corresponding inability to meet cash obligations would be small. Such considerations could influence a choice between automating a production system or maintaining a labor-intensive operation.

FORECASTING TECHNIQUES

In discussing forecasting or pro forma projections, questions are frequently asked about where the numbers come from. The concern expressed is that it often appears that the numbers are made up. The answer is that, by definition, the numbers are made up. Projections have to do with assumptions about the future, and in the absence of a crystal ball, the projected future reality is indeed fictitious. However, it is important to recognize that it is fabricated within a very carefully constructed set of constraints. The objective of the forecasting process is to reduce the risk of error to the extent possible by considering every possible way of assuring that the projections will be true representations of the future reality they are designed to portray.

The basic considerations for forecasting have already been examined in the discussion of breakeven analysis. For example, breakeven cannot possibly be considered without the dual concern for gross profit and fixed expenses. The additional important factor which must be included in order to create useful forecasts is the rate at which sales are projected to develop. There are a variety of ways this can be done. One of the quickest, most useful, and frequently most accurate ways is to create a curve on a graph (see Figure 8-9). The simple curve illustrated is representative of the growth and development pattern for a wide variety of business operations. It will commence at the origin, or even somewhat further along the horizontal axis, unless the business is able to start operations with substantial sales already in hand—say, through a substantial contract. Such pre-sold business has been common in firms that deal in government-sponsored R&D and frequently for manufacturing organizations. Retail sales operations, on the other hand, are not as likely to have sales commence until they have actually opened their doors for business.

The slope of the growth curve is a function of the rate of customer acceptance and/or the rate at which sales will be developed.

Figure 8-9. Typical sales growth curves.

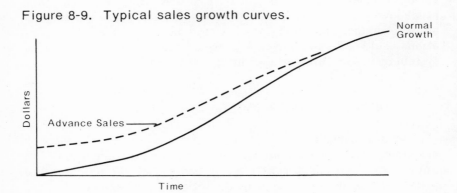

There are a variety of ways the validity of the slope of the curve can be tested. One way is to consider either the number of units or the number of customers that a particular slope would represent. It may be helpful here to refine assumptions by thinking through the process once again—considering the rate at which it is reasonable to attract customers, the average unit sale per customer, and the repeat purchase cycle, if any. If there is a repeat cycle, then the growth rate can become geometric. If there is no repeat cycle, then it is reasonable to assume that the growth curve will be arithmetic.

If units are being used as an element of feasibility determination, they should be measured against production capacity. Production capacity typically has two facets: an absolute capacity and a rate of production. If the organization is a retail outlet, the same rate of processing must be used as a factor in feasibility consideration. In other words, sales could not occur at a rate faster than products can be produced or processed through the retail system. These rates represent outside constraints on the possible volume of business. Further, it is perfectly reasonable to assume that a developing organization will experience a learning curve, in terms of developing capability and understanding, which affects the rate at which sales can be processed or products produced and which naturally acts as an additional constraint on the growth curve of the venture.

In creating a growth curve, then, there are two important factors to balance. One is the capacity for rate of growth, which is an internal constraint, and the other is the rate of customer acceptance, which is an external constraint. It is very important to spend a good deal of time going through a numbers-pushing exercise at this point. The better validated the numbers are, the more viable and therefore valuable will be the projections.

Once the sales curve has been established, it is generally useful to create a second, more pessimistic curve. The purpose of this second curve is to help to determine the impact on the business if the original assumptions do not work, if growth does not occur as rapidly as originally projected or desired. Calculating this so-called worst case provides valuable insight into the downside risk which is typically associated with any venture. The difference between the normal expected growth curve and the worst-case or more pessimistic growth curve will indicate the contingency reserve or extra amount of working capital that will be required in order to get to the second breakeven point (Figure 8-10).

Figure 8-10. Typical sales growth curve with worst case alternative.

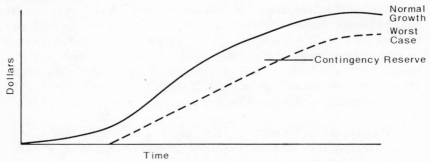

Some important questions to ask about sales levels are:

- How fast will sales grow, or will they decline or stabilize?
- How rapidly can new customers be developed?
- What is the frequency of repeat sales? Can that also be increased?
- What is the frequency of repeat sales? Can that also be increased?
- What is the state of the economy in general, in the specific industry?
- Are there cyclical trends in the industry? How will they affect the specific business?
- What is the nature of the competition? Is it getting stronger, is it declining, or is new competition entering the market?

Another approach to either testing the reasonableness of a projected growth curve or constructing a growth curve is to calculate how many new customers can be added per month, how many old customers will be retained in terms of the frequency of repeat sales, and the average dollar sale per customer. An example is:

	Month					
	1	*2*	*3*	*4*	*5*	*6*
Number of Customers	10	15	20	30	45	50
New	10	5	5	10	15	5
Old	0	10	15	20	30	45

Assuming that the business will never lose a customer (an outrageous assumption), that frequency of repeat sales is one per month, and that the average sale per customer is $75, gross sales for this example will grow as shown in the table.

Month	Average Sale per Customer		Total Customers		Repeat Sales	Gross Sales
1	$75	×	10	×	1	$ 750
2	75	×	15	×	1	1,125
3	75	×	20	×	1	1,500
4	75	×	30	×	1	2,250
5	75	×	45	×	1	3,375
6	75	×	50	×	1	3,750

Plotting these projections will yield a growth curve (Figure 8-11). Adding a breakeven line to this chart will indicate when the business will reach breakeven.

In summary, it is important to test all assumptions used in forecasting sales growth from as many different angles as possible, including the rate of customer development, the unit of sales processed, or any other measures that may be relevant for the particular venture under consideration. The objective is to create the most accurate representation of the future that is possible given the information available in the present. Any techniques that can be utilized to help refine or qualify those assumptions will repay the trouble taken many times over. The more accurate the assump-

Figure 8-11. Projected sales growth curve.

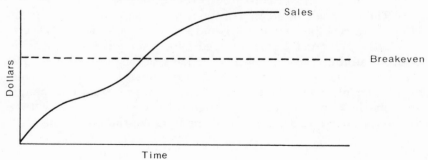

tions, the more accurate the forecast and the less risk associated with the implementation of the business plan.

SUMMARY

This discussion of financial mechanics has included a whole potpourri of techniques and ideas which are not necessarily related in any sequential or organized manner, but which are all interrelated and all interdependent. The secrets of success in achieving the dual objective of improving both forecasting and control within the business organization are imagination and resourcefulness in applying and utilizing the techniques shown here and others which may seem relevant for the business under consideration. In addition, conclusions reached through these activities should be discussed with various advisors, consultants, accountants, bankers, attorneys, and any other individuals who may be available to the management principals and who are willing to devote some thought to the business operation and provide some opinions. The variety of answers derived from the application of analytic techniques and the variety of opinions solicited from the different advisors available to the business will not necessarily be accurate, and many may be in conflict with each other. The point is, they all may be useful, particularly even because of the different answers that they may provide.

It is the managing principals' responsibility to take all this information, give it careful consideration and evaluation, and then make their decisions based on what seems most reasonable to them. The more alternatives, the more different ways of looking at the situation, and the more different opinions, the better the quality of the final decision is likely to be.

The downside of all this is that getting so many different answers is very likely to be a discouraging process. The answer to that is simply, don't be discouraged by it, take advantage of it instead. Planning and control are the keys to business success. The techniques and processes outlined here clearly provide the mechanics for planning and control. The rest of the equation, then, is to apply these techniques in a thoughtful and reasonable way, then follow the course of action that seems to make the most sense.

Chapter 9:
The Mechanics of Management

Once the plan has been constructed, it must be made to function. There are two important reasons why any plan may not work. The first is management failure, due to either inadequate controls or an inadequate management style. The second has to do with the fulfillment of environmental expectations.

Management success or failure is a variable which, by definition, is affected by the effectiveness of the management team. Some of the control techniques discussed in this chapter are tools facilitating effective management. Management style refers to the approach management uses in dealing with the workers within the organization. The whole issue of management style and human relations is, by itself, an important determinant of the effectiveness of any business organization, and it is particularly critical in small firms. Although an in-depth discussion of the philosophy, approach, and techniques needed for success in this area would extend considerably beyond the space limitations of this book, some basic guidelines are offered in this chapter.

While the other critical determinant, the fulfillment of the environmental expectations, is totally outside the control of the management team, the negative impact of their nonfulfillment can be anticipated. This has been an underlying concern throughout the discussion on the various planning activities, especially of strategic or long-range and contingency planning.

MANAGEMENT AND CONTROL

Once the effort has been expended in creating a plan, the real challenge and responsibilities follow in two important categories. The first is to direct activities in such a way as to fulfill the expectations of the plan. The second is to monitor those activities in order to determine whether or not the venture is proceeding as anticipated. Control itself comes in two forms: budget or financial control and people control. The process is completely circular, as noted earlier, with planning, organizing, directing, and controlling activities forming a perpetual sequence:

These four functions are all interrelated, and they must be seen that way. None can proceed effectively without the other three. Each of the four categories represent equally powerful tools of management. One cannot be emphasized at the expense of the others.

Since planning has been the major topic of discussion throughout the text, it is not particularly useful to re-examine this concept here. Organizing has also been included in the earlier discussions, though somewhat less specifically. Organization refers to both a process and a structure. The process is division by analysis of the particular business into the functions or activities that must be performed and the assignment of each task or function to specific individuals. The structure itself of these functional assignments can be formalized into an organization chart that clearly describes the assignment of responsibility within the organization and the flow of authority and reporting relationships that must accompany it.

Organizing ability is universally accepted as an essential characteristic of a successful manager. Much of the planning activities described provide the substance and the framework for organization. If the planning activities have been thoughtfully carried out, the various tasks that need to be performed will have been clearly identified, as will the various resources necessary for their accomplishment. The next requirement is to bring these resources together and put them into place. The utilization of capital resources has been carefully described in the plan itself. However, for most businesses at the planning stage, the people resources may have been defined at an abstract level. The reason is that, until the plan is actually nearing implementation, the business cannot begin to focus on specific individuals outside the critical management team members themselves.

An important function of organization is to begin to assign these abstractly described functions and subfunctions to specific members of the organization according to their respective abilities, capacities, and interests, being careful not to overload the better-qualified individuals. This will bring into play questions of authority and responsibility, which are particularly relevant in embryonic, developing organizations. If an individual is made responsible for a certain job, it is essential to give that person the authority necessary to do it.

In small businesses, particularly new ones, the delegation of authority may become a difficult issue. Many managers of these developing organizations will seek to retain all authority for themselves. These managers may be true entrepreneurs, but the same characteristics that make them successful as entrepreneurs starting up their ventures (single-handedly overcoming the multitude of obstacles and problems cropping up to inhibit that progress, making decisions, and implementing those decisions) are not necessarily good characteristics once the organization is under way. The major difficulty these individuals begin to encounter is that of delegation. The entrepreneur is good at starting businesses, because he himself in some way is able to take care of all the different functions that need to be performed. He makes sure that these tasks are done, in part by doing a lot of them himself. As the business gets bigger, the sheer dynamics of organizational complexity begin to impose a very real limit on how many of these activities he can continue to perform himself, and so he is forced to either put a cap on further growth or begin to develop a middle management infrastructure and share the work.

In order to organize and delegate the work of the organization there must be personnel. Identifying and securing those individuals involves the function of staffing. Staffing is finding the right person for the right job, and is a logical component of organization.

In the planning and early organizing stages, management establishes positions and decides which duties and responsibilities belong to each. Staffing, then, is getting the actual individuals to fill those positions. As the organization develops in size and complexity, staffing becomes a separate and important function requiring continual attention as new employees are needed to replace those who leave and to fill new positions that open as a result of organizational growth. Hiring the best employees for each job and keeping these people efficient and loyal is an important function in any organization and is especially critical in a very small organization.

If a tiny organization employs five people and one of them is not suited for the job or in other ways is a personnel problem, that individual represents 20 percent of the workforce which is nonproductive. The problem doesn't stop there, however, because that individual will undoubtedly interfere with the work of the others. If that interference represents a 25 percent reduction in the efficiency of each of the other workers, then that will represent in total another person's value lost to inefficiencies. These two people units of the workforce, then, being in a nonproductive status, represent a loss of productivity of 40 percent of the total workforce. If this were a factory employing 1,000 workers and 40 percent of the workforce, or 400 workers, were unproductive, immediate and drastic action would be taken to cure this problem. However, in the small organization this same 40 percent loss of efficiency may go unnoticed or, if noticed, uncorrected for a variety of reasons.

Supervision logically follows staffing and carries with it the double dimension of both the directing and controlling functions. There are at least three aspects to it that are important even in tiny firms. First of all, to supervise implies observation, to see that duties are being performed or that work is being done correctly. The style of that observation can have an enormous impact on the productivity of the workers. (This is further developed under the topic of control itself.) The second aspect of supervision is training or remedial training, teaching someone how to do something the first time and correcting bad habits or inefficient or ineffective ways of performing activities. The first step, observation, will frequently point out the need for the second step, remedial or corrective training.

The third dimension of supervision involves upgrading the work, making improvements, constantly determining new or better ways of performing the activities of the firm. This function will require constant attention in a developing firm, because the sheer dynamics of growth will constantly impose new responsibilities on the workforce, and these responsibilities must be constantly reassessed in order to assure that the individuals who are responsible for the activities have the capabilities required for their effective performance and that new work is not naturally gravitating to the most competent employees, thereby unfairly penalizing their good performance by overloading them with additional tasks.

Supervision, to the extent that it requires an ongoing direct monitoring of employees' activities, is time-consuming, and time spent in this activity cannot be spent in others. Many top managers find themselves feeling more like babysitters than executives. When these feelings begin to occur, it is another sign that they have failed to properly delegate responsibility.

Along with delegating tasks and supervising work to assure that the tasks are being performed, management must be flexible to respond to changing situations and unusual or unanticipated problems. The technique for dealing with this is management by exception. Management by exception involves the establishment of decision rules to deal with anticipated problems or tasks, with the clear understanding that situations that do not fit the decision rules are to be treated as exceptions.

The establishment of decision rules or agreements is a key component of delegating authority. Everyone understands what will be done, what is desired, and what is permitted in specific situations. Then, when the circumstances do not fit the decision rules, those problems are passed along to upper levels of management until they get to the point where some individual with the necessary level of authority and scope of responsibility can make the intelligent decision they require. A major unexpected expense, an accident, a peculiar customer complaint, or some other unusual activity will clearly need to be dealt with in a different way than routine problem solving. Managers must be prepared to help their employees with such situations, or they themselves should wrestle with the customer, client, machine, or material that presents this special problem.

Directing carries with it the implications for control. Control has two important dimensions: it is both subjective and objective. The subjective component of control deals with the management of the human resources; the objective dimension of control involves the quantitative evaluation of processes within the operation.

Objective control requires setting standards or objectives for accomplishment, maintaining current operating records for comparison with the standard, and acting promptly when operations deviate too much from the goal established. These control systems deal with measurable quantities such as money, units of production, or sales. In these categories, control involves an investigation into the reasons why actual performance deviates from the budgeted norm, or why the operation is not performing as expected. Control focuses on deviation, and deviations identify problems. Control may be on an hourly, daily, weekly, monthly, or even quarterly basis, depending on how critical that aspect of the operation is to the total business. The actual mechanics of objective control were discussed under "Budget Deviation Analysis" in Chapter 8.

Control represents a major weakness in many small businesses. The owner/manager will proceed along on a hunch basis, intuitively trying to get a sense of whether the business is doing all right or not. This seat-of-the-pants management style carries with it some serious disadvantages. Instincts may be wrong. Businesses grow beyond the ability of any single person to be able to comprehend and always be aware of all the nuances of all the activities. Control systems are information systems, and information is the heart of any good management system.

The second critical dimension of management control is the control of the human resources of the organization. For most contemporary organizations, especially those with growth potential, this calls for the delegation of authority and responsibility to the lowest levels feasible within the organization. The underlying assumptions are simple. If competent people are hired, they will be able to do the work that is required. If they are provided with challenging responsibilities, they will respond with enthusiasm and creativity, generally performing well beyond the technical relationship of a fair day's work for a fair day's pay.

The secret lies in psychological gratification in addition to monetary rewards. This does not suggest in any way that employees should not be well paid—they should. Economies or efficiencies were never achieved by leaving employees feeling that they are slightly underpaid. They will respond to this feeling by slightly underworking. Small organizations especially cannot afford to have individuals simply hanging around. The success of the organization comes from the maximum utilization of its scarce resources, and, again, people are the major resource of most organizations. In small organizations, their optimal utilization is especially critical. It makes a difference, first, between failure and survival, and then, between survival and success. The additional output, the additional effort, the additional creativity, the additional concern will not only make the difference between failure and survival but lead to growth and success.

There are some well-established methods available to help achieve optimum utilization of human resources, notably management by exception and management by objectives. Management by exception has been very briefly described in the foregoing discussion. Management by objectives will be briefly described after the following introductory remarks.

MANAGEMENT STYLE

Two individuals can take the same assets, cash, machinery, facilities, products, and people, and one will develop a successful business, the other a failure. The difference lies in applied-management and leadership skills.

Management and leadership skills can be developed. Like the acquisition of any other skills, their development must go through a series of stages before competence is achieved. First, a conceptual or philosophical understanding must be developed. Then, these conceptual understandings must be translated into action. Finally, actual skills are developed and refined through conscious exercise and practice.

It is usually much more difficult to learn behavioral skills than to acquire physical skills. Physical skills, such as playing tennis or operating a machine, are accessible to relatively objective evaluation. Others can observe the physical movements and tell whether or not the individual is performing correctly. Evaluating behavioral skills, on the other hand, is highly subjective, and effectiveness must be measured over time.

Another important difference between developing behavioral skills and physical skills is that different personalities may require different approaches to achieve the same results for behavioral skills, whereas physical activities are performed in much the same way, irrespective of individual personality differences. For example, the management technique or style that may work for one individual may not work for another, and in developing management processes or management strategies, it is important to keep this in mind. There is not a set pattern of behavior that will cure management problems or lead to effective management. Instead, there are ideas each person has to modify in the way that best suits him, his business situation, his own personality, and the type of workers within the business.

It must be added that there is an important similarity between the acquisition of behavioral skills and the acquisition of physical skills. The similarity is that training and practice can greatly improve both. For any business, this area of management responsibility must be clearly recognized and given appropriate priority. The importance of this must be re-emphasized continually, because it typically represents an area of weakness, especially for technically sophisticated entrepreneurs. These individuals tend to feel that, because they well understand the mechanics of their business, the other aspects of management will simply follow automatically. Unfortunately, for many of these technical entrepreneurs, the cost of this error in judgment has been the failure of the business.

In carrying out management activities, there are at least three areas of skill that are critical to the process: technical, human, and conceptual.

1. Technical skill—the ability to use knowledge, methods, techniques, and equipment necessary for the performance of specific tasks. Acquired from experience, education, and training.

2. Human skill—the ability and judgment in working with and through people, including an understanding of motivation and the application of effective leadership.

3. Conceptual skill—the ability to understand the complexities of the overall organization and how the various parts of the organization fit together, interact, and contribute to or inhibit the effective operation of the rest of the organization. This knowledge encourages decision making within the framework of the total organization rather than only on the basis of the goals and needs of one component of the business operation.

Any of these areas of skill can become disproportionately important at the expense of the others, thus seriously inhibiting the organization's effectiveness. An imbalance of technical skills leads to an overemphasis on the process aspects of the business and tends to ignore the general management needs of the organization. The application of conceptual skills helps to bring this kind of distorted emphasis back into perspective and places it in the context of the total organization. An overemphasis on the human skills has a tendency to seek improvements in relationships at the expense of getting the necessary work done within the organization. However, insufficient emphasis on the human skills, especially in a small organization, ignores the needs of the workers and tends to reduce their opportunity for involvement in the organization.

In most cases, organizational effectiveness is enhanced by encouraging the participation of the employees in the decision making and actions of the firm. Understanding and meeting employee needs provides managers of embryonic and developing small businesses with some especially powerful motivational techniques. Within limits, maximizing the satisfaction of employees can directly contribute to maximizing the achievement of the organizational goals. Again, however, this can only occur within the context of the organization's total objectives.

Once the tasks that need to be performed within the organization have been identified and delegated, the next problem is getting people to do them. Getting anyone to do something that he is not naturally going to do by himself involves the application of power. There are two kinds of power that are available to leaders or managers within an organization. One is the traditional hierarchial right to tell others what to do. This is the traditional, classical management, or Theory X approach, and is justified by the assumption that the organization buys a portion of the subordinate's time. Insofar as they're aware of that assumption, the subordinates usually feel obliged to contribute only that amount of time and energy and interest to the organizational purposes.

Another source of power is grounded in respect and acceptance. It suggests that subordinates are willing to do what they are told to do and that they look to the leader or the manager as the resource that will help them accomplish more. From the manager's point of view, this becomes a process of letting the subordinates accomplish the organizational purposes, of helping them accomplish the organizational process, rather than making them perform various duties. This "letting" instead of "making" is the Theory Y approach to management.

Theory Y is increasingly recognized by behavioralists as an important motivational tool, a way to increase the productivity of workers without increasing costs. Small embryonic and developing businesses can and must achieve maximum efficiencies from their workforce if they are to maintain their competitive edge. Theory Y is an essential tool for the accomplishment of this purpose in many organizations.

Not only is the Theory X approach of making people work self-limiting in that they will only do as much as they are required to do, it has an additional cost in that it requires a great deal of supervision in order to make sure that everyone is doing what he's supposed to do. Theory Y, on the other hand, the approach of letting people participate in the work of the organization, not only

increases the productivity of the individual worker, but also reduces the amount of supervision required. In most small businesses, this is a practical necessity. The owner/manager simply
doesn't have the time to directly and closely supervise all the workers within the organization. They will wind up being self-con-
trolled either by sheer default or by intention.

The objective, then, is to develop a system that will encourage
employees' self-control to the maximum extent. Management by
objectives (MBO) is a method of accomplishing this. The MBO process involves identifying, clarifying, and integrating individual
and organizational goals and showing that the individuals are
going to best achieve their personal objectives through the performance of activities that contribute to the organizational objectives.

MANAGEMENT BY OBJECTIVES

Management by objectives, commonly referred to as MBO,
represents a sharing of the activities within the business. It ac-
knowledges that subordinates have some intelligence and are contributing to the success of the organization along with the management. Sharing the full range of activities—the decision making as
well as the work—gives employees a sense of accomplishment as
well as a weekly paycheck. For many employees this sense of
shared accomplishment becomes just as important as, and in some
cases far more important than, the actual amount of money they
receive as salary.

Along with the motivational implications of MBO goes a process of management development. As the business grows, it will
need to develop a layer of middle management, which will gradually assume more and more responsibility. This can be done
through the MBO process. Over time, as employees assume responsibilities for the various tasks and for their own self-supervision,
they can gradually learn to acquire additional levels of responsibility and thus develop in accordance with the increasing complexity of the organization itself. In this way they are increasingly able
to handle more and more complex demands and so are able to
respond to these demands as they grow within the organization.
The MBO framework can be a process for explicitly structuring
this growth program.

Applying management by objectives involves participation in
and sharing of important management functions by workers at all

levels within the organization. Generally, the approach will involve the identification of goals for individuals, for groups, and for the entire organization. Conversely, the goal sets for individuals are subsets of the goal sets for groups, which are themselves goal subsets of the entire organization's goals. Subordinates and superiors jointly determine and agree upon the results they seek to achieve along with the standards that will be used to measure these results.

Periodic reviews are made by superiors and subordinates to evaluate projects and results against the previously set objectives. The process encourages certain important steps, including clear establishment and agreement of results sought, so-called ownership or acceptance of goals, and the basis for measurement of performance and contribution.

The last factor, measuring results, can in itself create giant problems in a small organization where people have multiple tasks to perform. Unless there is a clear agreement as to the expected outcome of these tasks, there may be a real disagreement as to how productive or effective the employees have been. One of the important results of the MBO process is to reduce this kind of ambiguity and confusion which could otherwise lead to serious disagreements about work expectations and performance.

A successful MBO process incorporates the development of plans necessary to achieve goals and encourages the adaptation of organizational structure to facilitate the implementation of these plans. To encourage success, different groups can share the necessary personnel, facilities and equipment, and other resources available. Successful implementation of MBO can help achieve commitment of all concerned to the task at hand. It can focus attention on the central functions of the managerial process. To be successful, MBO must have complete commitment of all involved, but especially the management principals of the business unit. A true sharing, a true delegation of authority as well as responsibility must occur. The opinions of subordinates must be sought, not as part of a con job, but because they are valued and their participation is appreciated.

It is the recognition of the accomplishments of subordinates that contributes so strongly to the motivational process. Most people go to work and expect to get paid; recognition is that extra dimension of pay that becomes especially rewarding for most. It is a form of psychic gratification—a recognition of work done, the ability to participate, to become part of the organization rather than being just another employee—that makes MBO such a power-ful motivational tool.

In a large organization such a process can minimize conflicts throughout the organization, encourage cooperation, and facilitate the successful achievement of organizational goals. In a small business, this form of sharing is critical. A small business needs an extra edge to give it a competitive advantage, and that extra edge can be the extra caring and the extra effort of its employees. Under MBO that extra edge comes through the recognition of subordinate employees as valuable assets of the organization and a willingness to let them know of their importance to the total business process.

The implementation of MBO can be seen as involving the following series of steps, which is summarized in Figure 9-1.

Step 1. The organization's goals are established, its particular objectives are clearly identified and explicitly stated, and measures of performance are specified. It is essential that both goals and standards are made completely clear so that everyone within the organization will understand these organizational expectations.

Step 2. Revisions in the organizational structure are made in order to accommodate the achievement of these organizational goals. If, for example, a new department is needed to perform a certain function, it would be created.

Step 3. The superior and the subordinate separately establish their expectations of the subordinate's work activities. This is a critical point in the MBO process, particularly because the subordinate must have an opportunity to think through the implications of this work without undue influence from his superior. Both must make their expectations explicit.

Step 4. The separate expectations developed in step 3 are brought together through a process of mutual agreement, an activity frequently characterized by negotiation. These negotiated understandings become the work objectives for the subordinate. The subordinate and the superior both agree that the job as defined makes a relevant contribution to the organizational objectives and represents a reasonable amount of work to be done. The subordinate is sharing a slice of the organizational activity which is clearly recognized and clearly understood.

These agreements are ordinarily formalized in writing on a standardized form so that they can be referred to in the future. Generally, both the supervisor and the subordinate would sign this work plan or form as a sort of contract. All the work plans, when added together, will represent the total work activities of the orga-

Figure 9-1. The MBO process.

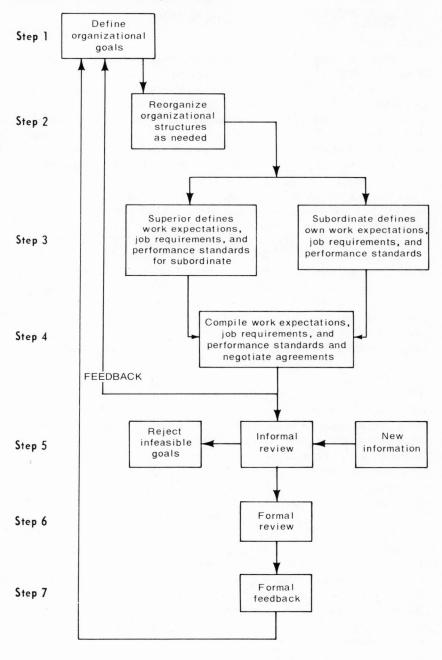

nization that are available and necessary to achieve the organization's goals.

There is a feedback loop between step 4 and step 1 at this point which may result in a modification of some of the organization's goals, or may influence or change the joint agreement or subordinates' goals in order to emphasize some organizational objectives. For example, it may turn out that some organizational objectives are infeasible given capability or resource limitations within the organization. The organizational objectives are the goals that are being worked toward; they must either be achieved or, if they are infeasible for some reason, be changed. This becomes a form of reality testing of the organization's goals and will help in determining whether or not they are achievable. If not, they must be modified.

Step 5. Interim results are measured through an ongoing informal review process. This is another important aspect of the MBO system. MBO is effective not from the Theory X point of view of trying to catch the employee in his failure to accomplish goals, but rather as a means of being sensitive to problems that the employee may be having in achieving the goals. The purpose is to help the subordinate achieve the goals in any way possible or to recognize problems that may be inhibiting the achievement of the goals.

The distinction here between Theory X and Theory Y is quite critical. The Theory X approach is to punish the employee for not achieving the goals. The Theory Y approach is to find out why the employee is not achieving the goals and help relieve or remove these barriers. After all, the underlying objective is to achieve the purposes of the organization, not to punish ineffective employees. Step 5 recognizes both the possibility that the introduction of new information may modify the goals or that some of the goals initially established were, in fact, infeasible. If they are infeasible, then it is jointly recognized and they are eliminated.

The importance of the informal review process is to provide, through a constant monitoring process, an ongoing opportunity to identify when plans are getting off the track or when circumstances arise where the subordinate may need some additional help. Ordinarily, through the informal review process, inefficiencies can be more easily recognized and are less threatening and less likely to result in confrontations than through the more formal review process.

Step 6. The formal review process is initiated on a regular periodic basis, often quarterly. It is essential that the subordinate and the superior sit down together with the work plan contract and jointly determine whether or not the goals have been achieved, and if not, why not. It is important that these deficiencies be analyzed—again, not in terms of the employee's failures, but rather because the failure to achieve the goals represents a setback to the achievement of the organizational purposes since, of course, the subordinate's goals are subsets of the organization's goals. It is the superior's role as the helper of the subordinate that becomes important. The formal review is typically incorporated into the original work plan that was signed by both the subordinate and the superior. The conclusions to that review would be written on the same plan, deviations noted, deficiencies recognized, and new strategies made explicit.

Step 7. The formal review documents are aggregated to provide a review of the total organizational performance. This will yield a picture of the cumulative impact of the achievements or deficiencies of the lower-level work plans. The results of this analysis are fed back into step 1 to complete the cycle and may result in the revision of the organizational goals and/or the establishment of new goals. This informational feedback linking system will continue as an ongoing dynamic flexible process, which will help ensure that new goals are incorporated into this system, that innovation is part of the system, that the orientation of personnel within the organization is toward the accomplishment of organizational goals and toward the achievement of goals that are jointly recognized and clearly accepted by all as being reasonable and achievable. Finally, individual participation is made explicit through the joint determination of the work plans and joint measurement of their accomplishment.

There are some limitations to MBO. Primary deficiencies in MBO systems have occurred when subordinates have been held liable for the nonachievement of goals, thus making it quickly clear to them that they are being measured, not on performance or achievement, but rather in terms of their deficiencies, whether these deficiencies were the result of their own ineptness or the result of some factors over which they had no control. Under such conditions, it becomes important to the subordinates to limit the goal-setting process to make sure that the goals established are as minimal as possible, and therefore as easily achievable as possible. This negative cycle of thinking will lead to the reinforcement of Theory X stereotypes, and rather than maximizing productivity, the MBO process would then be a limitation. Used wisely, however, MBO can be a powerful management tool and make a strong contribution to the success of the business.

SUMMARY

Unless they are supported and carried out by proactive enlightened management, the best plans in the world are unlikely to fulfill any of their potential. Management capability is a skill that can be developed, but it requires conscious attention and active participation. Management by objectives has been described as a logical and systematic process for the achievement of organizational goals. MBO represents both a management attitude and a series of activities that can result in improved productivity of all employees within the organization. It is attitudinal in that it represents a true commitment to the idea that employees within the organization can contribute to the design of the work task and to the establishment of goals. It is mechanical in that a series of steps can be followed to help develop an MBO program and monitor its progress and effectiveness. It is a system that initially will require a certain degree of learning for both managers and subordinates and in many cases will require a change of behavior patterns for each. If the inconvenience of these changes can be tolerated, MBO can be put into place and used as an effective motivator to improve the organizational climate, improve individual productivity, and increase profits—all valid objectives for any business.

In short, planning and management are the keys to business success.

Appendix A:

A Business Plan for the Battleworks Furniture Company, Inc.

(COVER SHEET)

A BUSINESS PLAN
FOR
THE BATTLEWORKS FURNITURE COMPANY, INC.
EAST PODUNK, NEW HAMPSHIRE

John M. Silver
President
(603) 555-1234

---

or:

A FINANCING PROPOSAL

Submitted to

The First National Bank
of East Podunk

by

THE BATTLEWORKS FURNITURE COMPANY, INC.
EAST PODUNK, NEW HAMPSHIRE

John M. Silver
President
(603) 555-1234

Table of Contents

Statement of Purpose

The Battleworks Furniture Company, Inc., is seeking a loan of $63,000 for eight years to purchase equipment and inventory, prepare operating space as needed, maintain necessary cash reserves, and provide adequate working capital to successfully launch a vertically integrated, custom, butcher-block furniture manufacturing and retail operation. This loan, together with an equity cash investment of $8,000, will be sufficient to finance the transition through the development phases so that the business can operate as a viable profitable enterprise.

or:

Statement of Purpose

This business plan has been developed by the Battleworks Furniture Company, Inc., as an operating guide to the development of a vertically integrated, custom, butcher-block furniture manufacturing and retail operation. The aggregate investment of $71,000 being provided from private sources is sufficient to purchase equipment and inventory, prepare operating space as needed, maintain necessary cash reserves, and provide adequate working capital to successfully launch this business. This document is for internal planning and operations purposes only, and is not to be released outside the operation.

4

I THE BUSINESS

Description of the Business

The Battleworks Furniture Company, Inc., is a combined manufacturing/retail operation engaged in the semicustom butcher-block furniture business. Battleworks has been designed to operate initially with a small labor force and low overhead, utilizing advantages of modern technology employed in an innovative and creative manner. Production will be tied to demand, so the common problem of attempting to second-guess future demand to determine what to produce is eliminated. The firm will be located in East Podunk, New Hampshire. The firm is vertically integrated, with manufacturing and retail operations occupying the same premises.

The firm plans to manufacture high-quality, contemporary furniture of wood. A definite market exists for this type of furniture and is currently being inadequately satisfied by retail operations offering finished products at high prices. These prices automatically exclude certain market segments that cannot or do not want to pay this amount. Their alternative currently exists in stores offering lower-quality products, finished and unfinished, at lower prices, a combination which offers a poor compromise. Within the East Podunk area, this gap exists between firms such as Sam's Exotic Furniture and Snobby Articles, Inc., both offering high-quality contemporary furniture at high prices, and other businesses such as Mal's Bargain Specials and the Cheapo Emporium, offering much lower quality at lower prices. Battleworks will fill this gap, offering quality at a reasonable price.

Once the gap in the existing delivery structure was identified, intensive market research was conducted to find the specific market segment or individuals who would be potential customers. This target segment group can be described as young, educated professionals who are married, have children, and reside either in the city itself or in the surrounding suburbs. The market strategy of the firm will be to intensively cultivate this market, informing them that they no longer need to compromise their desires. The target market segment will be advised of this opportunity through a highly selective direct mail campaign of quality brochures describing the product and through selective advertising in periodicals and magazines specifically serving the market segment. At

5

the present time the market is deliberately restricted to the greater East Podunk area, constrained by the size limitations of the firm. As the firm grows, the market area will be expanded accordingly.

Battleworks will be especially competitive, both through production and design efficiencies and through the application of innovative concepts in an industry which has historically been change resistant. Currently, technology is available that has not been utilized in the furniture industry, such as the use of ultrasonic sound waves to facilitate almost instantaneous drying of glue, thereby eliminating the traditional overnight delays for curing and thus dramatically reducing the production cycle time. Battleworks is being created by an engineer with the deliberate intention of incorporating such innovative technology as a way of increasing operating efficiencies and decreasing labor costs, thus giving the firm a competitive advantage over more conventional operations, without a corresponding sacrifice in quality.

The furniture industry is characterized by a large number of small firms, the largest of which controls only three and one-half percent of the total market. This structure, coupled with the relatively low absolute dollar entry costs (in terms of plant and equipment), permits the entry of a new small firm without the threat of being shut out by a large firm. Traditionally, furniture has been assembled in certain areas of the country such as Grand Rapids, Michigan, and increasingly now in North Carolina, and then shipped by rail or truck to various wholesale and retail distributors throughout the country. There are some problems inherent in this process. A customer must select from the products actually available for sale at a given location. In addition, special orders must pass through a long and cumbersome channel and so have an inordinately long cycle time. Because of this, if customers do not find the item or the finish or the color that is desired in one store, then they are likely to continue shopping in other stores until they find a product more appropriate or suitable to their needs. The alternative, for the retailers especially, is to maintain larger and larger inventories. This has the combined important consequences of high inventory carrying costs and the sheer amount of space required to store a large amount of furniture. An additional problem is the cost of freight, which is an important component of the final retail price.

In designing the Battleworks operations plan, it was important to identify these particular problems endemic to the industry and seek solutions that could be incorporated in a relatively low-cost operation. The two keys to this dilemma appear to be vertical integration and semicustomized production. Through vertical integration, the manufacturing and retail operations are completely associated and, in fact, will occupy the same premises. There will, by definition, be no delivery time or cost between manufacturer and retailer. The second problem, that of providing a variety of sizes, shapes, colors, and finishes, is resolved through semi-custom manufacturing. Standardized parts are to be manufactured to inventory. Then, when a customer desires a particular size, style, or type of wood, the base components are gathered from inventory and assembled, tops or other major dimensional pieces cut to specification, and the total product finished and/or, as is increasingly the case in much furniture manufacturing, wood veneer finishes laminated onto the final product. All of this can be done quite quickly and so merely represents the final assembly stage of any furniture manufacturing operation. The advantage, however, is that it is done strictly in response to demand, so that final-inventory anticipation is never a problem. Storage costs are eliminated, and the customer will always be able to receive exactly the style, color, and/or finish desired without compromise, working merely from floor samples and photographs.

A firm such as Battleworks has tremendous competitive advantages over more conventional operations. This firm will have complete flexiblity and can be immediately responsive to changes in demand, being relieved of long production cycles or from being stuck with large inventories of obsolete merchandise. Vertical integration offers economies of shipping and handling, and wholesaling and inventory costs are minimized or eliminated. Thus, Battleworks can operate in this industry as a new firm and achieve significant cost advantages, giving it the capability of being very price competitive with larger established operations.

Market and Competition Analysis

An in-depth analysis of the furniture industry competition structure and market segments in the target Standard Metropolitan Statistical Area has indicated the existence of an undersatisfied target market of sufficient size to warrant exploitation by the Battleworks Furniture Company. As noted earlier, the existing market delivery structure offers either quality finished products at high prices, which automatically exclude certain market segments that cannot or do not want to pay this amount, or alternatively offers lower-quality products, finished and unfinished, at lower prices, a combination which provides a poor compromise.

Once the gap in the existing delivery structure was identified, intensive market research was undertaken to identify the specific market segment of individuals who would be potential customers. These individuals can be described as young, educated professionals, who are married,

7

have children, and are either suburban or city dwellers. As indicators of market sufficiency, within the target SMSA there are 1,136,474 individuals employed who are 16 years old and over. Of this total, 416,732, or over one-third (36.6 percent), can be classified as white-collar workers (not including the 260,400 workers who are clerical and related types). Using education as a second indicator of market potential, of the 1,529,168 persons 25 years old and over within the SMSA, 181,358 have completed one to three years of college, and 240,937 have completed four years or more of college, for a total of 422,295, or 27.6 percent of the total. In using income as a barometer of market sufficiency, of the 661,650 families in the target SMSA, 306,045, or 46.25 percent, earn over $12,000, and 199,139, or 30 percent of the total, earn $15,000 or more. Finally, using age as a determining characteristic, of the 2,753,700 total individuals living in the SMSA, 420,677, or 15.28 percent, are between 20 and 44 years of age.

COMPETITION. In assessing the nature of the competition in the target SMSA, two separate views must be taken. The first view would be a consideration of all of the stores marketing furniture. For example, there are over 350 furniture stores listed in the Yellow Pages for the city alone, not including a variety of additional stores scattered throughout the suburbs. Of this total, however, only 14 are felt to be direct competitors, and of these 14, the following five are felt to be the closest in terms of type of furniture offered, style of operation, price, and potential customers: The Ardvark, Union Square Furniture, Spiffys, Smith's Furniture Emporium, and Joe's Store. Of these five, the first two stores offer the same high-quality contemporary furniture as Battleworks, have convenient and accessible locations, and advertise competitively; however, their prices are considerably higher than those that would be charged by Battleworks for the same type and quality goods. The other three stores are similarly priced and equally accessible but have furniture of lower quality. The corresponding lower-quality image is reflected in their storefronts, signs, and general marketing approaches utilized. Battleworks steps into the gap between these competitors, offering quality at a reasonable price.

A market study was conducted of retail firms within the target SMSA selling furniture similar to that proposed by Battleworks and to a market segment similar to that addressed by Battleworks. The data shown were selected as representative of the volume of specific items in these stores. They do not indicate the total volume of these stores, nor do they suggest that Battleworks, though selling similar items, will necessarily achieve these volumes. These data are included to support the unit sales volumes used to project reasonable sales levels for Battleworks.

Competition Analysis

Store	Item	# Sold per Month	Price	Battleworks Price, Similar or Better Quality
A	3' x 5' Dining Table	20	$75	$75
	3' x 6' Bookcase	30	$80–92	$75
	Desk Pedestal—Single	10	$55	$75
B	Platform Bed—Queen	13	$358–400	$150–250
	39" Child Bed	10	$120–135	$100
	3' x 5' Dining Table	8	$150	$100
C	Bed—Queen Plain	6	$245–290	$150–250
D	Bed—Queen	10	$300–320	$150–250
	Oak Coffee Table	8	$250	$125
	3' x 5' Butcher-block Table	5	$225	$125
	3' x 6' Bookcase	10	$110	$75

Products

Battleworks will be manufacturing, and selling at retail, finely crafted contemporary furniture at reasonable prices. Products are to be made on the premises in the firm's own workshop. Only choice selected hardwoods will be used, and samples of wooden furniture will be on display in the showroom. Modifications to current designs and/or special executions in selected woods and custom work will be available on a limited basis. Even though the workshop will be small, it will be one of the best-equipped on the East Coast. With the appropriate equipment and a high level of pride, craftsmanship and quality can be maintained to the advantage and satisfaction of both cabinetmaker and consumer. The trestle table is a good example of this. Proposed to be crafted of solid oak or rock maple (sometimes in solid walnut or teak), it is designed for today's use but with a potential to be tomorrow's heirloom.

BEDS. Beds will be available in a variety of styles and sizes:

Platform bed—available in queen or double, in solid walnut or teak. Bases are solid with matching legs. King size available on special request.

Studio bed—a small platform bed with open corners; accommodates a cot-size mattress. Framed in solid wood with matching solid legs. Decorative fabric cover. This bed can be used for casual seating.

Studio bunk bed—actually two studio beds in a ladder arrangement that permits stacking or future separation for individual use. The result is two beds which, when separated, do not look like a bunk bed in halves. The ladder arrangement is additionally designed to accommodate one storage drawer under the bunk without hardware.

Bunk beds—while more conventional than the studio bunk, these beds are unusual in that the ends are ladders. Crafted in solid oak and available in walnut or teak on special request.

Headboards—these are available separately, crafted of finest matched veneers or of solid wood with three inserts of real cane. Headboards may be either wall-mounted or bed-mounted.

Storage units are designed to fit under beds; one unit fits nicely beneath the studio, while two units can be accommodated by a double, queen-size, or king-size bed. All have fronts and handles of solid oak, walnut, or teak and a removable center divider. Each unit has hidden wheels that permit easy rolling on carpets or hard floors. The smooth sides of the straight legs on the bed act as guides; thus no hardware is needed, and the units can be added at any time to a bed previously purchased. Mattresses will be available of high-quality, high-density polyurethane foam with an eight-ounce ticking cover.

SEATING. Sofas, loveseats, and chairs will be available with solid ends and backs. Seating prices will not include the fabric but will include the cushions. Fabric coverings will be available and finished work provided at additional cost. Cushions are to be reversible with zippers and separate muslin covers for maximum utility and ease of cleaning.

Dining chair—a simple chair in solid oak with natural cane seat and back, available as a side chair or armchair. Will unobtrusively complement any table, but has the good looks, clean lines, and workmanship to stand on its own merits.

TABLES. Table tops are sold on a square-foot basis. The price includes the attachment of legs. Legs are available in two styles, and each style is the same price in a given wood. Connecting trestle rails will be available and are optional for tables under five feet and recommended for those over five feet.

Bench table—eighteen inches high and eighteen inches wide. This unit is suitable for sitting on or using as a coffee table. It will be offered in oak with matching or contrasting dowel plugs. Other sizes and woods to be available on request.

Parsons table—made on request in various woods and sizes.

Trestle table—complete table is priced as sum of parts.

Round table—tops measured across the diameter. Wood vases come in two sizes, small and large.

OTHER PIECES.   In addition to the items described, other pieces will be made regularly, for example, table tops, upholstered benches, etc., whose volume does not warrant special attention but for which capability can be easily maintained.

A special note about all table tops: All tops are to be nominally one and one-half inch thick and of solid hardwood. Tops may be requested in any size within the range permitted. Length, width, and diameter tolerances are normally held to plus or minus one inch, but this tolerance can be held tighter on request. This leeway of an inch is very helpful in permitting the more careful selection of lumber to go in a given top and permits less waste, thus keeping costs down. On request, a limited series of veneer tops are available at usually lower cost.

A special note about furniture: All pieces are made of the finest kiln-dried stock available. The oak used is generally northern red oak from New England. The maple is rock maple from New England also, but occasionally both will be obtained from West Virginia. Black walnut and black cherry will come from the Midwest. The bulk of the teak comes from Thailand, but some is obtained from Burma. All mahoganies to be used are generally African ribbon or Honduras.

A note about finish: All finishes are durable, hand-rubbed satin oil finish. This finish is easily renewed and must be oiled occasionally. The instructions on care will be given with each purchase. A more durable synthetic finish is available on request.

Manufacturing/Operations

The Battleworks Furniture Company is to be a small vertically integrated manufacturing/retail establishment. The integration of the manufacturing and retail operations is seen as a highly efficient way to reduce channel time, along with storage, handling, and freight costs, all of which add up to a significant competitive advantage for Battleworks relative to more conventional forms of operations. The plant layout and work flow process have been carefully designed to maximize the use of available space and minimize redundancy in handling, repeat operations, and other inefficiencies seemingly inherent in many such woodworking operations (see Appendix I).

Furniture will be manufactured and stored in inventory in unassembled form. The styles available, assembled and finished, will be on display in the retail area. When a customer has made a selection, the parts for that item will be taken from inventory and assembled and finished to the customer's desire. Under these conditions, furniture can be available for delivery within three days, the time period comparable to stores holding assembled prefinished furniture in inventory. This plan obviates the need for maintaining large inventories of finished goods while preserving the capability of offering an almost infinite variety of finishes to complement or match any existing decor (a capability that often is not satisfied by even the largest inventory reserves of finished goods).

The inventory flexibility represented by the proposed operational strategy is an extremely significant factor in the success of this relatively small-scale operation. It offers the capability of custom manufacturing, but practically eliminates the time delays normally associated with that type of operation. It also relieves the work flow problems normally part of a custom manufacturing operation; that is, rather than producing individual items, batch processing techniques can be used, reducing set-up time and considerably improving the efficiency of the total production process. By having a relatively limited range of styles and by manufacturing parts for inventory, the firm can plan and maintain a consistent work flow and stable workforce while assuring that the workforce will be fully utilized at all times. Finally, because of the limited labor invested in the unassembled inventory, and because the expensive finish (veneer) is not applied until the product is actually sold, this operation offers an opportunity to maximize the limited resources of time, material, and funds by producing only those final products which are actually sold. A mistake in inventory planning under conventional operational methodology could be disastrous for a small-scale operation and, in fact, cause failure of the firm. Under the strategy represented by the Battleworks plan, the danger represented by this problem is greatly minimized.

The operations plan enables Battleworks to be completely flexible and immediately responsive to changes in demand, being relieved of long production cycles and from the danger of being stuck with large in-

ventories of obsolete merchandise. The vertical integration offers economies in that shipping, handling, wholesale, and inventory costs are minimized or eliminated. The work flow process and plant layout shown in
Appendix I to this plan indicate the careful efficiencies designed into the
operation. In addition, it should be emphasized that a very particular
combination of equipment is being planned which will ensure maximum
capability with the least number of items. The equipment selected is expensive and of extremely high quality; however, the economies available
through its use will far more than offset these price considerations.
Through the operations strategy, this new firm can achieve significant
cost advantages giving it the capability of being very price competitive
with larger established operations.

Location

Battleworks has identified two potential locations as being particularly
appropriate for the type, style, and size of operation contemplated.

LOCATION A. Vacant storefront operation located on a well-traveled
main thoroughfare linking the downtown areas of the city with the more
prestigious westerly suburbs. The building is of masonry construction,
reasonably attractive, sound and secure, and has display windows facing
the street and a large overhead door access fronting a sidestreet, as well
as ample parking to the sides and rear. Twenty-five hundred feet of floor
space are available on the main floor, and the same amount of space is
available in the basement, which could be utilized for the storage of inventory components. The store was previously used as a retail tire outlet,
operations of which were discontinued because of insufficient customer
demand for that type of operation in that location. There is no negative
reputation known to be associated with this location. Traffic counts and
traffic surveys indicate both the volume and appropriateness of potential
customers traveling this route to make the retail visibility desirable, in addition to the accessibility represented by the location. The rent of this facility is known to be $200 per month, with the understanding that heat
and other utilities would be provided by the occupant.

LOCATION B. A portion of an old factory building is available in an area
undergoing considerable commercial revitalization. This building and
two others, each being well over 100 years old and empty for the last 20
years, are being subdivided and leased to small contemporary manufacturing and specialty retail operations, all of which are complements to

13

each other in that they are attractive to the same target market segments. This is seen increasingly as an area where smart young professional shoppers would find a variety of interesting products at reasonable prices that they could afford and feel comfortable paying. A potential disadvantage is that the buildings are not on well-traveled thoroughfares and could be difficult to find. Parking is somewhat limited as well. The space available to Battleworks is a second-floor location, accessible to customers by a wide flight of low-rise stairs and providing access for raw materials and other large items through a freight elevator. The area is easily secured against potential theft, has all utilities provided, and various amounts of space are available for an average price of $6.00 per square foot.

Marketing Plan

Given both sufficiency and accessibility of the target market as described in the market/competition analysis, and given the identified gap in the existing delivery structure, a marketing strategy has been defined which will intensively cultivate this market segment, informing them that they no longer need to compromise their desires. The target market segment will be informed of this opportunity through a highly selective direct mail campaign of quality brochures describing the products, and through selective advertising in periodicals, magazines, and newspapers serving this market segment. At the present point in time, the market is restricted to the Greater Podunk area and is constrained by the initial size limitations of the firm. As the firm grows, the market area will be expanded accordingly. The specific components of the marketing plan are presented in the following description, and additional backup information is provided in Appendix II.

1. *Photo displays.* Quality-image 8 × 10 photographic prints mounted on white cardboard mat will be placed on display in noncompeting stores that have good window space not in use or whose "product" is a service and which may therefore be willing to rent the space for a quality display (for example, jewelry stores at night, or a fabric store). Battleworks will seek to avoid paying cash and offer to pay in credits toward goods or fixtures which could be billed.

2. *Direct mail.* A brochure will be prepared showing fine pen-and-ink reproductions of goods with a descriptive soft-sell high-quality presentation and a low-tone cover letter. Photos of representative furniture will be included. Mailings will be made to: (a) friends of present cus-

tomers, (b) old customers, informing them of new products, (c) members of faculty wives clubs, faculty members, and professional associations, (d) parents whose children attend the better day schools, day care centers, and private schools, (e) other special groups, for example, those who might be interested in purchasing seconds or potential commercial customers.

3. *Samples.* Free samples of certain goods will be made available as display items or as building fixtures in exchange for having the recipient inform customers about who made the particular products, and possibly in exchange for mailing lists and other forms of support:

- To daycare centers in limited numbers, sturdy but nice toys would be provided; for example, a good wooden scooter or a wagon.
- To realty agents of large developments, furniture may be provided for the rental office in exchange for putting out literature on the premises for prospective tenants.
- To art and theater shows, free furniture would be provided for use as stage props in exchange for putting the Battleworks name in the theater program.

4. *Normal advertising.* A limited number of small, unobtrusive, clean pen-and-ink-type advertisements will be placed in local media, in the handbooks of graduate schools, and in free community papers in more affluent suburbs. In addition, a very limited amount of advertising will be done at a local FM radio station that plays classical music throughout the day and evening.

5. *Referrals.* Referrals come through existing customers who have purchased furniture and inform their friends of its source and by exchanging demonstration and sample pieces with noncompeting craftsmen and having reciprocal displays available at each respective place of business.

6. *Limited showings for special interest groups.*

7. *Education.* Information and literature will be provided in the showroom designed to educate customers on furniture construction, how to identify quality furniture, and the woodworking practices utilized at Battleworks.

It is clearly understood that the mere manufacture of quality furniture and its availability at a reasonable price are not sufficient to ensure the success of Battleworks. In addition to these critical but not sufficient requirements of success, Battleworks proposes to launch a carefully designed, methodical, staged marketing campaign, structured to achieve maximum benefit with the limited resources available to the firm. Further details on the marketing strategy are included in Appendix II.

Future Change Strategies

Once Battleworks has successfully made the transition from a conceptual model to an operating reality and unknown quantities have been defined and other assumptions of the model tested and revised as needed, the organization proposes to expand in two directions.

The first will be the gradual development of commercial sales. The butcher-block style of furniture which is proposed to be the basic product line of Battleworks is attractive and durable and increasingly seen as appropriate for contemporary business firms, especially in reception areas, employee leisure areas, and other such commercial space that requires comfort, attractiveness, and durability in its furniture. Battleworks will be in a position to be completely competitive with other sources of supply, in terms of both price and quality, and as the organization develops, it will have the capacity to take on such sales.

The second dimension of projected expansion is the development of satellite storefronts. The creation of one or more satellite stores has the potential to increase sales volume dramatically. The satellite store will be a retail showroom operation employing one salesperson. It will have on display a selection of Battleworks furniture and sales literature.

Since the satellite store would be strictly a sales operation (all manufacturing would continue to be done at the primary Battleworks location), it would occupy relatively little space. Given a satellite store's modest space requirements, it can be in a high-traffic location affording maximum exposure without prohibitively high rent. The satellite store would have a selection of furniture representative of Battleworks' total product line, which would be complemented by large photographs and other such sales aids. A competent salesperson would be able to satisfy most customers' needs and, in the few instances where it would be necessary, customers could always be referred to the primary store location.

Such an operation could contribute significantly to Battleworks' sales and profits. Aside from the materials costs and the salary of one salesperson, most of the organization's normal operating costs will continue to be carried by the primary location. The satellite store could thus contribute significant income while incurring only a low level of direct cost.

Both of these strategies would be put into operation only if the development of the business itself warrants this and the additional projected required funding is available.

Management Team

The firm will be under the management of Mr. John M. Silver, President of the Battleworks Furniture Company, Inc. Mr. Silver is extremely well qualified to manage such an operation, having undergraduate training in engineering and personal interests that have led him to experiment with the application of advanced engineering technology to the centuries-old craft of furniture building in wood. This includes such methods as the application of ultrasonic technology in combination with new forms of bonding materials to produce structures stronger and less expensive than previously possible. Various articles of furniture have been produced by Mr. Silver using such technology, and given to friends as presents.

Mr. Silver gained management experience while in the Navy where he attained the rank of lieutenant and had responsibility for over 300 men. His duty in the Navy made excellent use of his engineering training, particularly when he was assigned major responsibility on the USS Delong. While in the Navy, Mr. Silver had further opportunity to utilize his woodworking skills, manufacturing various articles of furniture for his friends and colleagues in the well-equipped woodworking shops available where he served. He has since received his MBA from the East Podunk Graduate School of Business.

The combination of experiences gained, supported by manufacturing operations responsibility at Johns-Manville, qualified him for a position on the faculty of the College of Engineering of the State University. Among other responsibilities, he assisted in the successful presentation of a proposal to the Engineering Council for Professional Development for accreditation. The State University is the first and only institution to be accredited in manufacturing engineering. The concept of manufacturing as an engineering discipline is relatively new, and the accreditation by the Council is a reflection of its belief that the solutions to many manufacturing problems are through the application of skilled engineering.

Mr. Silver, as part of his MBA studies, performed a major, in-depth study of the furniture industry as research for his Master's Thesis. Through this research, complemented by his personal interest in small-scale furniture manufacturing and retail operations, he has gained extensive knowledge of the operation of the industry, the nature of the competition, problems to avoid, and requirements for successful entry into the industry.

Mr. Silver, as principal of the firm, has arranged for professional outside support to assist him during his planning implementation phase and to provide a source of continuing advice and counsel once the business has been established. Arrangements are currently under way to secure the services of a major CPA firm, and Smith, Fargell and Wasp, a Podunk-based law firm, provide legal counsel.

Mr. Silver will be performing all the management team functions initially. As the business develops, he anticipates the need to develop a production manager while retaining the sales and marketing responsibilities himself. This one additional individual will be the only anticipated addition to the management team throughout the time period covered by this plan, although the need for additional personnel at future points in the development of the business is identified and shown on the accompanying organization chart.

Operating Personnel

The initial workforce of the firm consists of two skilled craftsmen, who will perform the majority of the manufacturing operation. This staff will be expanded only as needed. Mr. Silver will directly supervise this operating staff and be responsible for all of the sales activity. The initial employees will have woodworking experience and be familiar with the style of operation necessary in a small semicustom fabrication shop. There is a sufficient supply of such talent in the area so that hiring appropriately experienced people will not represent a difficulty. As noted, additional craftsmen can be added if and when required by the volume of work.

In addition to the production workforce, one clerk/secretary will be hired. This person will be responsible for the required correspondence, billing activities, bookkeeping, and other normal office activities. It is expected that one person will be sufficient to perform these functions, at least initially. At such point in time as the work load requires an additional person, one will be hired. Market wages and normal benefits will be standard for all staff personnel.

ORGANIZATION CHART
BATTLEWORKS FURNITURE COMPANY, INC.

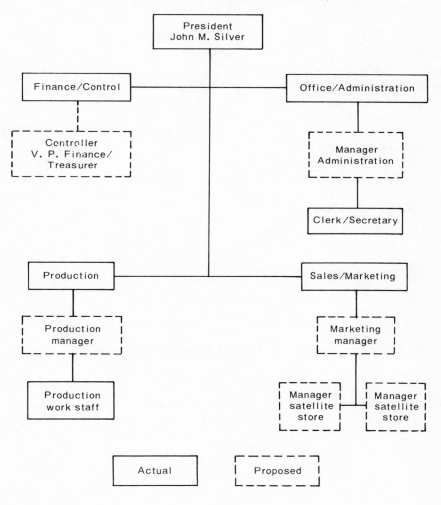

19

Battleworks Furniture Company, Inc.
Venture Development Schedule

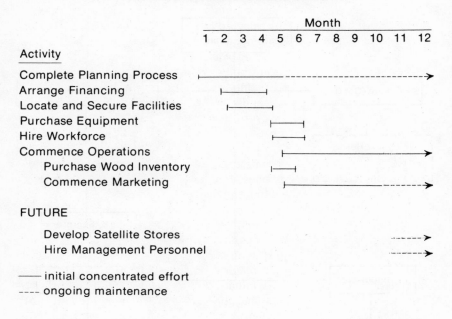

	Month
	1 2 3 4 5 6 7 8 9 10 11 12

Activity

Complete Planning Process

Arrange Financing

Locate and Secure Facilities

Purchase Equipment

Hire Workforce

Commence Operations

    Purchase Wood Inventory

    Commence Marketing

FUTURE

    Develop Satellite Stores

    Hire Management Personnel

—— initial concentrated effort

---- ongoing maintenance

Proposed Uses of Funds Requested

Tools and equipment	$17,000
Legal and organization	600
Hardwoods inventory	6,000
Plywoods inventory	4,000
Semifinished inventory	1,200
Other inventory	5,000
Supplies and office materials	1,000
Working capital	28,200
Contingency	8,000
TOTAL	$71,000

The tools and the equipment are the mainstay of the production operation. The equipment listed is necessary to have a complete shop. Included are high-quality, special-purpose items which together will repre-

sent the optimum combination of quality equipment required for a full range of production activities, providing for a maximum amount of automation in the process and a minimum of hand-oriented operations.

Items were specifically selected to assure that this shop will be well balanced in order to assure smooth efficient operation of the manufacturing process. The list provided was derived from extensive planning discussions with J. F. Munroe Company, distributor of woodworking machinery. It is supported by a listing of the equipment used by the Podunk Partition Company (see Appendix IV), a fine modern custom furniture shop which has the reputation of being one of the best-equipped, best-run shops in the area.

It should be noted that while the equipment is listed at retail, it is expected that many of the items can be purchased at a discount or even second-hand. This cannot be accomplished, however, until funds are available for actual negotiations to finalize an on-the-spot cash deal.

Wood inventories, representing a major portion of the investment, are in quantities sufficient for initial levels of production and sufficient to secure reasonable quantity discounts, yet not so excessive as to tie up cash for inordinate periods of time or to represent serious storage problems. Working capital, a third major investment category, is sufficient to support the firm through its initial stages of development until it has passed its breakeven point. The contingency reserve is for conditions outside the purview of the plan as it is presently envisioned. The funds shown are conservative and yet adequate to cover the full range of costs that will be encountered in commencing and developing this business.

Critical Risks and Problems

The project shown here seems to be feasible as described. The factors that could be serious feasibility constraints are essentially the untested variables at this point. Of concern here should be the following:

1. The ability of Mr. Silver to organize and operate a business of this type.
2. The actual extent of production economies available through the process described.
3. The rate of business acceptance (it may not be accepted at all).
4. The introduction of competition of exactly the same type, directed at exactly the same market segments.
5. Technological difficulties in production.

These variables can actually be tested only in application. However, the limited initial investments in the business, the staged development philosophy, and the fact that there is sound evidence in support of the underlying assumptions substantially mitigate the risk of failure.

Summary

The Battleworks Furniture Company, Inc., will be a manufacturing and retail operation producing contemporary furniture made from wood, utilizing advanced production techniques. The planned manufacture of unassembled products for inventory offers the capability of providing an infinite range of finishes with a minimum of inventory. Short production cycle time will enable the company to respond immediately to changes in market demand without having to sacrifice large inventories that could suddenly become obsolete. Vertical integration brings economies of operation by eliminating shipping, handling, and middleman costs.

The product pricing strategy fills an existing gap in the target SMSA. The marketing strategy has identified individuals who are affected by the existence of this void, and they will be reached in a direct manner. The marketing plan represents a low-cost, highly effective way of accomplishing these marketing purposes.

The expertise and experience of the President in engineering, production, and business administration assure that the business will be run effectively and efficiently. Conservative income projections demonstrate that the firm will operate at a profit, even under less than favorable conditions. The corresponding cash flow analysis demonstrates that the financial structure proposed will be adequate to satisfy the working capital needs of the business, purchase the required equipment, and service any potential debt.

All these factors combine to clearly show that the firm will be a viable, profitable enterprise.

II FINANCIAL DATA

Sources and Applications of Funds

APPLICATIONS

Tools and equipment	$17,000
Legal and organization	600
Hardwoods inventory	6,000
Plywoods inventory	4,000
Pre-finished inventory	1,200
Other inventory	5,000
Supplies and office materials	1,000
Working capital	28,200
Contingency	8,000
	$71,000

SOURCES

Equity funds available	$ 8,000
Requested loan	63,000
	$71,000

SECURITY

Equipment, chattel, and store inventory
Signature: John M. Silver

Capital Equipment List
Equipment Selection

Major Equipment and Normal Accessories	Model	List Price
Rockwell Delta 9″ Circular Saw	34–647	$ 360
Rockwell Delta Uniplane	22–300	590
Rockwell Delta Shaper	43–301	800
Rockwell Delta Unidrill	15–107	575
Rockwell Delta 12″ Radial Saw	33–489	575
Rockwell Delta Combination Sander	31–715	520
Rockwell Delta Overarm Router	43–502	800
SCM Joiner	F–4	1,705
SCM Surfacer	S–63	3,230
SCM 24″ Band Saw	C–600	1,130
Samco Stroke Sander	LL–2500	1,700
Newton Twin Spindle Horizontal Borer	B–100	500
Sand-Rite Contour Sander	DD–63	260
Workrite High-Frequency Electronic Welder	4000	1,040
Rockwell Delta 28-Gallon Vacuum Cleaner	49–255	55
Rockwell Delta 6″ Tool Grinder	23–636	170
		$14,010

Minor Shop Equipment

Assorted power hand tools		$ 650
Hand tools, clamps, etc.		300
Jig, fixtures, patterns, etc.		500
		$ 1,450

Other Equipment

Sewing machine and accessories		$ 500
Conductivity meter		100
		$ 600
	Subtotal	$16,060
Transportation (some equipment is F.O.B. factory)		940
		$17,000

Pro Forma Balance Sheet
as of Commencement of Business

Assets

Current Assets
Cash	$27,150
Inventory	15,700
Rent Deposit & First Month's Rent	2,000
Prepaid Insurance	1,800
Prepaid Marketing	1,150
Utilities Deposit	200
Total Current Assets	$48,000

Fixed Assets
Leasehold Improvements	$ 6,000
Tools and Equipment	17,000
Total Fixed Assets	$23,000
TOTAL ASSETS	$71,000

Liabilities & Net Worth

Current Liabilities
Current Portion of Long-term Debt	$ 2,885

Long-term Liabilities
Long-term Debt	60,115
Total Liabilities	$63,000
Shareholders Equity	$ 8,000
TOTAL LIABILITIES & NET WORTH	$71,000

25

Breakeven Analysis

Fixed costs   = $55,824 (per annum)
($4,652 per month)

Variable costs   = 55% (.55)

Contribution margin   = 45% (.45)

thus:

$$B/E = FC \div \frac{CM}{100}$$

$$B/E = \$55{,}824 \div .45$$

$$B/E = \$124{,}053$$

$$B/E \text{ per month} = \$10{,}338$$

Customers Needed Per Month at Breakeven

Assumptions:

Average unit selling price   = $175

Average customer repeat sales = 2 × per annum

Average revenue per customer
per month   = $29.16

Average number of customers needed
per month   = $\dfrac{\$10{,}338}{\$29.16} = 354.53$

PRO FORMA INCOME FORECASTS

Financial Projections

The figures used in the sales projections are extremely conservative and are based on several worst-case assumptions. Though unlikely, these figures are possible and are used so as to show the firm's ability to repay the loan from profits. When in operation, the firm expects to do considerably better in reducing costs and increasing profitability.

It is projected that the business will reach its breakeven point monthly sales (60 units at an average price of $175, or $10,338) in the seventh month, under the most conservative assumptions. These projections are based on a detailed analysis of the market structure and supported by a marketing strategy designed to impact the target market segments under a selective saturation plan (see Appendix II). It will be further seen that the breakeven point will drop after the first annual operating period, due to a planned decrease in variable marketing costs once the business is established.

Battleworks Furniture Company, Inc., Pro Forma Income Statements, Annual Summary, First Three Years

	Year 1	Year 2	Year 3
Net Sales	94,500	196,000	216,000
Cost of Goods Sold	51,975	107,800	118,800
Gross Profit	42,525	88,200	97,200
Expenses			
Gross Wages	16,800	16,800	16,800
Marketing	12,700	6,000	4,200
Rent	6,000	6,000	6,000
Administation	6,000	6,000	6,000
Utilities	1,200	1,200	1,200
Insurance	1,800	1,800	1,800
Legal & Accounting	2,000	2,000	2,000
Depreciation	3,396	3,396	3,396
Interest	4,728	4,512	4,512
Miscellaneous	1,200	600	600
Total Expenses	55,824	48,308	46,508
Net Profit (Loss)	(13,299)	39,892	50,692
Cumulative Profit (Loss)	(13,299)	26,593	77,285

Battleworks Furniture Company, Inc., Pro Forma Income Statement, First Year of Operations

	Month: 1	2	3	4	5	6	7	8	9	10	11	12	Total
Net Sales		1,200	3,300	6,000	7,000	8,000	10,000	11,000	11,000	12,000	12,000	13,000	94,500
Cost of Goods Sold		660	1,815	3,300	3,850	4,400	5,500	6,050	6,050	6,600	6,600	7,150	51,975
Gross Profit		540	1,485	2,700	3,150	3,600	4,500	4,950	4,950	5,400	5,400	5,850	42,525
Expenses													
Gross Wages	1,400	1,400	1,400	1,400	1,400	1,400	1,400	1,400	1,400	1,400	1,400	1,400	16,800
Marketing	1,150	1,350	1,350	1,350	1,350	1,350	800	800	800	800	800	800	12,700
Rent	500	500	500	500	500	500	500	500	500	500	500	500	6,000
Administration	500	500	500	500	500	500	500	500	500	500	500	500	6,000
Utilities	100	100	100	100	100	100	100	100	100	100	100	100	1,200
Insurance	150	150	150	150	150	150	150	150	150	150	150	150	1,800
Legal & Accounting	150	150	150	150	150	150	150	150	150	150	150	350	2,000
Depreciation	283	283	283	283	283	283	283	283	283	283	283	283	3,396
Interest	394	394	394	394	394	394	394	394	394	394	394	394	4,728
Miscellaneous	350	350	50	50	50	50	50	50	50	50	50	50	1,200
Total Expenses	4,977	5,177	4,877	4,877	4,877	4,877	4,327	4,327	4,327	4,327	4,327	4,527	55,824
Net Profit (Loss)	(4,977)	(4,637)	(3,392)	(2,177)	(1,727)	(1,277)	173	623	623	1,073	1,073	1,323	(13,299)
Cumulative Profit (Loss)	(4,977)	(9,614)	(13,006)	(15,183)	(16,910)	(18,187)	(18,014)	(17,391)	(16,768)	(15,695)	(14,622)	(13,299)	

Battleworks Furniture Company, Inc., Pro Forma Income Statement, Second Year, by Quarter

	First Quarter	Second Quarter	Third Quarter	Fourth Quarter	Total
Net Sales	42,000	49,000	51,000	54,000	196,000
Cost of Goods Sold	23,100	26,950	28,050	29,700	107,800
Gross Profit	18,900	22,050	22,950	24,300	88,200
Expenses					
Gross Wages	4,200	4,200	4,200	4,200	16,800
Marketing	1,950	1,950	1,050	1,050	6,000
Rent	1,500	1,500	1,500	1,500	6,000
Administration	1,500	1,500	1,500	1,500	6,000
Utilities	300	300	300	300	1,200
Insurance	450	450	450	450	1,800
Legal & Accounting	450	450	450	650	2,000
Depreciation	849	849	849	849	3,396
Interest	1,128	1,128	1,128	1,128	4,512
Miscellaneous	150	150	150	150	600
Total Expenses	12,477	12,477	11,577	11,777	48,308
Net Profit	6,423	9,573	11,373	12,523	39,892
Cumulative Profit	6,423	15,996	27,369	39,892	

Battleworks Furniture Company, Inc.,
Pro Forma Income Statement,
Third Year, by Quarter

	First Quarter	Second Quarter	Third Quarter	Fourth Quarter	Total
Net Sales	54,000	54,000	54,000	54,000	216,000
Cost of Goods Sold	29,700	29,700	29,700	29,700	118,800
Gross Profit	24,300	24,300	24,300	24,300	97,200
Expenses					
Gross Wages	4,200	4,200	4,200	4,200	16,800
Marketing	1,050	1,050	1,050	1,050	4,200
Rent	1,500	1,500	1,500	1,500	6,000
Administration	1,500	1,500	1,500	1,500	6,000
Utilities	300	300	300	300	1,200
Insurance	450	450	450	450	1,800
Legal & Accounting	450	450	450	650	2,000
Depreciation	849	849	849	849	3,396
Interest	1,128	1,128	1,128	1,128	4,512
Miscellaneous	150	150	150	150	600
Total Expenses	11,577	11,577	11,577	11,777	46,508
Net Profit	12,723	12,723	12,723	12,523	50,692
Cumulative Profit	12,723	25,446	38,169	50,692	

Battleworks Furniture Company, Inc.,
Pro Forma Income Statement,
Notes of Explanation

1. Cost of Goods Sold: 55%, materials and variable expenses.
2. Gross Wages: Two manufacturing personnel, one office.
3. Marketing: 1st Month, $800 over normal.
   2nd Month to 6th Month, $1,000/month over normal.
4. Rent: Projected in absence of actual site.
5. Administration: President.
6. Utilities: Electric and telephone.
7. Insurance: Public liability, fire and theft.
8. Depreciation: Straight line, equipment and leasehold, 5 years.
9. Interest: $63,000, 8 years, 7.5%.

PRO FORMA CASH FLOW ANALYSIS

Battleworks Furniture Company, Inc., Pro Forma Cash Flow Analysis, Three-Year Summary

	Year 1	Year 2	Year 3
Cash Receipts			
Sales	37,720	78,400	86,400
Accounts Receivable	48,980	107,400	129,600
Total Cash Receipts	86,700	185,800	216,000
Cash Disbursements			
Materials	52,975	107,800	118,800
Gross Wages	16,800	16,800	16,800
Marketing	12,700	6,000	4,200
Rent	6,000	6,000	6,000
Administration	6,000	6,000	6,000
Utilities	1,200	1,200	1,200
Insurance	1,800	2,000	2,000
Legal & Accounting	2,000	1,800	1,800
Loan Amortization	7,614	10,500	10,500
Miscellaneous	1,200	600	600
Total Disbursements	108,289	158,700	167,900
Net Cash Flow	(21,589)	27,100	48,100

Battleworks Furniture Company, Inc., Pro Forma Cash Flow Analysis, First Year of Operations

	Month:												
	1	2	3	4	5	6	7	8	9	10	11	12	Total
Cash Receipts													
Sales		400	1,320	2,400	2,800	3,200	4,000	4,400	4,400	4,800	4,800	5,200	37,720
Accounts Receivable			800	1,980	3,600	4,200	4,800	6,000	6,600	6,600	7,200	7,200	48,980
Total Cash Receipts		400	2,120	4,380	6,400	7,400	8,800	10,400	11,000	11,400	12,000	12,400	86,700
Cash Disbursements													
Materials	1,000	660	1,815	3,300	3,850	4,400	5,500	6,050	6,050	6,600	6,600	7,150	52,975
Gross Wages	1,400	1,400	1,400	1,400	1,400	1,400	1,400	1,400	1,400	1,400	1,400	1,400	16,800
Marketing	1,150	1,350	1,350	1,350	1,350	1,350	800	800	800	800	800	800	12,700
Rent	500	500	500	500	500	500	500	500	500	500	500	500	6,000
Administration	500	500	500	500	500	500	500	500	500	500	500	500	6,000
Utilities	100	100	100	100	100	100	100	100	100	100	100	100	1,200
Insurance	900						900						1,800
Legal & Accounting				1,000						1,000			2,000
Loan Amortization	394	394	394	394	394	394	875	875	875	875	875	875	7,614
Miscellaneous	350	350	50	50	50	50	50	50	50	50	50	50	1,200
Total Disbursements	6,294	5,254	6,109	8,594	8,144	8,694	10,625	10,275	10,275	11,825	10,825	11,375	108,289
Net Cash Flow	(6,294)	(4,854)	(3,989)	(4,214)	(1,744)	(1,294)	(1,825)	125	725	(425)	1,175	1,025	(21,589)
Cumulative Cash Flow	(6,294)	(11,148)	(15,137)	(19,351)	(21,095)	(22,389)	(24,214)	(24,089)	(23,364)	(23,789)	(22,614)	(21,589)	(21,589)

Battleworks Furniture Company, Inc.,
Pro Forma Cash Flow Analysis,
Second Year, by Quarter

	First Quarter	Second Quarter	Third Quarter	Fourth Quarter	Total
Cash Reciepts					
Sales	16,800	19,600	20,400	21,600	78,400
Accounts Receivable	22,200	25,200	29,400	30,600	107,400
Total Cash Receipts	39,000	44,800	49,800	52,200	185,800
Cash Disbursements					
Materials	23,100	26,950	28,050	29,700	107,800
Gross Wages	4,200	4,200	4,200	4,200	16,800
Marketing	1,950	1,950	1,050	1,050	6,000
Rent	1,500	1,500	1,500	1,500	6,000
Administration	1,500	1,500	1,500	1,500	6,000
Utilities	300	300	300	300	1,200
Insurance		1,000		1,000	2,000
Legal & Accounting	900		900		1,800
Loan Amortization	2,625	2,625	2,625	2,625	10,500
Miscellaneous	150	150	150	150	600
Total Disbursements	36,225	40,175	40,275	42,025	158,700
Net Cash Flow	2,775	4,625	9,525	10,175	27,100
Cumulative Cash Flow	2,775	7,400	16,925	27,100	

Battleworks Furniture Company, Inc.,
Pro Forma Cash Flow Analysis,
Third Year, by Quarter

	First Quarter	Second Quarter	Third Quarter	Fourth Quarter	Total
Cash Receipts					
Sales	21,600	21,600	21,600	21,600	86,400
Accounts Receivable	32,400	32,400	32,400	32,400	129,600
Total Cash Receipts	54,000	54,000	54,000	54,000	216,000
Cash Disbursements					
Materials	29,700	29,700	29,700	29,700	118,800
Gross Wages	4,200	4,200	4,200	4,200	16,800
Marketing	1,050	1,050	1,050	1,050	4,200
Rent	1,500	1,500	1,500	1,500	6,000
Administration	1,500	1,500	1,500	1,500	6,000
Utilities	300	300	300	300	1,200
Insurance		1,000		1,000	2,000
Legal & Accounting	900		900		1,800
Loan Amortization	2,625	2,625	2,625	2,625	10,500
Miscellaneous	150	150	150	150	600
Total Disbursements	41,925	42,025	41,925	42,025	167,900
Net Cash Flow	12,075	11,975	12,075	11,975	48,100
Cumulative Cash Flow	12,075	24,050	36,125	48,100	

Pro Forma Cash Flow Analysis,
Notes of Explanation

1. Sales: 40% cash, 60% 30 days accounts receivable.
2. Materials: Replacement inventories.
3. Gross Wages: Two manufacturing personnel, one office.
4. Marketing: 1st Month, $800 over normal.
   2nd Month to 6th Month, $1,000/month over normal.
   7th Month to 12th Month, $450/month over normal.
5. Rent: Estimated in absence of actual site.
6. Administration: President's salary.
7. Insurance: Public liability, fire and theft, semiannual premium.
8. Legal & Accounting: Preparation of semiannual audits and reports.
9. Loan Amortization: $63,000, 8 years, 7.5%. Moratorium on principal, interest shown for only first 6 months.

PRO FORMA BALANCE SHEETS

**Battleworks Furniture Company, Inc.,
Pro Forma Balance Sheet,
Year 1, by Quarter**

	First Quarter	Second Quarter	Third Quarter	Fourth Quarter
Assets				
Current Assets				
Cash	12,013	4,761	3,786	5,561
Accounts Receivable	800	4,200	6,600	7,200
Inventory	14,300	14,700	15,000	14,100
Rent Deposit	1,500	1,500	1,500	1,500
Prepaid Insurance	300		450	
Utilities Deposit	200	200	200	200
Total Current Assets	29,113	25,361	27,536	28,561
Fixed Assets				
Leasehold Improvement	6,000	6,000	6,000	6,000
Less: Depreciation	222	444	666	888
Net: Leasehold	5,778	5,556	5,334	5,112
Tools & Equipment	17,000	17,000	17,000	17,000
Less: Depreciation	627	1,254	1,881	2,508
Net: Tools & Equipment	16,373	15,746	15,119	14,492
Total Fixed Assets	22,151	21,302	20,453	19,604
TOTAL ASSETS	51,264	46,663	47,989	48,165
Liabilities & Net Worth				
Current Liabilities				
Current Long-term Debt			1,443	1,443
Accounts Payable			6,050	7,150
Total Current Liabilities			7,493	8,593
Long-term Liabilities				
Long-term Debt	63,000	63,000	61,557	60,114
TOTAL LIABILITIES	63,000	63,000	69,050	68,707
Shareholders Equity	(11,736)	(16,337)	(21,061)	(20,542)
TOTAL LIABILITIES & NET WORTH	51,264	46,663	47,989	48,165

Battleworks Furniture Company, Inc.,
Pro Forma Balance Sheets,
End of Years 2 and 3

	Year 2	Year 3
Assets		
Current Assets		
Cash	32,661	80,761
Accounts Receivable	10,200	10,800
Inventory	15,500	15,700
Rent Deposit	1,500	1,500
Prepaid Insurance	500	500
Utilities Deposit	200	200
Total Current Assets	60,561	109,461
Fixed Assets		
Leasehold Improvement	6,000	6,000
Less: Depreciation	1,776	2,664
Net: Leasehold	4,224	3,336
Tools & Equipment	17,000	17,000
Less: Depreciation	5,016	7,524
Net: Tools & Equipment	11,984	9,476
Total Fixed Assets	16,208	12,812
TOTAL ASSETS	76,769	122,273
Liabilities & Net Worth		
Current Liabilities		
Current Long-term Debt	5,772	5,772
Accounts Payable	9,900	9,900
Total Current Liabilities	15,672	15,672
Long-term Liabilities		
Long-term Debt	54,242	48,570
TOTAL LIABILITIES	69,914	64,242
Shareholders Equity	6,855	58,031
TOTAL LIABILITIES & NET WORTH	76,769	122,273

APPENDIX I
PLANT LAYOUT AND WORK FLOW

PLANT LAYOUT

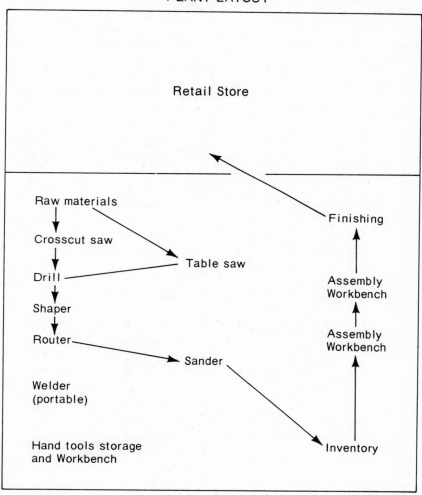

WORK FLOW CHART

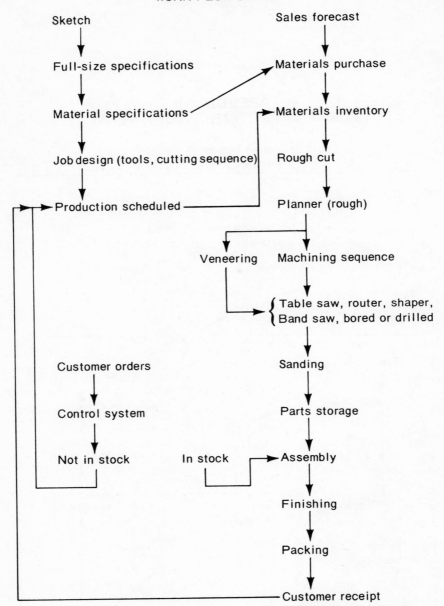

APPENDIX II
MARKETING PLAN

Breakdown of Marketing Costs

Photo Displays	$400 per month
Direct Mail	$300 per month
Samples	$200 per month
Normal Advertising	$200 per month
Education Literature	$ 50 per month

Costing of Direct Mail

- Envelope containing 12 photos of products with cover letter and cover stock.
- Photo sheets are 5½″ × 8½″ halftones, printed on two sides.
- Cover letter is 8½″ × 11″ letter folded.
- Cover stock is 8½″ × 11″ folded with 2 creases, printed on two sides. Print outside: firm name and logo; print inside: price list and description.

COSTS

Sheet Printing: 12 5½″ × 8½″ sheets (single) is the equivalent of 3 8½″ × 11″ sheets (on two sides) cut in half.
- $315

Photo Costs: 12 set-ups and one view of each
- $642

Cover Stock: Equivalent of ½ of 16″ × 11″ stock, 2,000 sheets or 1,000 sheets. Additional cost of second-side printing $20.
- $95

Cover Letter: 8½″ × 11″ sheet creased once for folding.
- $50

Envelopes:
- $60

Total cost of materials = $1,144 or $.572 per mailing (for 12 items)

Postage = 1,000

Total cost of mailing $2,144

NOTES
- Over half the cost ($624) is for photography, which is nonrecurring for an item.
- Once the initial printing is done, the original plates can be reused at a later date and the printing charge is lower.
- Cost of mailing to 200 people per month is $130.40 including postage.

Advertising-Printing

Printing

Job to be of A-1 quality from a printing standpoint.
Halftone plating on excellent paper.

Cost

Assuming original black/white glossy print supplied.
Paper supplied by printer, 8½" x 11".
Assumes all printing as per 1 sheet; not mixed per order.

Printed on two sides

1,000 copies of 1 sheet	$65
Second 1,000 copies of 1 sheet	$40

Printed on one side

1,000 copies of 1 sheet	$47
Second 1,000 copies of 1 sheet	$20

Cover stock

Heavy fine-quality cover stock printed with firm's name, address, and corporate symbols; on one side.
Scored for hand folding, sheet 11" x 17".

One-side printing, 1,000 copies of 1 sheet	$75
Second 1,000 copies of 1 sheet	$45

Calling cards

Choice of ink and papers at top-quality level.
1,000 copies $13.95.

Printed Matter Format

Planned

- As photos will be contacts of 4" x 5" negatives, they will fit on 5½" x 8½", which is a half sheet, and still leave room for small descriptive printing on stock.
- Cover stock will be similar to printed stock but slightly heavier. Also, since printed stock is half size, cover stock will be 8½" x 11" (a normal-size sheet), opening horizontally with 8½" side. Interior should have price list printed.
- Using smaller format permits showing two views of same item at cost of extra photo only.

Advertising–Photography

Black and White

$48 set-up charge
$ 4 per view (photographer)
$ 1 per copy (of same photograph)
Reorders
$ 5 per view
$ 1 per copy

Set-up charge includes the photography of the event and the proof sheets; the proof sheets are permanent and are the property of the customer (min. size 2½″ sq., max. size 4″ x 5″).

Sample Format
Pricing and Margins

ITEM: TWIN-SIZE BED

	Price	Margin over Cost of Materials	Percent
Finished bed with mattress	$100	$49.46	49.5%
Unfinished bed with mattress	90	41.46	46.1%
Finished bed without mattress	75	51.46	68.6%
Unfinished bed without mattress	65	43.46	66.9%
Mattress only	40	13.00	32.5%

Notes:
- Mattress assumed to be fire-retarded polyurethane.
- Cover not assumed to be fire-retarded—price to retard is negligible, but firm price was unavailable.
- Finished versus unfinished materials—$2 difference (finishing oil).
- Unfinished is ready for coating or paint; surface is sanded smooth.
- As finish used is basically a rubbed oil finish, it can be done easily by unskilled labor (e.g., high school students) if it becomes more pressing to use firm's skilled labor elsewhere.
- Figures quoted assume a minimum of 8 beds made per production run.

Sample Format
Product Cost Planning Typical Product

ITEM: TWIN-SIZE BED

Lumber Used in Construction	Cu. In.	
2 sides—2 × 75″ × 1″ × 5″	750	
2 × 78″ × 1″ × 1″	156	
2 ends —4 × 3″ × 1″ × 41″	492	
4 × 3″ × 1″ × 18″	216	
2 end braces—2 × 1″ × 39″ × 3″	228	
	1,842	12.792 bd. ft.

Plywood Used in Construction		
3 supports—3 × ⅜″ × 24″ × 39″	1,053	7.313 bd. ft.

Assume 50% wastage of initial lumber: 12.792—began as 25.584 bd. ft.
Assume 10% wastage of initial plywood: 7.313—began as 8.126 bd. ft.
Assume lumber is white oak $5/4$ milled to $4/4$, length selected, width selected, with top, bottom, and edges planed, by lumber yard.

Typical price $.64/bd. ft.
- Lumber @ $.64/bd. ft. for 25.584 bd. ft. $16.38
- Plywood @ $.50/bd. ft. for 7.313 bd. ft.   3.66
                                              $20.04

Supplies and miscellaneous parts
    (screws, glue, oil, etc.)   3.50
        Total Manufactured Material Cost $23.54

Mattress—polyurethane foam 6″ × 75″ × 39″ $10.00+ $5.00 if fire-retarded
    plus purchased cover with zipper   12.00

                        Mattress Cost: $22.00 $45.54
                                                   +$5.00 if fire-
                                                    retarded

Sample Format
Manufacturing Planning

ITEM: TWIN-SIZE BED

Subassembly	Specs.	Mfg. Labor
2 sides	2 × 75″ × 1″ × 5″	10 min.
	2 × 78″ × 1″ × 1″	6 min.
2 ends	4 × 3″ × 1″ × 41″	12 min.
	4 × 3″ × 1″ × 18″	12 min.
3 mattress supports	⅜″ ×39″ × 24″	9 min.
2 end braces	2 × 1″ × 39″ ×3″	3 min.
1 mattress	6″ × 39″ × 75″	
		52 min.

Total finishing time: 40 minutes (2 coats, 20 minutes each)
Miscellaneous parts: 4 screws, 4 threaded tubes, glue, 8 wood screws.

Typical Educational Literature

BED—TWIN SIZE

Hi! The purpose of this little note is to assist you in the purchase of furniture, which everybody buys, but which most folks could use a little help on. If this information is of assistance, let us know and we will continue to try to improve it based on your recommendations.

Features	Us	Them	Them

1. Solid wood—is it made of solid wood, not plywood, chipboard, or pressed sawdust, but real wood?

2. Thickness of wood—it's silly to pay for wood that's too thick, but remember wood 1 inch thick is 33% thicker than wood ¾ inch thick and costs ⅓ more. We prefer to think of 1 inch wood as ⅓ better than ¾ inch.

3. Are nails required to hold it together? Are they exposed? Look for nail holes filled with colored putty. Ask us, we'll tell you where to look.

4. How are the joints? Are they tight? Can you see the excess glue? The glue line should be thin, crisp, and smooth to the touch.

5. Feel the mattress. How thick is it? A six-inch mattress is 50% more mattress than a four-inch mattress. Which comes with the bed? Is it extra and how much? If polyurethane, which kind? There are two kinds of mattresses, regular and flame-retarded. We always use the flame-retarded. Some say latex is better than polyurethane, others disagree. We're not sure, but we're sure latex burns and the stuff we're using doesn't.

etc.

11. Price—what is being charged for what you're getting? Review the first ten items and compare the results with #11. Good luck in your purchase.

P.S. Ask the store personnel here and elsewhere about the composition of the goods you're considering; they should know it, and you have a right to know. If they won't tell you, ask us; we know. Also, for those who want to check our advice, we have reference books.

APPENDIX III
BACKGROUND OF PRINCIPAL

Resume of John M. Silver
President
Battleworks Furniture Company, Inc.

EDUCATION

19xx–19xx   East Podunk Graduate School of Business Administration, Master of Business Administration, June 19xx. General Management major, with Small Business Management minor.

19xx–19xx   State University, Bachelor of Science, June 19xx. Major: Engineering Management; Minor: Entrepreneurship. Dean's List three semesters.

BUSINESS EXPERIENCE

19xx–19xx   Johns-Manville Corporation, Wheeling, West Virginia Manager, Interdigital Fibre Division; general management responsibility for operating division employing 200 production workers and annual budget of $2,700,000. Interface management team responsibility with general division management, Controller's Division and technical representative liaison to marketing division. Responsible for the full range of production operations.

19xx–19xx	Fargilworth Corporation, East Orange, New Jersey
	Supervisor for production group, 25 employees. Responsibilities included production supervision for the production and distribution of custom-designed, handmade walnut and mahogany toothbrushes, including production scheduling, inventory maintenance, raw materials purchasing, personnel and training, and operations accounting.

MILITARY   Honorable Discharge

19xx–19xx   United States Navy
Lieutenant
Various assignments including executive and engineering officer of the U.S.S. Canine; awarded National Defense Service Medal and three bronze stars.

PERSONAL BACKGROUND

Grew up in New Hampshire. Work experience in a wide variety of jobs while attending college. Interests include polo and woodworking.

APPENDIX IV
EQUIPMENT LIST, SIMILAR OPERATION

Podunk Partition Company

- Three-man custom industrial and architectural shop—no regular retail.
- In operation for fourth year.
- Approximately 2,000 sq. ft.
- Lots of raw material stored.

Major Equipment Observed

- Model S-50 SCM 20″ planer
- Model 800 SCM 32″ wheel band saw
- Small band saw
- Drill press (large)
- 2 table saws with extensions
- Model F-3 SCM 12″ joiner plus horizontal borer attached
- Radial arm saw
- Model T-100 SCM shaper
- High-frequency gluing machine—2″ penetration capacity
- Air compressor for spraying and nail gun
- Router
- Lots of power hand tools—locked in 2 large 4′ × 5′ and 6′ × 4′ safes at night

Source: Chris Fredericks, co-owner.

- Owner in trade for 22 years.
- Owner very cooperative, gave considerable time (e.g., an entire morning for one of the visits) and advice on the selection of tools, equipment, job estimation, and wood characteristics for various purposes, and on problems of the business in general.

Appendix B:
Sources of Financing for New Business

A great deal has been written about raising funds for a new business, including such sources as debt capital, venture capital, trade credit, friends, relatives, associates, and a variety of others. It is not the purpose here to go into great detail concerning any of these alternatives, but instead to provide a general overview as the basis for further consideration and research, or at least to provide the basis for knowledgeable questioning of bankers and other financial intermediaries and advisors.

The key problems facing businesses, and especially new businesses, are where they will get the necessary funds, how they should go about getting them, what they must give in return, and what kind of proposal will be required. If the planning process has been carefully followed, many of the questions that will need to be answered will have already been dealt with from the better perspective of management decision making. If a careful and thoughtful approach has been used up to this point, the work of preparing a financing proposal for the solicitation of appropriate funds is substantially completed.

After a new business has been planned and organized conceptually, financial strategy is the next important consideration before the business can be implemented and developed. Very simply, money or capital is required to get just about any kind of business started. Generally, most of these funds come from sources other than the business principals themselves, although the very initial financing is usually provided by the owners. This would include the funding that is required to get the business through the planning stage and, if a new product is involved, probably through the development stage of the prototype as well. As the venture begins to show some actual viability and is nearly ready to get started, then it may be possible to use outside funding to the benefit of all concerned.

Historical sources of funding are:

Commercial banks
Mortgage institutions
Insurance companies
Commercial credit companies and factors
Pension funds
Mutual funds
Investment bankers
Venture capital investors

Investors or lenders are often seen as overly tightfisted by new companies (and often existing companies) seeking their help. These financiers, however, are not in a position to give anything away. They are generally the managers of other people's money and, in keeping with their fiduciary responsibilities, expect and require a fair return on their investments. Most financing from commercial banks is in the form of loans whose lenders expect their return in the form of interest. Equity investors, those who deal in stock or other forms of ownership in a company, expect capital gains—in other words, as the business grows and gains in value, their investment will gain in value because they own a share of the company. Both the lenders and the investors all want the new business to succeed. If the new business succeeds, they succeed in their investment objectives. If the new business fails, they are likely to lose their money, the downside risk any investor must always consider.

Financing for a new business is obtained by renting, leasing, or buying funds. Loans or short-term debt funds are rented by paying interest. Money is leased through debentures or bonds with relatively long fixed payback periods. Money is bought through stock offerings. It is important to recognize that once a portion of the company is sold, it belongs to another individual, and along with these ownership rights are also included a share in the operating proceeds and a permanent share in the decision making within the business. Other intermediate combinations of financing include convertible debentures and warrants which essentially provide options to buy equity in a business.

Most business loans come from commercial banks. They can be divided into three categories:

1. *Short-term financing*—usually through notes to be paid within one year or less and paid in one sum.

2. *Intermediate-term financing*—from one to five years, usually repaid with an installment loan on a monthly basis.
3. *Long-term financing*—five years or more, especially used for the purchase of capital assets that have a long useful life period, such as real estate and buildings, and similar in form to a mortgage loan.

Loans may be *secured* or *unsecured*. A secured loan is one that is backed up by collateral, such as liens against property, savings accounts, investments, or sometimes co-signed by another individual who may have additional assets or additional credit. The collateral thus pledged, theoretically at least, will be taken by the lender in the event of a default on the loan. An unsecured loan is a loan that is not backed up by collateral. Unsecured loans are typically used for short-term lending and are generally available only to individuals who have proved themselves to be creditworthy. In other words, such loans are made simply because the lender has faith in the borrower's ability to repay the loan. A typical borrowing relationship may start out on a secured basis and, as the business develops and the owners prove themselves to be responsible, may gradually become unsecured.

Most funds for small- and medium-size businesses do not come directly from conventional lenders and investors, but are the result of selling transactions utilizing interbusiness credit. This trade credit represents the transfer of risk from one venture to another. A business experiencing difficulty in borrowing funds at a reasonable rate, or in fact borrowing them at any rate, can be financed indirectly in the same capital market at lower rates through an intermediary position of another firm with a better credit standing. In this way, trade credit is an important alternative route for financing. It is not only the largest single source for many smaller businesses, but also tends to be one of the easiest to tap. In fact, trade credit frequently expands in response to a tight money economy. As the small business's own receivables begin to shorten, it is often able to make up the deficit impact on its cash flow by lengthening its payables to its suppliers.

On the other hand, trade credit is not automatically available to all new businesses. As with more conventional forms of borrowing, a new business can generally expect to start out on a cash-in-front or C.O.D. basis with its trade suppliers. As the new business begins to develop a relationship with the supplier, and the supplier begins to develop some confidence in the new business's ability to run itself effectively (and to survive), then the new business may be able to gradually begin using trade credit through accounts payable with the supplier.

Equity is generally seen by most bankers to be a necessary prerequisite for any loan. While there are many different sources of equity available to businesses in general, in reality most of these sources are simply not available to small businesses. Equity is ownership, and for most new small businesses that equity is provided from the personal savings or personal assets of the people who are starting these businesses, their friends and relatives, and the retained earnings of the business. When these funds come from outside the immediate principals, they are frequently provided to give emotional support by family and friends, not to show confidence in the business itself. There are two important problems facing small businesses seeking equity funds from outside these very immediate sources: (1) professional investors are simply not interested in the majority of smaller, ordinary, unsophisticated situations, and (2) nonprofessional investors may carry with them such a collection of headaches that the ultimate cost of the funds may far exceed their value. Since it is only the nonprofessional investors, then, who are likely to be available to a new small business, it is critical that the relationship be workable over time. The business must make sure it won't wind up with an investor who gets scared and wants to bail out at a critical moment in the venture's development or who suddenly decides that he wants an increasingly important management or decision-making role because of the funds he has committed.

In locating equity funds from outside the immediate family and friends, it often makes sense to use middlemen who are in an especially advantageous position to know of possible sources and who are sophisticated enough to know when the resulting deals are favorable to both parties involved. These middlemen include tax lawyers or accountants with wealthy clients, management consultants, investment banking houses, commercial banks, brokerage firms, and patent attorneys. They usually charge a finder's fee ranging from 3 percent for large amounts to 5 or 10 percent for smaller amounts. Working with a professional broker of this kind will very probably save an immense amount of time and trouble by automatically excluding certain investors who simply would not be interested in the deal, by identifying others who might, and by helping to make sure that the relationship will be on the proper footing when the investment transaction actually occurs.

It is important to re-emphasize that professional venture capital investors are simply not going to be interested in the vast majority of deals. Their principal interest is in high-technology business ventures, especially where a new product is able to clearly demonstrate appeal to a specifically identified target market segment. Typically, professional venture capital firms will immediately reject 90 percent of the proposals submitted to them, take a second glance at and reject an additional 3 percent, and perform an in-depth analysis of the remaining one percent. In the end, they have historically funded less than one-half of one percent of the proposals presented to them. The reasons for this high level of selectivity are the extraordinary amounts of risk perceived by the venture capitalist, the lack of interest in the technology or the business activity concerned, or the lack of confidence in the business principals themselves. Many potential business developers casually talk about securing venture capital without having the faintest understanding of how seriously the odds are loaded against their ever being able to do so. For most small businesses, this venture capital simply does not exist.

In discussing small business financing it is important to acknowledge the role of the Small Business Administration. Since its inception in 1953, the SBA has been an important secondary source of financing for higher-risk small businesses that, though potentially viable, do not meet normal lending criteria. In addition to financial assistance, the SBA also provides management training and counseling and various forms of purchasing assistance. The SBA defines a small business as one that is independently owned and operated, is not dominant in its field, and meets a variety of criteria that are established by law. There are local SBA offices in most cities, and any questions concerning eligibility requirements or application procedures can generally be answered with a brief visit or telephone call.

For qualified businesses, the SBA may either participate with a bank or some other lender in a loan or guarantee up to 90 percent of a loan made by a bank or some other lending agency. If the bank or other lender cannot or will not provide funds under either of these methods, the SBA by law can consider lending certain amounts as direct government loans if funds are available. In reality, the demand for direct loans traditionally exceeds the SBA's available funds and, as a result, most of the SBA's lending is done in cooperation with banks. SBA loans may be used for business construction, expansion, or conversion, for the purchase of machinery, equipment, facilities, supplies, or materials, and as working capital. Excluded are businesses engaged in speculative activities, newspapers, radio and television stations and other forms of media, and businesses generally engaged in gambling. Under certain disaster-loan recovery programs, owners of small and large businesses, homeowners, and renters may be eligible to apply for SBA disaster-loan assistance.

Finally, in considering financing alternatives, it is important to suit the proposed financing to the need. If the business has a requirement for seasonal working capital to be invested in an inventory buildup prior to a busy selling season, short-term debt is appropriate. If there are long-term needs—say, if the business is going through a growth period and must in-

Typical Sources of Financing for Smaller Businesses

1 Owners, relatives, friends	8 Leasing companies
2 Private investors	9 Finance companies
3 Trade credit	10 Life insurance companies
4 Profits	11 SBA
5 Commercial banks	12 SBICs
6 Savings banks	13 LDCs
7 Commercial credit companies	14 Consumer finance companies

FINANCING NEEDED	Equity (Personal)	Equity (Other)	Long-term Debt	Mortgage	Secured	Unsecured	Intermediate-term Debt	Short-term Debt	A/R Financing	Field Warehousing	Unsecured	Personal	A/R Factoring	Line of Credit	Accounts Payable	Floor Planning	Second Mortgage
Start-up																	
Organizational Expenses (Legal, Deposits, Development)	1,14	2	5,11				5,11					14					
Initial Inventory	1	2	5,11				5,11										
Capital Expenditures																	
Plant/Real Estate	1	2,12 13	6,10 11	7													
Equipment	1	2,12 13			5,7 8,10												
Fixtures	1	2					5,11	5,11									
Working Capital	1	2					5,11	5,11				14					
Seasonal																	
Inventory								5,7		1,7		14		5,11	3	7	
Accounts Receivable								5,7	5,7 9				5,7 9				
Payroll/Supplies											5,11	14		5,11			
Marketing								5,7			5,11	14		5,11			
Growth																	
Inventory	1,4	2			7	5,11											9,14
Equipment	1,4	2,12 13			7,8 5,11	5,11											9,14
Physical Improvements	1,4	2		6	5,11		5,11										9,14
Working Capital	1,4	2					5,11										9,14

TYPE OF FINANCING

vest in additional working capital—an intermediate-term loan may be required. If the business is making a substantial investment in capital assets, then long-term lending may be most appropriate, although leasing is a frequently overlooked alternative that should also normally be considered. Equity may be required by any lenders in order to improve debt-to-worth relationships or because of the unusual risk typically associated with a brand-new business. The matrix shown here shows appropriate relationships between the type of business need, potential sources of financing, and the possible forms of financing that are appropriate for each type of need.

The best advice for anyone who is considering becoming involved with any type of financing is to thoroughly discuss the needs and alternatives with professional accountants, attorneys, and bankers. Fully understand the implications of each alternative and follow the advice of these experts. The general rule to follow is the same as for any other aspect of management decision making: list all the alternatives, evaluate their pros and cons, and then select the course of action most appropriate for that particular activity.

Index

AMACOM Executive Books—Paperbacks

John Applegath	Working Free	$6.95
John D. Arnold	The Art of Decision Making: 7 Steps to Achieving More Effective Results	$6.95
Alec Benn	The 27 Most Common Mistakes in Advertising	$5.95
Dudley Bennett	TA and the Manager	$6.95
Don Berliner	Want a Job? Get Some Experience ...	$5.95
Blake & Mouton	Productivity—The Human Side	$5.95
Borst & Montana	Managing Nonprofit Organizations	$6.95
George A. Brakeley	Tested Ways to Successful Fund Raising	$8.95
Ronald D. Brown	From Selling to Managing	$5.95
Richard E. Byrd	A Guide to Personal Risk Taking	$5.95
Logan Cheek	Zero-Base Budgeting Comes of Age	$6.95
William A. Cohen	The Executive's Guide to Finding a Superior Job	$5.95
Ken Cooper	Bodybusiness	$5.95
James J. Cribbin	Effective Managerial Leadership	$6.95
William Dowling	Effective Management & the Behavioral Sciences	$8.95
Richard J. Dunsing	You and I Have Simply Got to Stop Meeting This Way	$5.95
Sidney Edlung	There Is a Better Way to Sell	$5.95
Elam & Paley	Marketing for the Nonmarketing Executive	$5.95
Norman L. Enger	Management Standards for Developing Information Systems	$6.95
John Fenton	The A to Z of Sales Management	$7.95
Figueroa & Winkler	A Business Information Guidebook	$9.95
Saul W. Gellerman	Motivation and Productivity	$6.95
Roger A. Golde	Muddling Through	$5.95
Hanan Berrian, Cribbin, & Donis	Success Strategies for the New Sales Manager	$8.95
Lois B. Hart	Moving Up! Women and Leadership	$6.95
Hart & Schleicher	A Conference and Workshop Planner's Manual	$15.95
Michael Hayes	Pay Yourself First	$6.95
Hilton & Knoblauch	On Television	$6.95
Herman R. Holtz	The $100 Billion Market	$10.95
Herman R. Holtz	Profit From Your Money-Making Ideas	$8.95
Charles L. Hughes	Goal Setting	$5.95
John W. Humble	How to Manage By Objectives	$5.95
Jones & Trentin	Budgeting (rev. ed.)	$12.95
Donald J. Kenney	Minicomputers	$7.95
William H. Krause	How to Get Started as a Manufacturers' Representative	$8.95
Sy Lazarus	Loud & Clear: A Guide to Effective Communication	$5.95